The Secrets of Southeast Asian Tex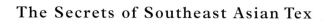

The Secrets of
Southeast Asian Textiles
Myth, Status and the Supernatural

The James H W Thompson Foundation Symposium Papers

Edited by Jane Puranananda

RIVER BOOKS

Published by The James H. W. Thompson Foundation
6 Soi Kasemsan 2, Rama I Road,
Bangkok 10330
Tel. (66) 2 216-7368
Fax. (66) 2 612-3744
www.jimthompsonhouse.com

First published and distributed in Thailand in 2007 by
River Books Co., Ltd
396 Maharaj Road, Tatien,
Bangkok 10200
Tel: (66) 2 225-4963, 2 225-0139, 2 622-1900
Fax: (66) 2 225-3861
Email: riverps@ksc.th.com
www.riverbooksbk.com

A River Books Production.
Copyright collective work © The James H W Thompson Foundation 2007
Copyright text and photographs © The James H W Thompson Foundation 2007,
except where indicated otherwise.

Publisher Narisa Chakrabongse
Design Narisa Chakrabongse and Suparat Sudcharoen
Production Paisarn Piemmettawat

ISBN 978-974-9863-38-1

Printed and bound in Thailand by Bangkok Printing Co., Ltd.

CONTENTS

6   Foreword

7   Introduction

9   Map of Southeast Asia

BHUTAN

Diana K. Myers   10   Parallels
Form and Function in Bhutanese and Southeast Asian Textiles

CAMBODIA

Gillian Green   28   Spirit Ships and Ships of the Soul
Images on Cambodian Celebratory Textile Hangings

INDONESIA

John Guy   40   Rama, Rajas and Courtesans
Indian Figurative Textiles in Indonesia

Roy W. Hamilton   58   Barkcloth Skirts from Southwestern Borneo

Robyn J. Maxwell   72   Piety and Protection
Talismanic Textiles in Islamic Southeast Asia

MYANMAR

Susan Conway   84   Shan Expressions of Power and Protection

Barbara G. Fraser
David W. Fraser   92   Hidden Threads
Structure and Status in Chin Textiles

Vibha Joshi   108   Redefinining Status and Identity
Naga Textiles

Piriya Krairiksh   122   Mon Ancestral Textiles

LAOS

Patricia Cheesman   134   Spirit Skirts of the Lao-Tai Peoples of Laos

Linda McIntosh   150   From Girl to Woman
Textiles in Contemporary Phuthai Society

THAILAND

Leedom Lefferts   160   Monks' Robes in Rural Northeast Thailand
Relic and Memory

Suriya Smutkupt   172   Female Lower Garment or Holy Manuscript Wrapper?
The Role of Women in a Buddhist Society

Thirabhand Chandrachareon   180   Royal Brocades in the Siamese Court

VIETNAM

Michael C. Howard   194   Religious and Status-Marking Functions of
Textiles among the Tai Peoples of Vietnam

FOREWORD

As part of the objectives of The James H. W. Thompson Foundation which are to encourage studies about Southeast Asia's rich cultural heritage, the Foundation organized a textile symposium in August, 2005 entitled *Status, Myth and the Supernatural – Unraveling the Secrets of Southeast Asian Textiles.* The symposium was held at the request of the many scholars and textile collectors who had attended the Foundation's first textile conference organized in 1999.

While the first conference *Through the Thread of Time – Southeast Asian Textiles* provided a general introduction to textiles by presenting papers on a wide range of topics, for the second conference it was decided to focus on a specific theme. The question posed to the speakers concerned the role that status, myth or the supernatural plays in the making and use of Southeast Asian Textiles. This publication contains the papers presented by the textile experts and scholars who were invited to answer this question. Their varied and colorful responses help document important traditions, beliefs and customs, many of which are disappearing as this publication is being printed.

The *Status, Myth and the Supernatural* symposium attracted over two hundred and fifty participants from all over the world. Fifteen scholars and textile experts presented fascinating papers on a variety of thought provoking topics. Many who attended the conference suggested that there be more discussions related to textiles and their function in society. Hopefully, this publication will help raise questions, stimulate discussion and encourage more research.

There are many people to thank for the success of the textile symposium and the publication of this work. Foundation President Professor William Klausner and Board Member William Booth had the vision to ensure that this project was carried out in manner that would meet the highest standards of the Jim Thompson legacy and of academic excellence. Foundation Board Member Eric Booth made major contributions to the organizing of the event through his highly appreciated support and suggestions. Thanks must be given to Supicha Teerasenee and her team at the Foundation for their assistance in overseeing the entire project and handling the many important administrative details.

In terms of preparing this publication, the Foundation is deeply appreciative of the advice and support of M. R. Narisa Chakrabongse and Paisarn Piammattawat of River Books. In addition, the assistance of Linda McIntosh, with her extensive textile expertise, has been of great value in the editing of this book. The advice and editorial suggestions of Liz Lu of the Thai Textile Society were also very much appreciated.

Warm thanks and deep appreciation go to the fifteen speakers who each, in their own way, made such a valuable contribution to *The Secrets of Southeast Asian Textiles – Myth, Status and the Supernatural.* Through their scholarship our understanding and appreciation of Southeast Asian textiles has been greatly enhanced.

Finally, this book is dedicated to Jim Thompson. The year 2006 marks the 100th anniversary of his birthday. This publication is a most fitting tribute to the man who fell in love with Thailand and built a marvelous teak home across a canal from his favorite silk weavers. His passion for Southeast Asian art has ensured that ongoing scholarship will continue through The James H. W. Thompson Foundation.

Jane Puranananda

INTRODUCTION

Due to their unique cultural origins, varied production methods and a vast array of designs, Southeast Asian textiles pose a myriad of intriguing questions about their origin, meaning and traditional use. In some cases the answers are only available through scholarly detective work and the piecing together of information from unusual sources. In other instances, information from the weavers and users of such textiles must be obtained by traveling to remote, even dangerous areas.

With each passing year the secrets that Southeast Asian textiles hold become more difficult to uncover. Disappearing traditions, social transformations and expanding markets for machine made cloth hamper our search to learn to learn the truth. In this volume the reader is invited to travel with fifteen textile experts and researchers on a journey throughout Southeast Asia and beyond as they ask and answer fascinating questions about textiles. For each question answered, for every explanation given, a host of new questions come to mind.

The first article in this work takes the reader beyond Southeast Asian to the little know kingdom of Bhutan. Traveling through Southeast Asia on her way to Bhutan, **Diane K. Myers** became struck by intriguing similarities between Bhutanese and Tai textiles. She takes on the challenging task of making comparisons between Bhutanese and Southeast Asian weavings and textile traditions. Her article points to a number of areas which are ripe for future study.

Next in alphabetical order we come to Cambodia where Khmer textiles scholar **Gillian Green** presents a thought provoking hypothesis on Khmer celebratory hangings. In particular, her search to answer why intricate seagoing vessels appear in these hangings often woven by women who were far from and unfamiliar with seaports leads to uncovering some long forgotten ideas about these textiles.

John Guy invites us to travel back in time to consider the implications of ancient textile trade between India and Indonesia. Rare Indian textile remnants dating to the 15th and 16th centuries provide insights into what types of imported cloth served as status markers for Indonesian nobility. However, what needs further analysis is how these cloths were used in ceremonies.

The reader is next invited to travel with **Roy W. Hamilton** to remote river areas in Borneo in order find the source of a series of bark cloth skirts collected in 1908. Of all the papers presented in this book, none more clearly demonstrates how quickly cultural memory can vanish. Hamilton could find no one who had any recollection of the skirts, however good detective work does result in some interesting discoveries.

Robyn J. Maxwell explains the fascinating link between the Muslim world and underlying indigenous beliefs of Southeast Asia through the influence of textiles. We see how Islamic symbols and calligraphy are employed to create talismanic protection for their Indonesian users.

Next we visit Myanmar where three different writers focus on minority groups. With **Susan Conway** we enter into the realm of the supernatural while visiting the Tai speaking Shans. Her study and research into shaman rituals record the use of textiles and tattoos in a supernatural context.

With co-authors **Barbara and David Fraser** we travel to western Myanmar where the writers explain how four different weaving techniques requiring exceptional skill help to serve as status markers in Chin society. Their dedication in studying detailed aspects of the Chin weavings documents an important page in the textile tradition.

Scholar **Vibha Joshi** invites us to consider how social change has affected the use of textiles among various Naga groups living in both Myanmar and India. She examines how textiles, including specific ones for those who had become headhunters, continue to provide status to the wearer, but in a new context.

Next, we travel to Laos with **Patricia Cheesman** who documents the weavings and use of spirit skirts imbued with supernatural powers. The author points to the striking homogeny in the structure, material and design of textiles which were used by male and female shamans of various Tai-Lao groups.

Based on recent field work, **Linda McIntosh** provides insights into the changing role of textiles and weaving among the Phuthai, a Tai group living in central and southern Laos. Economic change and government policy are playing a significant role in the changing status of women who must adapt their textile traditions to meet modern demands.

Although **Piriya Krairiksh** presents a topic listed under Thailand, in fact, the information presented is based on research by a team of scholars from Thammasat University's Thai Studies program and covers Mon peoples living in both Thailand and Myanmar. His paper demonstrates the importance of cross-border research, particularly in the case of minority groups where customs and languages are rapidly disappearing.

Leedom Leeferts shares with readers the ceremonies held in rural northeastern Thai villages in order to demonstrate how the robes worn by the village monks become markers of status and power to the men who wear them. We see how the robes hold meaning as relics of the Buddha but are also intimately connected with remembrance of the deceased relatives.

Our next paper by **Suriya Smutkupt** also focuses on Buddhism, textiles and status in another Thai context. Here, the author highlights an apparent enigma by posing the questions of how textiles traditionally woven to cover the lower half of a woman's body could be modified in use to cover sacred Buddhist manuscripts.

Thirabhand Chandracharoen examines the traditional use of imported and locally made brocades in the Siamese court. Employed to enhance the power of monarchs as divine rulers, distribution of these sumptuous textiles was strictly controlled according to rank and status of the wearer in the court.

Minority Tai groups in Vietnam have a long and fascinating heritage according to **Michael C. Howard** who finds links between present-day cultures and the Bronze Age. In searching among the patterns and designs of modern Tai weavers, he hopes to uncover secrets about the meaning of symbols used in ancient times.

The enormously varied selection of papers presented in this book points to the complexity and diversity of Southeast Asian textiles. Only through dedication, ingenuity, determination, and extensive field research have scholars and textile experts been able to present their ideas and theories about the meaning, use and social significance of textiles. For each clue that is uncovered or new idea proposed more questions are raised.

As in all types of scholarly research, interpretations and ideas amongst experts differ. For example, one scholar traces traditions that go back to the Bronze Age among one group while another scholar finds that the memory of a custom has disappeared in less than a century in another group. In some cases textile traditions have adapted to modern change and thereby flourished. Yet, in many cases social transformation and new technology have resulted in the end of such traditions. Above all, the purpose of publishing this book is to share the ideas of the writers, and hope that the questions they raise will continue to stimulate research and scholarship in an important field because there are still many secrets to unravel.

BHUTAN

INDIA

BANGLADESH

DHAKA

Bay of Bengal

MYANMAR

CHINA

VIETNAM

HANOI

Gulf of Tonkin

LAOS

HAINAN DAO

RANGOON

VIENTIANE

THAILAND

BANGKOK

CAMBODIA

PHNOM PENH

Gulf of Thailand

ANDAMAN ISLANDS (INDIA)

MERGUI ARCHIPELAGO

ANDAMAN SEA

SOUTH CHINA SEA

Strait of Malacca

MALAYSIA

KUALA LUMPUR

BRUNEI

BANDAR SERI BEGAWAN

MALAYSIA

SINGAPORE

SUMATRA

BORNEO

INDIAN OCEAN

N

INDONESIA

JAVA SEA

JAKARTA

BALI SEA

JAVA

Parallels: *Form and Function in Bhutanese and Southeast Asian Textiles*

Diana K. Myers

Indigenous textile traditions reflect Bhutan's position as a geographical and cultural crossroads between Tibet and Southeast Asia (1). The kingdom's links to other parts of the Buddhist Himalaya are readily seen, for example, in architecture, festivals, and religious textiles, which, while uniquely Bhutanese, share clear similarities with those in regions to the north and west. Importantly, too, most textiles for sacred use are the province of men, who stitch, embroider, and appliqué furnishings for temples and household shrines. Bhutan's links with regions to the south and east are not as obvious and have been studied less. However, the topography, climate, and ecology of eastern Bhutan are much like Southeast Asia's – and Bhutanese say that the east is where their weaving traditions are oldest (2). Work at looms is closely associated with women, and the variety of cloth that they weave for everyday purposes demonstrates that Bhutan is the western frontier of some important "Southeast Asian" cultural features. This paper focuses selectively on textile traditions in eastern and north central Bhutan to: 1) review evidence of links to Southeast Asia; 2) examine what women's dress reveals about early cultural traditions and gender; and 3) suggest key areas for more research.

Bhutan and Southeast Asia

Cultural links: history, language and trade

The exhibition catalog *From the Land of the Thunder Dragon: Textile Arts of Bhutan* outlined the common cultural histories of peoples now living in Bhutan, northeast India, and as far away as Laos and Indonesia.[1] The array of ethnic groups that speak Tibeto-Burman languages is one manifestation of this distant collective past: Bhutanese share a linguistic heritage with people who live in Assam and Arunachal Pradesh, Burma, and northern Thailand.[2] It is generally agreed that one ancestral homeland of these groups was in what is now eastern Tibet, although the timing and chronology of the earliest outward migrations are lost in prehistory. Spurred onward for political, economic, and other reasons, Tibeto-Burman speakers intermingled with other populations as they made their ways over centuries to their current homes.

In most of mainland Southeast Asia today, Tibeto-Burman peoples are interspersed among the majority Tai, whose cultures also shaped textile traditions in Bhutan. For example, one group of Tai – the Shan – reached Assam from northern Burma some 1500 years ago and by A.D. 1228 they had established an empire in what is now northeast India. For the next 600 years, this dynasty was a potent political and cultural presence on Bhutan's frontier. In the 18th century, other Tai such as the Singpho and Khampti settled in northeast India as well.

Significantly, ancient migrations contributed to a distinctive textile culture in northeast India, and in Bhutan. In these areas, weaving is the domain of women, rather than men, and not confined to caste or other occupational groups, as it is in much of the rest of India and South Asia. Late 19th century British writers observed that the weaving of cotton and silk cloth was a widespread household industry in Assam, as it still is in Bhutan. Local fabrics figured prominently in Assamese trade and in tax payments, which was also the case in Bhutan until recently. Fine textiles were likewise an important element of the tribute and gifts exchanged among states and authorities throughout the area.[3]

Also, parts of central and eastern Bhutan, adjacent Tibet, and adjacent India belonged to a single political and cultural area starting in the 9th century, when Tibetan settlers brought Mahayana Buddhism to these regions south of the Himalayas. At least until the mid-1600s Tawang in Arunachal Pradesh (India) was a key center of power, and the enduring legacy of intercultural contacts during this historical period is still seen in language, ritual, myth, and clothing.

Buddhism itself is the basis for other important cultural connections and shared textile traditions. Mahayana Buddhists in Bhutan and Theravada practitioners in Southeast Asia all adorn statues of the Buddha

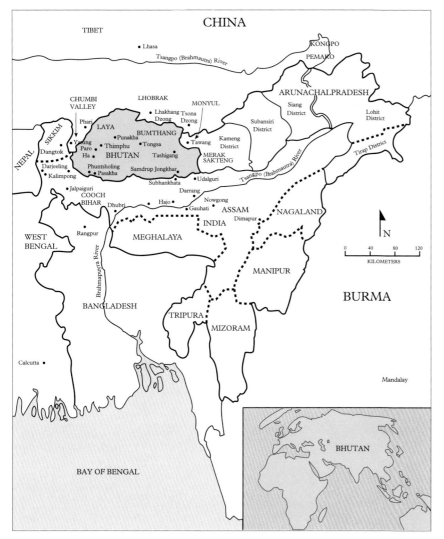

1 Bhutan, Northeast India and Southeast Asia. Ancient migrations of Tibeto-Burman and Tai-speaking peoples helped to populate these regions, where weaving is a household industry and the domain of women. *(Myers and Bean 1994)*

2 Regions of Bhutan. Bhutan's most sophisticated textile traditions are associated with north central and eastern Bhutan, where weaving was an early indigenous art. *(Myers and Bean 1994)*

3 Like several dozen ethnic groups in northeast India and Southeast Asia who also speak Tibeto-Burman languages, the Bhutanese use a body-tension loom with a continuous warp. Weaving a panel of wild silk decorated with supplementary warps, Radi, Tashigang District, Bhutan. *(Photo: DKM)*

4 Bast fibers were the earliest weaving materials in Bhutan, as they were in Southeast Asia. Some eastern Bhutanese continue to use nettle and hemp, which grow wild in the temperate hills. Hand-twisting nettle fiber, Rangjung, Tashigang District, Bhutan. *(Photo: DKM)*

with offerings of cloth; display long, narrow banners around sacred sites; and produce textiles as very important types of gifts presented to monks and to temples. White is the color of purity, and reds, oranges, and golds are the province of the clergy. Religion also shaped shared textile-related beliefs. Thus, in Thailand, Burma, and Bhutan, a man would not intentionally walk under a woman's wrapped garment that is drying on a line. Bhutanese explain this taboo as reflecting the sanctity of a person's head and women's perceived spiritual inferiority to men – hence, the potential pollution. Finally, religion took Bhutanese beyond their homeland. For centuries, devout pilgrims visited Buddhist sites in India; to pay their expenses, they traded at markets in the Himalayan foothills and Brahmaputra River Valley, mingling freely with people from Assam and more distant places.

Weaving links: technologies, beliefs and designs
Bhutanese legends about the origins of weaving all speak of noble women or princesses who came from the east and north. Such stories are consistent with the ancient migration routes of Tibeto-Burman-language-speaking

peoples. Common technologies for producing clothabound among several dozen of these groups who are linguistic cousins of the Bhutanese. The most important of these technologies is the body-tension loom with a continuous warp **(3)**, on which weavers mainly produce plainweave fabrics that are warp-faced and some twills.[4] In contrast, the Tai majority in Southeast Asia use a frame loom worked with foot treadles, although Gittinger and Lefferts have made a convincing case that this is a relatively recent historical change.[5]

Similar natural resources from Bhutan to the Philippines probably explain the shared use of certain fibers, but common methods of preparing yarns may be more persuasive evidence of substantive cultural links. Bhutanese say that their earliest garments were made from nettle and from hemp, which is a very ancient textile fiber throughout the region and in southern China. These bast fibers are now used only by a handful of communities in northern Thailand, the Shan states of Burma, and in Bhutan, where both hemp and nettle grow wild in abundance. Current methods of fiber preparation – soaking, drying, splitting with a fingernail, bleaching with ash water, and hand-twisting into a

5a and **b** This Bhutanese woman's dress (a left) and Phu Tai blanket (b right) show extraordinary parallels in their supplementary-warp patterning and colour palettes. **(a)** Woman's dress, *jadrima* (yellow and white patterning on a red ground), mid-20th century. Private collection. *(Photo: DKM)*

(b) Thailand/Laos, collection of Patricia Cheesman. Reproduced from Fig. 2.2, pl. 60, Gittinger 1992. *(Image courtesy Mattiebelle Gittinger)*

yarn **(4)** – are quite similar among the Bhutanese, Thailand's Lisu, and possibly others. Also, Bhutanese continue to use the drop spindle to spin, and to tighten the twist of commercial yarns while they tend livestock or walk in the hills. This early, practical technology is likewise found among the Naga in northeast India, some Indonesians in Flores and Timor, and in other relatively isolated communities. Other common tools of relatively more recent origin, such as the cotton gin, are also known.[6]

Significantly, too, throughout much of the region, weaving and dyeing skills are seen as intrinsically female and highly admired. In Bhutan, northeast India, and parts of Thailand and Laos, similar taboos associate women's creative role as weavers with their reproductive role as mothers. Thus, women in Bhutan and in Mishmi and other communities in northeast India are prohibited from weaving for at least three days after they give birth. Another regional belief is that interfering with the weaving process can have dire consequences for a woman's fertility. Bhutanese, for example, say that if a woman steps over the warp or a pattern-shed rod for picking out designs, she will never marry or will have a mute child –

while Tai in northeast Thailand and southern Laos say that a man should not touch a warped loom on which an unmarried young woman is weaving.[7] Finally, from Bhutan to northeast Thailand to Sumba in eastern Indonesia one hears that yarns should be coloured in a private place, away from pregnant or menstruating women, and never in the presence of men, and especially in Buddhist regions, monks.[8]

Weavers in the Himalayan kingdom and Southeast Asia also share several methods of decorating cloth, and some associated tools and processes. One example is a diamond twill weave, some of whose local names refer to the "eye" that the pattern resembles. Another example is continuous supplementary-weft and -warp patterning where weavers use slender wooden rods and extra heddles to lift ground warps in the proper sequence. There are extraordinarily parallels, for example, in the design format and technique – as well as the colour combinations – of the supplementary-warp patterning in some Bhutanese and Phu Tai textiles **(5a and b)**. Visually similar patterns on other Southeast Asian textiles are often created with supplementary wefts, indicating how weavers transposed and preserved these patterns once made on backstrap looms when frame looms came into vogue (e.g. **14b**). A third example is the continuous supplementary-weft patterning on textiles such as Tai head and shoulder cloths which is easily compared with that on traditional women's belts and ceremonial lap covers from eastern Bhutan (**6a** and **b**). Finally, women in Thailand, Burma, northeast India, and Bhutan all produced very intricate discontinuous supplementary-weft patterns, customarily with the help of a porcupine quill (**7a** and **b**).

A specific, intriguing technical parallel occurs in textiles made by Bhutanese and by four Chin groups in Burma. The finished designs resemble chain and cross stitches, but are created by sophisticated manipulation of pattern yarns on the loom. In Bhutan, the technique called *thrima* involves inserting a discontinuous pattern yarn behind two sets of paired warps, and crossing its ends on the face of the fabric. The yarn ends are then passed behind the warps so that they cross again, and brought back to the face of the fabric. Patterns made in the warp direction, or diagonally, resemble a cross stitch (**8a** and **b**). Alternatively, the pattern weft ends may be looped around the warp in the weft direction to create what resembles a chain stitch or countered twining.

A comparable technique, discussed in David and Barbara Fraser's recently published *Mantles of Merit,* is used by the Laytu, Khami, Khumi and Mro Chin in Burma. These weavers also wrap pattern yarns around ground warps to produce very similar designs with a structure that the Frasers call "false embroidery" (**9a** and **b**).[9] Neither Bhutanese nor Chin pattern yarns worked in these ways are visible on the reverse of the warp-faced textiles that they decorate. Although the patterning techniques are not identical, their complexity and distinctive character point to the possibility of an ancient relationship.

While textiles from the larger region do show a common repertoire of surface designs, it is very difficult to compare the meanings of most shared motifs, much less to draw conclusions about the significance of their appearance in textiles made by diverse communities. Even when distant cultural groups give a motif the same local name, this name often refers to what a design looks like rather than to what it represents. Today, Bhutanese say that many of their motifs are strictly decorative and often give different meanings to the same motif. These interpretations vary according to a person's age, sex, regional origin, education, and other factors. More field studies are clearly essential to understand what, if any, deeper significance a particular motif may have today, and to whom.[10]

6a and **b** Dense, continuous supplementary-weft patterning associated with traditional eastern Bhutanese textiles such as this woman's belt (**a** top) and ceremonial multipurpose textile (**b**) recalls the decoration of various Tai textiles, including head and shoulder cloths. **(a)** Detail, woman's belt *(kera),* mid-20th century. *(Photo: DKM)* **(b)** *Chagsi pangkheb,* early 20th century, Phillips *(Collection, Peabody Essex Museum (E74570)).* Fig. 5.48. *(Myers and Bean 1994)*

7a and **b** Weavers throughout the region still use porcupine quills to manipulate discontinous pattern yarns. (**a** right) Chin weaver, Burma: Fig. 29, p. 163, *(Lehman 1963)* (**b**) In Bhutan, a slender metal pick can now serve the same function. Chosung Lhamo is inserting pattern wefts that alternately pass underneath ground warps and lie on the surface of the cloth, a technique called *sapma*. *(Photo: DKM)*

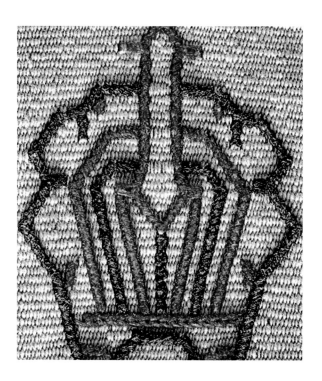

8a and **b** The patterning style called *kushu* originated in Lhuntshi District in north central Bhutan. It features two techniques of working with discontinuous supplementary wefts. *Sapma* pattern yarns appear to lie flat on the surface of the cloth (**8a**: above). Pattern yarns worked in the more complex technique, *thrima,* are wrapped around ground warps and interworked so that motifs are raised above the surface of the cloth and resemble cross and cross stitches. (**8b** left) Detail showing *thrima* patterning, *kushung* (tunic). *(Cover of Myers and Bean 1994)*

15

9a and **b** The Khami, Khumi, and Mro Chin in Burma use extra yarns to produce patterns that are structurally and visually similar to the Bhutanese technique called *thrima*. *(Fraser and Fraser 2005. (a) Fig. 79b, p. 52) (b) Fig. 312, p. 164)*

10a-d The content and arrangement of certain common motifs suggest ancient relationships between peoples who now live in Bhutan and in Southeast Asia. For example, rows of birds, elephants, and horses appear together in a variety of textiles, including some woven in north central Bhutan a hundred or more years ago and jackets worn today by a small group of women in eastern Bhutan. *(Merak Sakteng)*
(a) Detail, (above) *Tai Lue* towel *(pha chet)*, Samoeng District, Chiang Mai Province, Thailand. *(Prangwatthankun and Cheesman 1988, p. 31)*
(b) Detail, ceremonial seat cover (c. 1900), Lhuntshi District, Bhutan.
(Private collection. *(Photo: DKM)*
(c) Detail, Tai towel *(pha chet)*. Collection of Siam Society, Bangkok, pl. 12.
(Fraser Lu 1988)
(d) Detail from contemporary woman's jacket (see **19**), Chorten Kora, Bhutan. *(Photo: DKM)*

For example, the prominent diamond that appears in Tai shoulder cloths, head cloths, and healing cloths is said to have protective powers. Very similar patterning appears in multipurpose textiles from eastern Bhutan that served as traditional lap covers *(chagsi pangkheb)*. The lap cover consists of one loom length (center panel) heavily decorated with supplementary-weft patterning that always features a central diamond **(6b)**. This panel is framed by the two halves of another loom length, often decorated with supplementary-warp as well as supplementary-weft patterning, that have been cut along the warp. This assembled construction is unique in Bhutan, and the textiles themselves are prized by Bhutanese, but even older weavers from the east say they do not know the significance of the textiles' structure or patterning. Perhaps they would have answered differently fifty, a hundred, or two hundred years ago, or perhaps not. Thus, one can only speculate about the nature of potential links with the Tai textiles or with Indonesian textiles whose side panels metaphorically contain the power represented by patterning in a center panel.

Anthropomorphic and animal figures, whose significance today is intriguing but obscure, point even more clearly to ancient cultural relationships. Specifically, one finds rows of elephants, fanciful birds, human figures, and horses on banners from southern Yunnan, towels from Thailand, tunics from Burma, women's jackets from northeast India, and various textiles from Bhutan **(10a-d)**. The latter include archaic women's garments, ceremonial seat covers, and multipurpose cloths decorated with lively horses, human figures, and/or long-tailed birds. Elephants also appear on a woman's jacket still worn in eastern Bhutan. While scholars have studied what these motifs mean in some Southeast Asian contexts, we do not know what the motifs represent in Bhutan. However, the ways that Bhutanese use some of the textiles today suggest that these images, deeply embedded in the past, are associated with potent concepts, as women's dress traditions show.

10b

10c

10d

17

Women's Dress and Social Order

Women's apparel in Bhutan speaks dramatically of affinities with areas to the southeast, whereas men's dress does not. A brief look at history helps explain this difference. Early sources often represent Bhutan as a kind of "wild and uncivilized Barbary awaiting the 'taming' effect, first of refugee princes and later of Buddhist lamas from Tibet."[11] The generic name for the land's earliest people is Monpa, loosely, "people of darkness," meaning they were not yet blessed with the illumination of Buddhism. While legends speak of Buddhist saints from India reaching Bhutan in the 7th century, recorded Bhutanese history really begins when a Tibetan prince settles in the hills of eastern Bhutan in the 9th century and converts the people there to Buddhism. This is the same area where Bhutanese say their weaving "comes from."

Over time, Buddhism continued to spread among peoples living on the southern slopes of the Himalayas. One story about a 13th century Tibetan lama who came to this area vividly illustrates how the untamed and threatening physical world (thought of as female) was subjugated by the power of religion (thought of as male).[12] In this legend, the lama pauses to dance on some land "with the form of a ... demoness lying on her back." He spots his future consort/wife as she is weaving on a river bank, and eventually she "puts aside her weaving, the symbol of local culture, to give herself to the lama, who stands for a higher, nobler cause". The story's imagery reinforces very powerfully the association of women with the unconverted, fertile land and with weaving.

Bhutan's medieval history culminates in the arrival in 1616 of a charismatic Tibetan statesman/lama, Shabdrung Ngawang Namgyal. By 1651, the Shabdrung, as he is known, unified what is now Bhutan as a Buddhist state whose political boundaries are basically unchanged and that is still administered from fortress-monasteries (dzong) of that period. Importantly, this was a critical point for eastern Bhutan, which from this time onward became more oriented toward new centres of power to the west, such as Tongsa, whose governor administered eastern Bhutan until the early 20th century. Still, the east retained a distinct character – in its language, its continued adherence to the earliest Mahayana Buddhist traditions that reached the area, and its textiles.

The Shabdrung also laid the foundations of a new social order that is still very relevant to Bhutanese life, and in which clothing is a major expression of ordered society.[13] Thus, Bhutanese must wear official, national dress to enter dzongs and temples. For men, this means the gho, a robe that Bhutanese say the Shabdrung introduced from Tibet, with modifications for Bhutan's warmer climate (11). A shoulder cloth (kabne) is an essential part of proper apparel; worn on the left, it is associated with the shawl worn by the Buddha's disciples and by monks. The shoulder cloth is never patterned with supplementary yarns and its color corresponds to the wearer's civil service rank, white being for ordinary people, stripes and other colors for officials. In contrast, a Bhutanese woman's shoulder cloth (rachu) can also be a practical textile for carrying a baby or bundle. Traditionally, this textile was red with supplementary-weft patterning at each fringed end. Nowadays there are many varieties of rachu, some of them very narrow and not always red, strictly for wear on formal occasions (12). Among Tai Buddhist groups, men and women also wear a variety of shoulder cloths, whose functions today are also linked to religious ceremony.

The origins of proper dress for Bhutanese women have been forgotten, but the garment women wear now evolved from what Bhutanese consider an indigenous, rather than imported, style. According to oral tradition in north central and eastern Bhutan, women once also wore simply tailored tunics and wrapped garments, both of which are found in Southeast Asia and northeast India. Long and short tunics are still worn, for example, by the Bugun in Arunachal Pradesh, some Chin groups, and the Karen in Burma and Thailand.

It was the wrapped garment, however, that became proper dress for Bhutanese women, sometime after the 17th century. The corners of the dress, called a kira, are secured at each shoulder and the garment is held in place with a woven belt (12a and b). Kira are typically made of three loom lengths joined together, a structure that orients the warp horizontally when the dress is worn (13). Garments made of two or more loom lengths and whose warp is oriented horizontally are likewise found throughout Assam and in Southeast Asia: some are pinned on one shoulder, others are wrapped under the arms or at the waist, and some are stitched at the warp ends to form tube skirts.

We are not sure when Bhutanese women began to wear a jacket, but tailored upper garments are or were worn with wrapped dress and with tunics, by both Tibeto-Burman and Tai language groups in Southeast Asia. The jacket that most Bhutanese women wear with their kira is rather loose with wide sleeves (12).

Gender-specific decorative techniques and patterns are known in Southeast Asia and are notable in Bhutan

11 Bhutanese men still wear tailored robes that originated in Tibet. A shoulder cloth *(kabne)* is an integral part of Bhutanese men's proper dress for formal occasions such as attending a festival or visiting a temple or government office. The red and white shoulder cloth (left) indicates that the wearer is a village headman. Yadi, Mongar District. *(Photo: DKM)*

12a and **b** Proper dress for Bhutanese women is a wrapped garment *(kira)*, pinned at the shoulders and worn with a blouse and jacket. Contemporary shoulder cloths for women *(rachu)* are strictly ceremonial.
a (above) Girls at festival. Gangtey Gompa. *(Photo: DKM)*
b (left) This woman holds a woven belt *(kera)*, made by her grandmother. Mhinji, Lhuntshi District. *(Photo: DKM)*

19

as well.[14] Although most Bhutanese cloth is unisex, three patterns are exclusively female:

1) Thara/thare (*Tsangla:* woven cotton): The generic meaning of this eastern Bhutanese term is 'woman's wrapped garment' (Dzongkha: *kira*), indicating that this warp-striped pattern (**13**) is very old. Warp stripes with similar colours and proportions also decorate women's garments throughout Southeast Asia, for example, among the Naga.

2) Montha (*Mon:* understood as indigenous Bhutanese weaving): Montha shows supplementary-warp patterning in a colour scheme that combines blue or black and white warp stripes (**14a**). *Thag* is the primary word for fabric, and, to Bhutanese, *mon* recalls Bhutan's early inhabitants who were not Buddhist. The patterning and colours of this fabric are echoed in Naga and Lao, as well as other textiles (**14b**).

Visitors to Bhutan may have seen *thara* and *montha* worn by male clowns at the important festivals *(tshechu)* that celebrate the conversion of the region to Buddhism in the 7th century. These characters carry a wooden phallus with which they tease women in the crowd and make suggestive motions. The clowns' behavior can be interpreted as alluding to the circumstances that cause pregnancy and vulnerability in childbirth, and, by extension, to women's precarious spiritual position on the margins of ordered society. In the past at archery contests, male dancers, representing women, sometimes wore *montha kira*, reinforcing the notion that this cloth is fundamentally female.

3) Kushuthara (wrapped garment decorated with *kushu* [regional technique of supplementary-weft patterning]): This textile's name refers to its distinctive patterning, called *kushu* (**15**). Kushu includes two decorative techniques. The simpler one *(sapma)* employs pattern wefts that alternately pass under one or more warps and float on the surface of the fabric. The more complex technique, *thrima*, was compared earlier with the patterning in certain Chin textiles.

Originally from Lhuntshi District in north central Bhutan, *kushu* patterning decorates various regional textiles in addition to *kira*, but not garments for men. The technique is very closely associated, for example, with an earlier form of regional woman's dress, the tunic called *kushung* (**16**). *Ku* means "nettle," underscoring the ancient origins of the garment as well as the patterning technique. Most surviving tunics are elaborately decorated, although a few, said to have been for daily wear, are quite plain.[15] *Kushung* are woven of nettle or cotton and have a long fringe at the lower edge. Just above the

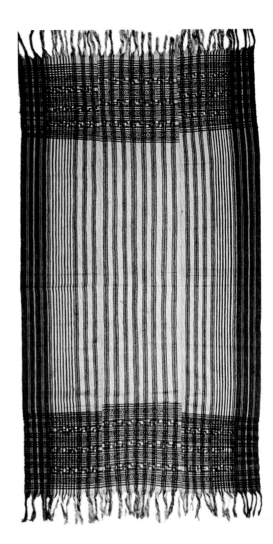

13 *Thare*, a warp-striped plainweave, is one of three types of cloth worn only by women. *Phillips Collection, Peabody Essex Museum (E200234). Fig. 5.22, Myers and Bean 1994.*

14a and **b** The Bhutanese supplementary-warp-patterned textile called *montha* (opposite page, top right) is likewise worn only by women. Its name indicates that the pattern is indigenous and very old. DKM **b**. *Montha* patterning and colors recall those in some Southeast Asian textiles, such as this woman's skirt from Laos (b opposite page, bottom), patterned with extra wefts. *(p. 115, Cheesman 1988)*

15 *Kushuthara*, a woman's garment from Lhuntshi District in north central Bhutan that is decorated with supplementary-weft patterns in the regional style called *kushu*. (opposite page, top left) This patterning was also applied to tunics once worn by women in this area (cf. Fig. 16). *Phillips Collection, Peabody Essex Museum (E73212). Fig. 5.24, Myers and Bean 1994.*

fringe, virtually all tunics show a third type of patterning whose parallels in Southeast Asia are unknown. This technique employs multiple pattern wefts, of bast fiber and of wool, in a single shed **(17)**. Skilled Bhutanese weavers say they can reproduce this patterning, but they do not use it today.

Tunics, their decoration, and their uses today provide insights into how one form of regional women's dress evolved in the context of the Buddhist state and social order that emerged in the 17th century. Many tunics have wonderful patterns that local people readily identify as birds, horses with a rider, or "horses carrying *torma* (Buddhist offering made of butter and flour)."[16] At the same time, most Bhutanese say that garments with human and animal figures are not suitable for wearing.[17] And, notably, as *kushu* patterning was applied to the new majority style of wrapped dress, these figures virtually disappeared. Only birds and horses continue to be seen in a few *kira* woven in the 20th century, and then as isolated motifs, and not in dramatic rows.[18]

In parts of central and eastern Bhutan, the early tunics called *kushung* are used now mainly to clothe ancestor figures in local temples. In several places, they are worn once a year in rituals to honor deities of place, whom Buddhists in Southeast Asia continue to venerate as well. The rituals *(pcha)* in north central Bhutan centre on local mountain deities who were converted long ago to be protectors of Buddhism. Their performance is considered critical for maintaining the well-being of the village. *Pcha* may require the temporary closure of household Buddhist altars. They take place away from the present village and involve non-Buddhist practices such as offering a bird or fish. As one means of recreating the setting when Buddhism arrived and local spirits were "subdued," men adopt what is described as 17th century garb and women dress in tunics. Significantly, the dress that participants wear should not be seen by any outsiders, including other Bhutanese. On these occasions, and for other ceremonies in the east, sexual taboos are suspended temporarily and participants are said to "hang their embarrassment on a tree" in order to participate.[19] These practices suggest early and continuing associations of women with deities of the land, with tunics, with human and animal motifs – and with a time long ago when society was ordered differently.

The only contemporary textile decorated with animal figures is found in eastern Bhutan, among one of several distinct, small groups who are not required to adopt proper dress as defined for most citizens. Women

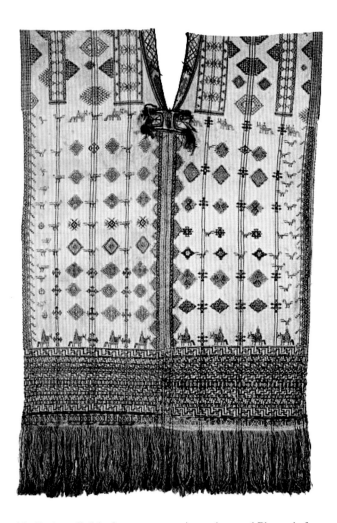

16 Tunics called *kushung* were worn in north central Bhutan before women adopted the majority style of wrapped dress (*kira;* cf. 15) and began decorating it in similar fashion. Today, archaic tunics dress ancestor figures in local temples and are worn for rituals to honor local mountain deities. *(Collection of The Textile Museum, Thimphu. Fig. 5.20, Myers and Bean 1994.)*

in the semi-nomadic herding communities of Merak and Sakteng on the kingdom's eastern border first wear a tunic rather than a *kira* **(18)**. They share this dress (*shingkha*, woman's over-the-head (under garment) with some of their neighbors in Arunachal Pradesh, who were part of the same political-cultural area until the mid-1600s. *Shingkha* are woven of wild silk and generally show narrow white warp stripes on a lac-dyed ground. Over these tunics, women on both sides of the border wear identical, hip-length jackets decorated with rows of horses, birds, and elephants **(19)**. This enduring style speaks of long-standing cultural relationships that have not been affected by current political boundaries.

17 Supplementary-weft patterning on the lower edge of a *kushung* tunic. Multiple, fine supplementary wefts, as many as eight or more in one shed, form distinctly raised pattern bands that are found only in this type of Bhutanese textile. The red pattern yarns are wool; the white yarns are bast fiber, somewhat shinier than the cotton ground. Possible parallels in Southeast Asia are unknown. *(Photo: DKM)*

19 Detail, Merak Sakteng woman's jacket. Rows of animal motifs are a signature characteristic of jackets worn by women of this minority group. *(Phto: DKM)*

18 The only women in Bhutan who wear tunics today live in the herding communities of Merak and Sakteng on Bhutan's eastern border. Warp-striped wild silk tunics and jackets, some identical to those in Bhutan, are worn by various groups in Arunachal Pradesh, India. Chorten Kora, Bhutan. *(Phto: DKM)*

Future research

In Southeast Asia there are many textiles, some of which carry patterns whose potency is not always obvious, and yet hold different kinds of special powers for their users. There is more to learn in this regard about Bhutanese textiles. There is evidence to propose that, for most Bhutanese today, tunics and patterns showing animal and human figures invoke complex ideas about women's nature: their creativity as givers of life to children and to cloth, their relationship with divinities of the land, their spiritual vulnerability in a Buddhist setting – and their association with a distant past. Field work could develop and explore this hypothesis.

Research in Bhutan could also investigate the uses of textiles that are fundamentally female in Buddhist contexts, a practice recently explored in Tai settings, where women's lower garments (pha sin) are found wrapping Buddhist manuscripts.[20] In Bhutan, thara, montha, garments patterned with kushu, and the tunic called kushung are likewise often seen around temples and altars. For example, pieces of these fabrics seem to be preferred for stitching square cloths (bundri) that protect sacred dance costumes when they are not in use and wrap manuscripts and sometimes ritual instruments such as drums in temples and family homes (20). Also, women's dresses decorated with kushu patterning, on a white or a blue ground, are often made into dramatic ceiling canopies that hang in a principal shrine room.

Many of these textiles were surely gifts to bring merit or presented in appreciation of prayers or rituals performed for the donor. As in Southeast Asia, convention requires that a gift textile be new – in Bhutan, this generally means loom lengths that are not yet stitched – meaning that even cloth that is otherwise suited only for women to wear does not have a gender connotation at the time of giving. The frequent use of thara, montha, and kushuthara in temples may thus simply reflect that fifty years or more ago this was the typical dress worn. Like the old lengths of now obsolete tax cloth that serve similar functions in temples, these textiles would have been some of the most common patterns being woven and not unusual to have on hand for a temple gift. This may also be true of the wrappers stitched from kushung tunic panels, which were possibly gifts of even earlier date.

Garments worn by someone who is ill or has passed away may be offered to a temple as well. And, on a practical note, Bhutanese point out that in the past villagers with few assets might only have been able to give their own garments. For similar reasons, villagers might have

20 Textiles that would only be worn by women were also once common gifts to temples, in Bhutan and in Southeast Asia. Some of the square cloths that wrap these Buddhist scriptures, stored in a Bhutanese temple, are made from thara and montha (cf. 13 and 14). (Photo: DKM)

recycled a woman's garment – be it a wrapped dress or tunic – that had been damaged beyond wearing, at least for use in a household shrine. Some examples seen may thus be cases of still serviceable textiles being put to new functions.

Research could explore these practices in more depth, as well as look at the other textiles put to use in Buddhist settings. While tax cloth and specially woven wrappers from the east (and now commercial fabrics) can also protect manuscripts, dance costumes, and ritual instruments, regional unisex clothing fabrics, such as plainweaves decorated with plaid patterns, seem little used in these ways. The absence in temples of the characteristically eastern-Bhutanese supplementary-warp-patterned textiles (e.g., 5a) is especially notable. Mentioned in written sources of the 18th century and worn by men and women, at least during the past century, these textiles were typically woven of wild silk, a more prestigious fiber than cotton – which perhaps meant that any loom lengths gifted to a temple were too precious to cut up and put to utilitarian use. Still, beautifully embellished *kushung* tunics and *kushuthara* were readily transformed. Moreover, Bhutanese say that the latter type of garment is particularly suited for temple canopies, and especially when it includes animal figures; several mid-20th century *kira* of this kind are believed to have been woven expressly as temple offerings (21). Again, it is uncertain whether use in a Buddhist setting might have, or have had, a symbolic function, such as transforming a fabric's unspoken associations.

In conclusion, although Bhutan is conventionally viewed as part of South Asia, the kingdom's textile traditions show important affinities with both Tibeto-Burman and Tai cultures in neighboring Southeast Asia. Common tools and technologies, some of which survive mainly in relatively isolated areas, firmly link weaving in the Himalayan kingdom with practices that probably spread along ancient migration routes. Distinctive patterning techniques associated with north central Bhutan and recently identified among some Chin groups may also be the legacies of long-ago proximity. The "femaleness" of weaving throughout the region is another area that invites ethnographic research, for instance, to better understand women's relationships with local divinities in contemporary Buddhist societies. And field work in Bhutan could help illuminate what appear to be the powerful associations of certain textiles and motifs. Given the rapid social changes that we know have occurred in recent centuries, many intriguing similarities will most likely remain unexplained – but ethnographic, historical, and textile studies should be able to uncover more information about textile structures, forms, and uses. This data in turn may provide evidence about how common features evolved, and will certainly lead to a better understanding of Bhutan's geo-cultural position as a meeting point of traditions from the south and east, as well as the north.

21 Animal motifs rarely appear in Bhutanese women's garments woven after 1900. This k*ira*, of the style called *ngosham* ('on a blue ground') shows horses and birds with other finely executed *kushu* patterning. It was woven around 1960-1970 in north central Bhutan. *(Collection of The Textile Museum, Thimphu; Photo: DKM)*

25

Footnotes

[1] Myers and Bean 1994, Chapter Two.

[2] Tibeto-Burman groups in northeast India include the Monpa, Sherdukpen, Bugun, Aka (Hrusso), Dhammai, Memba, Khamba, Mishmi, and Naga. Tibeto-Burman groups in Southeast Asia include the Kachin, Chin, Karen, Lisu, Akha and Lahu.

[3] E.g., *Provincial Gazeteer of Assam* 1906, 60.

[4] Elwin 1959a is still one of the best sources on the peoples, follore, and textiles and other crafts of northeast India. Among Tibeto Burman-language speakers in the larger region, only the Akha and Lahu do not exclusively use a body tension loom.

[5] Gittinger and Lefferts 1992, 30-35. Bhutan, Thailand, and Indonesia also share card looms, but it isn't clear how long the Bhutanese have used this technology, which might also have been introduced from Tibet.

[6] See Elwin 1959a, 5-6 (northeast India); Fraser-Lu 1989, 22-23 (Southeast Asia); and Jacobs 1990, 44-45 (Naga). See also Mueggler 1998 on practices in Yunnan.

[7] Gittinger and Lefferts 1992, 69; also Fraser-Lu 1989, 73.

[8] On Southeast Asia, see Fraser-Lu 1989, 27-28 and Maxwell 1990 (2003), 144-146.

[9] Fraser and Fraser 2005, 52 (figs. 79a and 79b) and 164 (fig 312). I am indebted to Mattiebelle Gittinger for bringing this very recent publication – and the patterning similarity – to my attention in time to mention it here.

[10] E.g., Gavin 2005.

[11] Aris 1990, 85-101.

[12] Myers and Bean 1990, 30-31.

[13] Much of Bhutan's "code of etiquette" concerns the proper ways to wear the national dress and manipulate shoulder cloths to express respect. It also describes proper ways of presenting gifts of cloth. (*Driglam namzhag* 1999) Bhutan formally adopted the *gho* and *kira* as national dress in 1989.

[14] See, e.g., Maxwell 1999, 86, on the Toraja.

[15] Tunic neck openings often show embroidery and appliqué, which typically cover patterns woven into the ground and are assumed to have been added at a later date as the garments took on a strictly ceremonial role. Myers 1995.

[16] However, imported Chinese silks decorated with formal patterns of birds, dragons, and mythological creatures have long been prized luxury items, stitched into men's robes and women's jackets.

[17] Under the patronage of Her Majesty Ashi Sangay Choden Wangchuck, a new appreciation of older textiles has developed in the past decade, and weavers are now reproducing women's garments and multipurpose cloths whose patterns include these motifs. The latter, woven in mulberry silk, are especially popular with tourists.

[18] For example, see Sonam Wangmo 1987, 141-43, for the annual festivities at a mountain that represents the "spiritual place" of Ama Jomo, a goddess/princess who co-founded the settlements of Merak and Sakteng in the 7th century.

[19] See Suriya Smutakupt. 2006. *Female Lower Garment or Holy Manuscript Wrapper? The Role of Women in Buddhist Society.*

References

Aris, Michael. 1990. *Man and Nature in the Buddhist Himalayas.* In Rustomji and Ramble 1990, 85-101.

Baruah, Tapan Kumar M. *The Idu Mishmis.* 1960. Shillong, on behalf of the Adviser to the Governor of Assam.

Cheesman, Patricia. 1988. *Lao Textiles: Ancient Symbols, Living Art.* Bangkok: White Lotus Co., Ltd.

_____. 2004. *Lao-Tai Textiles: The Textiles of Xam Nuea and Muang Phuan.* Bangkok: Studio Naenna Co. Ltd.

Conway, Susan. N.d. *Power Dressing: Lanna Shan Siam 19th Century Court Dress.* Exhibition catalogue. Bangkok: The James H. W. Thompson Foundation.

Dell, Elizabeth and Sandra Dudley, eds. 2002. *Textiles from Burma.* London: Philip Wilson Publishers, in association with The James Green Centre for World Art, Brighton.

Driglam Namzhag (Bhutanese Etiquette): A Manual. 1999. Thimphu, Bhutan: National Library.

Elwin, Verrier. 1959a. *The Art of the Northeast Frontier of India.* Shillong, India: On behalf of the Adviser to the Governor of Assam.

Elwin, Verrier, ed. 1959b. *India's North-East Frontier in the Nineteenth Century.* Madras, India: Oxford University Press.

Fraser, David W. and Barbara G. Fraser. 2005. *Mantles of Merit: Chin Textiles from Myanmar, India and Bangladesh.* Bangkok: River Books.

Fraser-Lu, Sylvia. 1989. *Handwoven Textiles of South-East Asia.* Paperback ed. Singapore: Oxford University Press.

Garner, Deborah Lindsay and Jay Bommer. "On the Trail of Khumi, Khami, and Mro Textiles," *Textile Museum Journal 38 and 39* (1999-2000).

Gavin, Traude. "Language Games: Iban Textile Designs in Their Cultural Context," *HALI 140* (May-June 2005).

Gittinger, Mattiebelle. 1979 (1991). *Splendid Symbols: Textiles and Tradition in Indonesia.* Oxford University Press, with the permission of The Textile Museum, Washington, DC.

Gittinger, Mattiebelle and Leedom Lefferts. 1992. *Textiles and the Tai Experience in Southeast Asia.* Washington, DC: The Textile Museum.

Jacobs, Julian. 1990. *Hill Peoples of Northeast India: The Nagas.* London: Thames and Hudson.

Lehman, F. K. 1963. *The Structure of Chin Society: A Tribal People of Burma Adapted to a Non-Western Civilization.* Illinois Studies in Anthropology No. 3. Urbana: University of Illinois Press.

Marshall, Rev. Harry Ignatious. 1922 (1997). *The Karen People of Burma: A Study in Anthropology and Etnology* (sic). Bangkok: White Lotus Press.

Maxwell, Robyn. 1990 (revised edition, 2003). *Textiles of Southeast Asia: Tradition, Trade and Transformation.* Australian National University and Oxford University Press of Australia.

Mueggler, Erik. The poetics of grief and the price of hemp in southwest China. *Journal of Asian Studies* 57: 4 (Nov. 1998).

Myers, Diana K. "Bhutanese Tunics: The Kushung and Shingkha of Bhutan," *HALI 16* (Dec. 1994/Jan. 1995).

Myers, Diana K. and Susan S. Bean, eds. 1994. *From the Land of the Thunder Dragon: Textile Arts of Bhutan.* Peabody Essex Museum, Salem, MA, and Serindia Publications, London.

Needham, Joseph, ed. 1986. *Society and Civilization in China.* Dieter Kuhn, Vol. V: Part 9, *Textile Technology: Spinning and Reeling.* Cambridge University Press.

Prangwatthanakun, Songsak and Patricia Cheesman. 1988 (second ed.). *Lan Na Textiles: Yuan Lue Lao.* Chiang Mai: Center for the Promotion of Arts and Culture, Chiang Mai University.

Provincial gazeteer of Assam. (1906) 1983. Compiled by Authority, Eastern Bengal and Assam Secretariat. Reprint. New Delhi: Cultural Publishing House.

Rustomji, Nari K. and Charles Ramble, eds. 1990. *Himayalan Environment and Culture.* Shimla: Indian Institute of Advanced Study, and New Delhi: Indus.

Sonam Kinga. 1999. *The Status of Women in Traditional and Modern Bhutan.* Thimphu: The Centre for Bhutan Studies.

Sonam Wangmo. 1990. *The Brokpas: A Semi-Nomadic People in Eastern Bhutan.* Reprint from Rustomji and Ramble 1990. Shimla: Indian Institute of Advanced Study.

Suriya Smutakupt. 2006. *Female Lower Garment or Holy Manuscript Wrapper? The Role of Women in Buddhist Society:* in Puranananda, Jane, ed. *The Secrets of Southeast Asian Textiles - Myth, Status and the Supernatural.*

Weavers for the local nobility of north central Bhutan preserved early design traditions from that region by sometimes incorporating figures of birds and horses in the patterning of very fine women's dresses. These examples are highly valued today. Detail, woman's dress *(kushuthara)*, c. early 20th century.
(Private collection; Photo: DKM)

Spirit Ship and Ships of the Soul
Images on Cambodian Celebratory Textile Hangings

Gillian Green

Cambodian handwoven silk textiles are justly famous. They are used for costume for both men and women and for hangings or canopies in temples. These hangings are patterned with pictorial and narrative themes. While one group of hangings features unambiguously Buddhist themes, there are those with additional enigmatic motifs that do not fit this category and therefore set them apart as a separate group. For the purposes of the hypothesis presented here they are called 'celebratory hangings'. There seem to be a mere handful of these antique textiles surviving in public and private institutions around the globe.

Very surprisingly, nothing has been recorded about their function and so in this article an attempt is made to address this issue. A hypothesis is put forward that the motifs on these celebratory hangings record a number of festivals celebrated in Cambodia at the end of the rainy season, around the end of October or beginning of November each year. The evidence is based on explo-ration of the meaning of individual motifs and groups of motifs and their relationship to historical events and cultural celebrations in Cambodia, and indeed Thailand, at that time of the year.

Researchers have to resort to hypothesis because there appears to be no ethnographic, historic or literary information recorded about the role these textiles may have played in Cambodian life in the nineteenth century, the time of their manufacture. Surprisingly, their characteristic motifs have not reappeared in contemporary weavers' repertoires since that time in contrast with the re-introduction of motifs on those other hangings with Buddhist themes. It is clear, however, that these celebratory hangings have a supra-mundane purpose because of the supreme technical and aesthetic skill invested in their creation.

Notwithstanding this lacuna, there are some certainties. Hangings are patterned by the method of resist dyeing the weft threads prior to weaving, a technique called

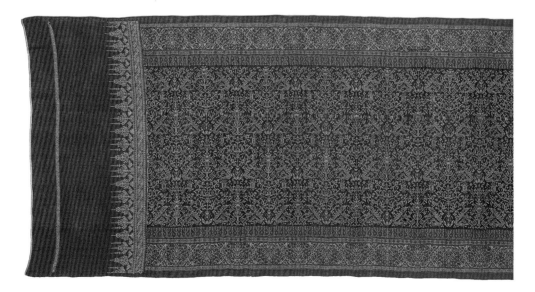

1 Ceremonial/celebratory hanging. 293 X 92 cm. Silk, uneven twill groundweave, resist-dyed weft *hol.* Gold metallic thread supplementary weave in end panels. Central field: Paired *nak*, birds, crabs, and fish, trees of life. A row of alternate three finial and one finial *yantra* appear in the end panels. A pair of birds appears at the base of the three finial *yantra.* Gift of Michael and Mary Abbot 1992.
(Courtesy of the National Gallery of Australia 92.219)

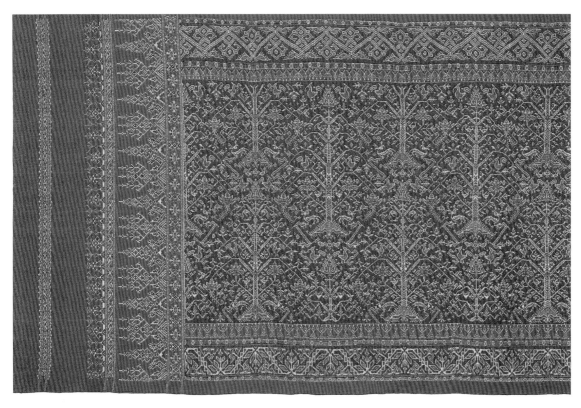

2 Ceremonial/celebratory hanging. 247.5 X 91.5 cm.
Silk, uneven twill groundweave, resist-dyed weft *hol.*
(Courtesy Fukuoka Art Museum)

hol in Khmer language, perhaps more familiar as weft
"ikat" or "*mat mee*" in Thai. Their distinctive 2/1 uneven
twill groundweave identifies them to be the products of
Cambodian weavers.[2] The textiles are said to be a hundred years old but could be much older, at least a half
century older as textiles with these technical characteristics are known to date from at least 1856.

Celebratory hangings are distinguished by the portrayal of a triad of motifs consisting of bird, snake and
tree of life and for the purposes of this argument this
triad defines the group.[3] This triad has an archaic universal cosmological significance by no means limited to
the Cambodian experience. **(1, 2, 3)**. In these hangings
birds sometimes single, sometimes paired, perch at tops
of trees-of-life or flutter either side of these trees accompanied by snakes – either as Cambodian-style *nak* or
Chinese-style dragons – also usually in pairs.
Superimposed on this backdrop in about half of the
textiles so far examined, ships ranging from archaic
Chinese junks and European steamers, to esoteric

3 Detail of fig 2.

29

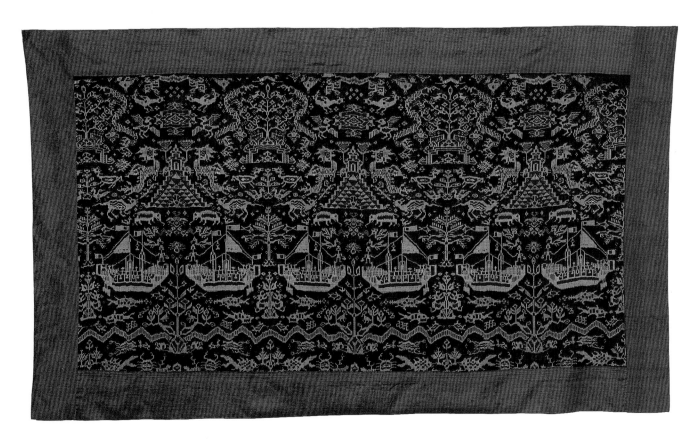

4 Ceremonial/celebratory hanging. Sailing ship style. 195 x 114 cm. Late 19th early 20th C. Silk, uneven twill groundweave, resist-dyed weft *hol*. Central field: The upper section contains two motifs – trees-of-life on a stepped pedestal and patchwork-filled stepped mounds. Each stepped mound has a small pavilion on the summit with two elephant heads peering out. The tree is enclosed by a pair of wavy snakes and the mound by pairs of dragon with (?) wings. Pairs of gold-coloured elephants, deer, butterflies and birds fill the background. A strange almost nomadic tribal motif appears between the trees-of-life in the uppermost register.

In a lower register is a sailing ship with external rudder, raised anchor, two masts, triangular sail, and three bi-coloured flags. A frontal figure stands on the bow holding an anchor in one hand and a length of rope linking him to the sail in the other. Three different pairs of confronted birds appear above the figure's head. Trees-of-life in three forms appear between the ships. Crabs, sawfish, whales, lobsters, fish, turtles, seaweed and flowering branches abound in this marine realm which is indicated by the wavy line. *(Courtesy the Honolulu Academy of Arts, Gift of the Christensen Fund, 2001, HAA11418.1)*

"symbolic" or "archaic" vessels, are depicted.[4] Birds here may be seen perching on the rigging of the ships while the *nak* are either floating free in the composition, often paired, or incorporated as part of the boat or other ritual or architectural structures.[5] Creatures such as crabs, lobsters, rays, and fish species including notably sawfish, appear in the composition indicating a watery environment. Terrestrial animals such as elephants and deer are also sometimes seen **(4, 5)**.

A paper published in 1975 by John Irwin, late head of the Indian and Southeast Collection at the V&A in London has been revelatory to trying to understand this triad and its possible place in the imagery on these textiles.[6] Though his paper sets out to discuss the imagery of the Asokan pillar, it moves into the area of cosmological imagery – the cosmic pillar and its avatars and its relationship to birds and water. Getting to the heart of the matter in a Cambodian context I interpret his discussion in this way. The cosmic pillar arises from the

water below the earth. It links this region to the heavens. A common manifestation of the cosmic pillar is the tree-of-life and in a Buddhist scheme, and amongst its different forms seen on these textiles are mounds, and *stupas* in the form of pagodas. The pillars, in whatever form, are accompanied by a bird or birds, and snakes (*nak*). In Irwin's argument the *hamsa* bird[7] atop the cosmic pillar (or tree-of-life) is instrumental in ensuring that water (the domain of earth spirits in the form of *nak* that reside in the waters from which the cosmic pillar arises) has a pivotal role in the annual cycle of rain and drought. It acts a sort of Master of Ceremonies ensuring that the water taken up into the sky by the sun and stored in clouds is released in the form of rain to sustain the earth.

In terms of the imagery that defines this group of textiles, the hypothesis proposes that the cosmological triad – bird, snake and tree of life – is iconic for this cyclic passage of water. It specifically indicates visually on these textiles that part of the year, usually late October into

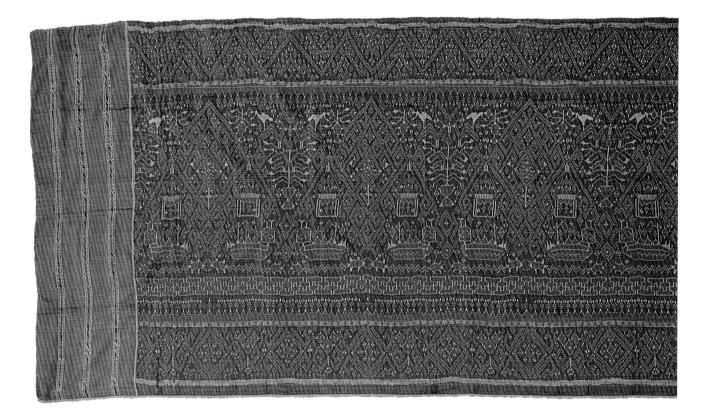

5 Ceremonial/celebratory hanging. Sailing ship and symbolic style ship motifs. 386 x 88 cm. 19th century. Silk, uneven twill ground-weave, resist-dyed weft *hol*. Central field: upper register has bi-conical form with a tree-of-life. Two pairs of birds appear above. Lower register features a ship with a large flag (?) at end. An architectural structure appears above it. Bold panels of "hook and fern" motifs separate each pair of ships. These are probably abstracted *nak* motifs as indicated by the yellow tips to the terminals. Fish and a wavy line representing water. *(Reproduced with permission of the Asian Civilisations Museum, Singapore)*

early November, which coincides with the end of the rainy season and the commencement of the dry season. If this is the case then it implies that these textiles played some role in Cambodian culture at that time.[8] A number of festivals take place at this time. One, with its animist origins, is *loy pratib* the launching of candle-filled model boats which return malevolent spirits to the under-world.[9] This period also coincides with a number of Buddhist celebrations. *Cen vossa* marks the end of the annual Buddhist monks' rainy season retreat. Soon after *the kathin*, the donation of gifts of new robes to the monks, takes place as well as the recitation of the Vessantara Jataka in the temples (*wats*), these being merit-earning occasions for participants.

As mentioned above, some of this group of celebratory hangings feature perhaps the most spectacular examples of Cambodian weaving skill, those with depictions of ships (*pidan rup duk*). While a number of varieties of ships and sailing vessels – named "symbolic",

"archaic" and "realistic" are depicted, the significance of only two forms is examined here.[10] These are motifs representing the model ships in the symbolic group referred to above, and secondly of Chinese-style junks and European steamers in the realistic group.

With regard to the model ships **(6, 7, 8)** in Thailand and Cambodia miniature ships made of banana leaves or bark loaded with candles, incense, food and textiles are launched on the swollen rivers at the end of the rainy season. Their purpose is to rid the community of evil spirits.[11] This practice reflects a cultural complex shared by communities as geographically diverse as China, mainland and insular Southeast Asia, Melanesia and Polynesia. So in hangings such as these it may be said that these textiles illustrate the setting adrift of these model boats.

With the second group, "realistic" ships be they Chinese-, Malay- or Thai-style junks or European steamers – evidence is now presented that in their case

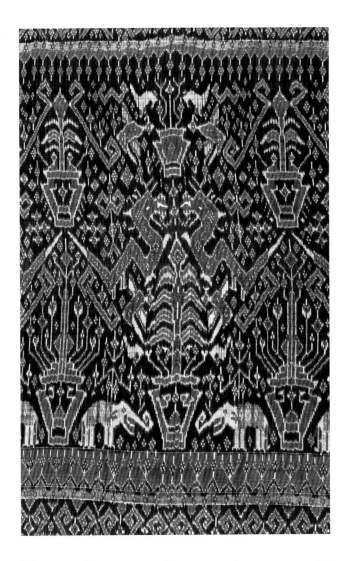

6 Ceremonial/celebratory hanging. Archaic ship style. Late 19th century. 294.6 X 83.8 cm. Silk, uneven twill groundweave, resist-dyed weft *hol*. Central field: upper register has model ships with tree-of-life masts and pairs of confronted birds. Pairs of confronted *nak* beneath. Lower register model ships one bearing incense alternates with one with a tree-of-life mast. Pairs of confronted elephants.
(Courtesy Edwina Nelon. Photograph Jim Nelon)

7 Ceremonial/celebratory hanging. Archaic ship style. 332 x 97 cm. Early 20th century. Silk, uneven twill groundweave, resist-dyed weft *hol*. Central field: upper register composed of two pairs of confronted *nak* each enclosing two large eyes (?). Middle register has a row of model ships loaded with incense or candles, possibly with *nak* head terminals. Lower register contains archaic ships with a superstructure enclosing a pair of confronted birds.
(Courtesy Tilleke and Gibbins 852CD)

8 Ceremonial/celebratory hanging. Archaic ship style. 333 X 94 cm, 19th century. Silk, uneven twill groundweave, resist-dyed weft *hol*. *(Courtesy Vichai and Lee J Chinalai)*

9 Ceremonial/celebratory hanging. Sailing ship style. Late 19th century. 243 x 150 cm (with border); 1.93 x 0.98 m (patterned section only). Silk, uneven twill groundweave, resist-dyed weft *hol*. Central field: the composition of this cloth consists of two similar principal repeat registers. Each register contains two component sub-registers. One is a sailing ship with masts, sails, small cabin, trailing dinghy and anchor and a pavilion beneath this. Pairs of dragons confront each other either side of the pavilion; paired birds perch either side; while a tree-of-life on a mound with a pair of confronted lions (?) deer and a tiny pair of green elephants between the pavilions. Birds perch on the lions' backs. A *phka ben* separates the sailing ships in the middle of the field. Pairs of birds, fish and sawfish abound, many of the birds perched on the ships. A row of *yantras* in supplementary weft forms a band between the central field and the end panels. *(Courtesy Vichai and Lee J Chinalai)*

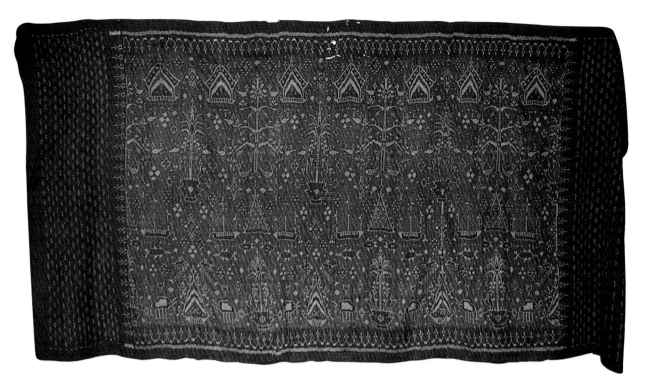

11 Detail of fig. 10.

10 Ceremonial/celebratory hanging. Sailing ship and symbolic ship style motifs. 188 x 92 cm. Late 19th century. Silk, uneven twill groundweave, resist-dyed weft *hol*. Central field: top register: simplified (?) *nak* headed (archaic style) ships/temples with central superstructure. Second register: trees-of-life on a mound alternating with model ships with central tree-masts and candles and incense; paired birds. Stars. Third register: sailing ships alternating with *phka ben*. Lowest register: model ships with central tree-masts alternating with? *Phka ben*/ships. Pairs of confronted *nak* and elephants. Stars, fish and saw fish appear in the background. *(Courtesy Patricia Cheesman)*

there is a completely different context to which they could belong while retaining that unifying link to the end of the rainy season ceremonies. Here, the events in which they play a celebratory role are more closely aligned with Buddhist belief yet retaining that animist backdrop **(9, 10, 11, 12)**.

The starting point of this research was a search for images which Cambodian weavers could have used as models for their masterly portrayal of these realistic historical ships. Rural women weavers would have needed to see images or indeed the real thing to have portrayed them in the minute detail with which they were depicted, especially in the fiendishly difficult technique of weft *hol*. Where could these models have been found? Mural paintings with images of ships at anchor on coastlines and estuaries are found in one particular Cambodian temple Wat Chadotes near Udong, the seat of the Cambodian royal court just prior to its relocation to Phnom Penh, forty kilometres to the south. **(13, 14, 15)**. They are dated to 1867. Realistic sailing vessels, both

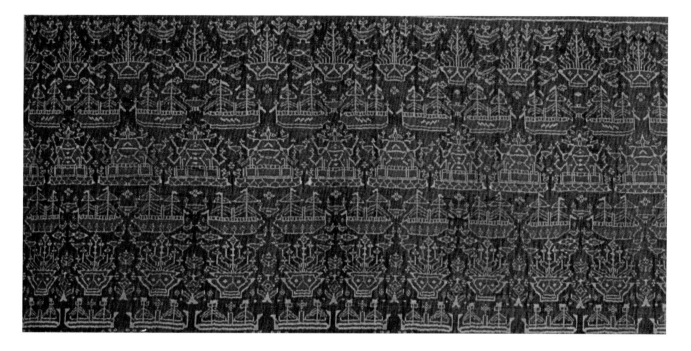

12 Ceremonial/celebratory hanging. Sailing ship and symbolic ship style. 182.9 x 81.9 cm. Early 20th C. Silk, uneven twill groundweave, resist-dyed weft *hol.* Central field: divided into two halves by a row of terrestrial pavilion structures along the warp axis. Upper section: top register has a row of model ships with candles and/or incense sticks. Either side and above are pairs of confronted birds and a pair of fish. Below this is a row of sailing ships with two masts.

Lower section: row of two-masted sailing ships with sails; pairs of fish and birds. Below this is a register of model ships with candles and/or incense with pairs of birds perched each side. Small tree-of-life in between. Below is a register of two-masted sailing ships with sails and flags. *(Courtesy Edwina Nelon. Photograph Jim Nelon)*

foreign as well as local dug out canoes, are depicted on these murals. In 1861 Henri Mouhot remarked on the numbers of Chinese junks and European ships in the Cambodian port of Kampot; and in 1922 George Groslier published a photo of a Chinese junk stranded high and dry in K. Chhnang also on the Sap River north of Udong a long way from the coast. So Cambodia, a country not noted for being a sea faring nation, does have ship images in place as well serving as a busy port of call for ships during the nineteenth century. An 1820 water colour by a European visitor shows that similar ships – Chinese junks and European style vessels sailed on the Chao Phraya River of Bangkok.[12]

Having identified some possible models, what was the reason that their images were woven into hangings? My proposition is based on textual evidence. This suggests that at least through the 19th century, more or less the likely age of these ship cloths, they may actually have commemorated Buddhist ritual and notions which share an association with ships at a material and spiritual level. The *ritual* refers to the reading of the Vessantara Jataka. And the *notion* refers to the transcendental "golden ships" which carry the sentient beings across the river of Samsara to Nirvana on the further shore.

What is the evidence for these associations? Gerolamo Gerini, an Italian military officer was a prolific recorder of Thai customs during his sojourn in the kingdom starting in 1881.[13] In 1892 he published a manuscript entitled "A retrospective view and account of the origin of the Thet Maha Chat ceremony or Exposition of the tale of the Great Birth as performed in Siam".[14] He notes that it had become the custom to recite the Vessantara Jataka at the end of the rainy season, at the end of the Buddhist retreat which concluded with the ceremony of *cen vossa*.

The importance of the recitation of the Jataka derives from Buddhist belief that Buddhists who desire to be reborn in the epoch of Maitreya, the Buddha of the Future, should attend recitations of the Vessantara Jataka as a way of attaining greater merit, sufficient to allow rebirth in this auspicious period. Gerini remarked that maybe this was the true reason why the exposition of this Jataka became so popular.

Traditionally the recitation was performed by a fully ordained monk in the temple but a novice could perform this rite for his family. This was a very meritorious act. By the nineteenth century if a crown prince became a novitiate, he would be called upon to undertake this

13 Mural, 19th century, Wat Chadotes, Cambodia.
(Courtesy Maisonneuve & Larose – Editions UNESCO)

14 Mural, 19th century, Wat Chadotes, Cambodia.
(Courtesy Maisonneuve & Larose – Editions UNESCO)

momentous task. Royal recitations occurred on three recorded occasions, in 1817, 1866 and 1891. A central feature of these rites was the construction of conically-shaped, layered, ritual offering tower (*krachat*), on which gifts to monks were placed prior to donation. On the latter two occasions life-size models of Chinese junks were constructed on which the *krachat* were sited in the same position that masts would appear in an ocean-going vessel. Another model junk constructed in masonry by royal decree of King Phra Nang Klao (r. 1824-1851) at Wat Yannawa in the Bangrak district of Bangkok, still exists today. The explanatory panel at this *wat* reads "[the monument] *sampao chedi* [junk and *stupa*] was built during the reign of King Rama III because His Majesty was concerned that the ship would become obsolete" **(16)**. It seems that the imagery implicit in these model ships filled with gifts symbolises the spirit of giving, the message of the Vessantara Jataka. Also embedded in the imagery could be a subtle signifier of prestige gifts imported from abroad by foreign ships.

There is a second context which employs a ship motif relating to a more transcendental aspect of Buddhist belief. "It [the ship] is metaphorically speaking the vehicle which will enable human beings to cross the ocean of rebirth, affliction and death, [Samsara] and reach a safe and peaceful haven [Nirvana]. It is built very differently from mundane, seagoing crafts. These – like all material and worldly things – perish ... but the 'Golden Vessel of the Law' is imperishable."[15] A ship in the image of a junk appears as one of the devices contained in the twenty first of 108 squares on the sole of the Buddhapada at Wat Pho in Bangkok. There is an aspect of the Vessantara Jataka which links it with the transcendental ship. In the eighth canto of one version of this Jataka, Prince Vessantara likens his accumulated perfections metaphorically to the structural features of the golden celestial boat with which he will cross the river of Samsara to Nirvana. "As a matter of course new features were gradually introduced into modern [nineteenth century] versifications of this passage of the [Vessantara Jataka] and in a measure as shipping progressed, the golden Vessel of the Law, was also improved in fittings and appearance ... when it was depicted as a Chinese junk, down to the present time [1892 CE], it passed through numerous transformations, and became successively a square rigged vessel, a frigate, a paddle steamer, a screw steamer, and an iron clad ..."[16]

Can these events and notions support the hypothesis concerning the function of Cambodia celebratory hangings, particularly those with ship images? Perhaps those cloths with the triad simply signified celebrations which

15 Mural, 19th century, Wat Chadotes, Cambodia. *(Courtesy Maisonneuve & Larose – Editions UNESCO)*

16 Model Chinese junk, rendered masonry (?). C. 1824-1851.
Wat Yannawa, Bangrak, Bangkok.

occurred at the end of the rainy season. Those with model ships recorded animist rituals at that time. Those with realistic ship motifs represented both the material ships with gifts and/or the transcendental golden ship of transmigration. Both these latter metaphors are expressions of Buddhist beliefs with an explicit connection with the Vessantara Jataka recited at that time.

That the weavers were Cambodian is evidenced by the technique with which the cloths were woven. The models that Cambodian weavers could have employed when called on to create these cloths were in place. There are those murals in a Cambodian temple at Udong and the ships that sailed into Kampot and other Cambodian locations. A small number of Cham Cambodian weavers renowned for their silk weft *hol* lived at Kampot. And of course there are the famous Cham Cambodian weavers who lived in Bangkok, near the Jim Thompson house, Bangkok was the port of call of ships of all kinds that visited on trading missions in the nineteenth century and for centuries earlier.

It is well attested to that Cambodian weavers, be they Khmer or Cham, wove silk *sampot hol chawng kbun* to order for the Thai court. So it is not too far a stretch of the hypothesis to suggest that these weavers may have been commissioned to create these cloths for use as mementoes or even backdrops for both Cambodian and Siamese end of rainy season celebrations. Whether these cloths were commissioned solely for the occasions of major royal events mentioned above in either or both kingdoms, or whether they were woven as part of annual ritual practice in a wider social context, can only be speculated on.

Whatever their history, it is easy to agree on the superb skill demonstrated by their weavers. Whatever the context, these few hardy survivors encode cultural practices that encompass archaic animist and contemporaneous Buddhist ritual which illuminate life in mainland Southeast Asia in the nineteenth century.

Bibliography

Gerini, G. (1892), *A Retrospective View and Account of the Origin of the Thet Maha Chat Ceremony or Exposition of the Tale of the Great Birth as Performed in Siam*, Bangkok Times Office, Bangkok.

Ginsburg, H. (2000). *Thai Art and Culture*, Silkworm Books, Bangkok.

Green G. (2003). *Traditional Textiles of Cambodia*, River Books, Bangkok.

__ "Spirit Ships. Ancient Images on Cambodian Narrative Textiles", *Arts of Asia*, May/June 2005: pp. 38-47.

Irwin J. (1976). 'Asokan' pillars: A Reassessment of the Evidence – 1V: Symbolism". Reprinted from the *Burlington Magazine*, Vol. CXVIII, November: pp. 733-753.

Nafilyan J. & G. (1997). *Peintures Murales, des Monasteres Bouddhiques au Cambodge*, Maisonneuve & Larose Editions UNESCO.

Footnotes

[1] Italics indicate transliterated Khmer language words.

[2] Neven twill weave is a ground-weave where a weft pick floats over two consecutive warps in a group of three then under the third, this repeated with the succeeding groups of three. This is notated as 2/1. This sequence may be recognised by two characteristics. One is that the crossing points of warp and weft become diagonally aligned with each successive weft pick. The second results in one third of the warp being visible on one side of the fabric and two thirds on the reverse. The opposite holds for the wefts. If the colours of warp and weft threads differ, this means that one face of the cloth reflects the colour of the proportionally dominant thread on that side and vice versa.

[3] The tree of life, stupas, pagodas, and Mount Meru are some of the representations of the cosmic pillar.

[4] Gillian Green, "*Traditional Textiles of Cambodia*" (2003): pp. 269-302.
__ "Spirit Ships. Ancient Images on Cambodian Narrative Textiles", *Arts of Asia*, May/June 2005: pp 38-47. In these publications I had defined this group solely on the basis of their ship motifs. This excluded a number of textiles which shared the triad of motifs but did not depict ships. The role of those cloths discussed in those publications is therefore extended here to include this group. The new extended group has been given the name of 'celebratory hangings'. The description of "symbolic", "archaic" and "realistic" is given in these publications.

[5] Comparison with other Cambodian silk textile patterns confirms the distinguishing motif details which characterise this group. While some hipwrappers *sampot* may have *nak* motifs they do not have accompanying birds and while other hangings may have birds in the pattern, they are not accompanied by snakes *nak*.

[6] John Irwin, 'Asokan' pillars: A Reassessment of the Evidence – 1V: Symbolism". Reprinted from the *Burlington Magazine*, Vol. CXVIII, November 1976: pp. 733-753.

[7] The *hamsa* bird is also called '*hong*'.

[8] In the cultural practices of its closest neighbours Thailand and Laos the end of rainy season is also the time of many celebrations.

[9] *Loy pratib* is called *loy kratong* in Thailand and Laos.

[10] Gillian Green, "*Traditional Textiles of Cambodia*" (2003): pp. 269-302.

[11] This custom, myth relates, was introduced by the Brahmin wife of a Siamese king, centuries ago.

[12] Henry Ginsburg, *Thai Art and Culture*, Silkworm Books (2000), p. 33.

[13] Gerini was a co-founder of the Siam Society in 1904.

[14] The terms '*mahachat*'; 'Great Birth'; and *Vetsandon* (in Thai language) refer to the Vessantara Jataka.

[15] Gerini, G. (1892). *A retrospective view and account of the origin of the Thet Maha Chat ceremony or Exposition of the tale of the Great Birth as performed in Siam*": 51.

Rama, Rajas and Courtesans
Indian Figurative Textiles in Indonesia

John Guy

All the clothes and things from Gujarat have trading value in Malacca, and in the kingdoms which trade with Malacca, Gujarati cloths were the most highly valued, followed by Bengali white cloths and all those from Coromandel.[1]

The earliest surviving evidence for Indian textiles in Southeast Asia appears in the form a of series of large painted cotton cloths produced in western India and recovered from the islands of Indonesia. In this paper I wish to present a group of early textiles found in Indonesia and review their significance against the archaeological record and the backdrop of historical trade, specifically the seminal role of Gujarati merchants in the growth of the Indian textiles-for-spices trade. The key Indian textile production centres for the Asian trade were western India, Bengal in the east, and the central and southern regions of the Coromandel Coast. For the textile trade to Southeast Asia the oldest group of Indian trade cloths which have survived are predominantly from Gujarat. The legacy of these cloths in Indonesia and their impact on regional textile traditions will be assessed, and some directions for further research suggested.

The presence of these cloths in rural communities in island Indonesia raises key questions – how were they used and what does that tells us about the ceremonial life and interests of those who owned such cloths. Do these cloths represent 'lost' textile designs no longer recorded in the Indian subcontinent, or were they made expressly for export as trade goods to Southeast Asia and therefore do not strictly constitute part of the Indian home market textile repertoire? It is certainly the case that they constitute an otherwise unrecorded body of Indian textile art. They very probably belong to a broader tradition of painted cotton display cloths, notably banners and narrative cloths intended to serve as a screen or backdrop on ceremonial occasions, or for theatrical performances.

These Gujarati textiles are readily identified. Their fibre, weave and dying techniques clearly belong in the western Indian cotton weaving tradition: the fabric is typically a coarse-weave reverse-spun cotton, variously dyed with a mordanted red lac or madder (providing a red ground), iron black (the block printed outline design) and a resist-dyed indigo blue. Their designs – though demonstrably western Indian – are not recorded in textiles surviving from the Indian sub-continent. Whether these types of cloths were ever produced for a home market is far from clear. In all probability they were, but the vicissitudes of the Indian subcontinent's history and climate have ensured that nothing remains. The designs preserved on these cloths relate to pictorial and stylistic traditions firmly belonging to the medieval art traditions of western India, and specifically Gujarat (1). Some of these links will be outlined, with dated analogies provided.

A number of these cloths have been subjected to accelerated radiocarbon 14 analysis, thereby establishing a series of calibrated date ranges which places the earliest extant group from Indonesia in the fourteenth and fifteenth centuries. These are not only the oldest securely dated textiles from Southeast Asia, they are also among the earliest dated Indian textiles extant. These dates, remarkably early for textiles surviving in a tropical environment, also raise the possibility that some other indigenous textiles produced in the region may also date from similarly early periods. This has radical implications for our understanding of the dating and survival of cloth in Southeast Asia.

Textiles in trade sources

Indian textiles have probably been traded to Southeast Asia for as long as Indian merchants are known to have sailed east. Early traders to Southeast Asia were high-risk adventurers in search of a common objective: a reliable and affordable source of the region's spices – cloves,

Detail (opposite page) of a ceremonial banner cloth, with a repeat design of a woman with parrot. Gujarat, for the Indonesian market. Painted mordant-dyed and resist-dyed cotton. Radio-carbon dated 1468 ± 45 years. Detail of (12).
(Collection H. & H. Neumann, Switzerland)

1 Relief decoration depicting designs familiar from textile samples. Queen Udayamati's stepwell, Raniki Vav, Gujarat, last quarter of the 11th century. *(Photo: John Guy)*

2 Fragment of Gujarati block-printed cotton with floral design, recovered at Fostat, Egypt. 14th-15th century. *(Cleveland Museum of Art)*

3 Detail of a geometric floral pattern cloth in the Gujarati-*patola* tradition. Block-printed cotton, probably produced on the Coromandel coast for the Indonesian market, c. 18th century. *(Photograph courtesy of Mary Kahlenberg, Sante Fe)*

nutmeg and mace – together with black pepper which originated in the Malabar Coast of south-west India. The spices were the exclusive products of a few isolated islands in eastern Indonesia, and Indian pepper was introduced to western Indonesia by around the tenth century, principally to supply the China market.

A key commodity used in the exchange system was Indian cloth. This took a number of forms. The luxurious Bengal muslin (evocatively described as 'woven air') that Pliny complained was impoverishing Rome undoubtedly also found its way to courts of Southeast Asia and China in the early centuries of the C. E. Evidence is scarce for the first millennium C. E., but the presence of Muslim and Hindu merchants in the port cities of Southeast Asia and China strongly points to Indian textiles circulating at this time.[2] The appearance of the term *gu bei* or *ji bei* for cotton in Chinese sources of the sixth century is significant, as it derives from the Malay *kapas,* itself a corruption of the Sanskrit word for cotton, *karpasa.* Around this time a Chinese term for cotton cloth – *thu lu pu* – a transliteration of the Sanskrit *tula* ('woven cloth') also appears in the record. These linguistic borrowings point to both Southeast Asian and Chinese cotton cloth in the middle first millennium being closely associated with India. Southeast Asia was also producing – and weaving – indigenous cotton by this time, but the elite would have expected to dress in Indian cotton, the finest available in the early Asian world.

The thirteenth century provides two Chinese sources of seminal importance for our understanding of the Indian cloth trade to both China and Southeast Asia. Zhao Rukua, the harbour-master of the port of Quanzhou (Marco Polo's 'Zayton') in Fujian, recorded in his *Zhufan zhi* ('Description of Barbarian Peoples') that 'foreign cloth' *(fan bu)* was available in his port, and lists the regions of India supplying cotton goods as Gujarat, Malwa, Malabar and the Coromandel Coast.[3] Other sources distinguish white and patterned cloths. At the close of the century Zhou Daguan, the Chinese observer of the royal city of Angkor, recorded that at the Khmer court "preference [was] given to the Indian weaving for its skill and delicacy."[4] Much of this trade was channelled through Srivijaya, the entrepot situated on the east coast of Sumatra. Arabic literature reveals that Arabic-speaking mariners and merchants were trading in western Indonesian waters from around the sixth century, and formed significant expatriate communities in the ports of the Malay peninsula and southern China during the later centuries of the first millennium.[5]

The emerging dominance of West Asian merchants is most clearly demonstrated by the widespread use of Arabic as the mariner's *lingua franca* for the Asian maritime diaspora, and by the swiftness with which the Arab Caliphate gold *dinar* established itself as the trading region's common currency. The *dinar* secured this position soon after its introduction in 695 and maintained it, largely unchallenged, until the eleventh century when Chinese copper coinage usurped its position. Gold *dinars* have been recovered along the entire maritime trade route, from the Persian Gulf to Sri Lanka, Champa and China, along with examples of Persian Gulf glazed pottery, most notably turquoise and green glazed earthenware jars now associated with the Basra region of Iraq.[6] The Arab (and Indian) *dhow* and the Malay *phrau* came to dominate the Asian sea trade, and it was these vessels which were instrumental in the distribution of Indian textiles to the remotest corners of insular Southeast Asia.

4   The corpse of Prince Tamu Umbu Huki Landu-djama 'lying-in-state' in the ceremonial house at Prai Yawang, Rindi, East Sumba, Indonesia, shrouded in Indian trade textiles, a Gujarati silk *patola* and a cotton block-printed *patola*-imitation, August 2005. *(Photograph courtesy of Georges Breguet)*

5 Detail of a ceremonial skirt-cloth *(dodot)*, with a patch-work design. Coromandel coast, for the Indonesian market. Painted mordant-dyed and resist-dyed cotton. *(Victoria and Albert Museum, London (IS 41-1988))*

A useful barometer of the geographical scope of Muslim traders is the distribution of tombstones belonging to members of their communities. From the fourteenth century, Gujarati white marble tombstones began appearing in Sumatra and Java (and elsewhere in the Indian Ocean diaspara), a clear indicator of the presence and sustained contact of Gujarati traders in the region. The dedications record that many of the tombstones were used by Gujarati and other Indians who had settled in Southeast Asia. One was Malik Ibrahim (d. 1419), an Indian Muslim who held high office in Gresik, Java, and another, Na'ina Hussam al-Din ibn Na'ina Amin, a Tamilian Kling merchant buried at Pasai, northern Sumatra.[7] In addition to the invaluable biographical information these tombstones yield on the ethnicity of these expatriate merchants, the designs which decorate these dated monuments also serve as a touchstone of motifs and styles prevalent at the time. Flowering trees and plantain are favoured devices, both of which are a recurring motif in the trade cloth repertoire **(6-8)**.

The surviving textile record itself makes it clear that the early Indian textile trade extended from the Red Sea to the Indonesian islands, with western India at the hub of this exchange. The fourteenth and fifteenth century radiocarbon 14 dated cloths presented in this paper bear witness to this trade. The pattern and mechanics of trade are vividly described at the beginning of the sixteenth century by Tomé Pires (d. 1540), an employee of the Portuguese Asian empire. Pires wrote the most detailed account of the Indian Ocean trade whilst stationed at Melaka (Malacca), newly conquered by the Portuguese in 1511. He was able to observe first-hand the interde-

pendence of the trading system, and the central role that Indian textiles played in securing supplies of Malukan (Moluccan) spices.

The axial role played by two great Asian ports, the Gujarati port of Cambay in western India and Melaka on the Malay peninsula, was clearly recognised by Pires in his *Suma Oriental*, which records his observations and insights for the period of his Melakan residency, 1511 to 1514:

> *Cambay chiefly stretches out her two arms, with her right arm she reaches out towards Aden, and with the other towards Malacca...Malacca cannot live without Cambay, nor Cambay without Malacca, if they are to be very rich and very prosperous. [From Gujarat] they bring cloths of thirty kinds, which are of value in these parts.*[8]

Arabs and Gujarati Muslims had a secure hold over the Western Indian Ocean and Arabian Sea trade, controlling the lucrative Persian Gulf and Red Sea routes. A great variety of goods travelled those routes, the major commodities being spices and semi-precious stones, printed textiles and dyestuffs employed in local textile production. The latter included Indian indigo (for blue) and lac (for red), together with sappanwood, itself an import from Southeast Asia. Many of these textiles were gathered from the Gujarati hinterland for international sale via Cambay (and its successor port in the seventeenth century, Surat), for shipment to the Red Sea ports to service the Arabian peninsula and Egyptian markets, and to the marts of Southeast Asia where they could be exchanged for the Malukan spices and forest products of the region. Cambay then was a crucial link in the chain of exchange that stretched from the Red Sea to Southeast Asia. From Melaka, where Pires claims a thousand Gujarati merchants lived and some four or five thousand Gujarati seamen visited each season, Indian textiles were disseminated throughout the Southeast Asian and East Asian trading network. Pires tells us that Gujarati Muslim traders:

> *have factors [agents] everywhere, who live and set up business... in places like Bengal, Pegu, Siam, Pedir, Kedah... there is no place where you do not see Gujarati merchants. Gujarati ships come to these kingdoms every year, one ship straight to each place.*[9]

In the preceding century, the sultans of Melaka had strengthened their place as the leading regional entrepot, successor to Srivijaya and rival to Banten, the great spice mart on Java's western coast. The adoption of Islam by Raja Kecil Besar in 1430 further hastened his port-city's integration into the greater Islamic trading system.

The largest and probably the oldest export market for the Gujarati textile weavers and dyers lay in the Arab lands. Archaeological finds of Gujarati printed cotton textiles in Lower Egypt - most in burial contexts - and at port locations such as Qusier al-Qadim on the Red Sea, point to an extensive and protracted international trade system at work in the pre-Islamic and early Islamic periods, in all probability dating from the early centuries C.E. **(2, 8, 13)**. A comparison with the decorative repertoire seen in medieval Gujarati architecture makes it clear that the designs of these export cloths were part of a shared vocabulary. The Queen's bathing place at Raniki Vav, northern Gujarat, dated to the late eleventh century **(1)**, rich in stonework patterns directly comparable to textiles of this and succeeding centuries, provides the most spectacular example of this.

Cloths destined for the Red Sea trade carry many designs now familiar from Indian trade cloths sourced in Southeast Asia. A Fostat fragment depicting intersecting circles and flowers has elements which were preserved in later Indonesian market cloths **(2)**; similarly a Sumatran-provenanced Indian cloth with a geometricized *patola*-inspired floral design belongs to a design tradition which leads straight back to the Queen's step-well at Raniki Vav **(1 and 3)**.[10] The dyed cottons of Gujarat were clearly exported to both markets, and in the pre-1500 period largely shared the same designs. The Indian textiles archaeologically recovered in Egypt with radiocarbon-14 dates span from the ninth century to the fifteenth.[11] The earliest radiocarbon-14 dates for Southeast Asian-provenanced examples established so far are from the fourteenth century. There is no reason to doubt that they were traded earlier and that their historical distribution paralleled the Red Sea trade. After all, ninth-century western Indonesia was already a prosperous and highly developed region and an important hub on the interna-

7 Detail of a ceremonial skirt-cloth *(dodot)*, with a forested landscape design. Gujarat, for the Indonesian market. Painted mordant-dyed and resist-dyed cotton. Radio-carbon dated 1457 ± 60 years. *(Collection H. & H. Neumann, Switzerland)*

8 Fragment of Gujarati block-printed cotton with wooded landscape design, recovered at Fostat, Egypt. Late 14th century. *(Photograph AEDTA, no.1355, Riboud Collection, Musee Guimet, Paris)*

9 Heirloom trade textiles *(maa')* displayed from communal house eaves during a Christian funerary ceremony, Tana Toradja, central Sulawesi, Indonesia, 1976. *(Photograph courtesy of Koninklijk Instituut voor de Tropen, Amsterdam)*

10 Illustration from a Vesanta Sutra manuscript, Gujarat. Gouache on paper, c.1500. *(Freer Gallery of Art, Smithsonian Institution, Washington)*

tional maritime trade routes.

In Egypt the Indian textiles that have survived are in fragmentary form, and have mostly been recovered in burial contexts, indicating their use as burial shrouds. Undoubtedly they had served as garments for the living and for use as domestic décor before being used to shroud the dead. Interesting parallels can be drawn with contemporary Indonesia where Indian textiles of heirloom status are still used to shroud the dead, as witnessed in 2005 at Rindi, eastern Sumba **(4)**. The deceased raja of Rindi, when laid-in-state for a period of public mourning, was draped in Indian trade textiles, heirloom objects of the royal household. This high-status funeral attracted some 3000 people from all the regions of Sumba, and horses as well as buffaloes were sacrificed.[12]

Cloths for the Raja Sultan

A relatively late Indian trade cloth from the western Indonesian market and attributed to the eighteenth century, has as its centrefield a patchwork design, providing a veritable catalogue of trade cloth patterns **(5)**. Cloths made of patchwork have a long tradition in the Islamic world as talismanic garments, typically worn by rulers and by warriors going into battle. This practise found its way into the repertoire of court dress in Central Java, as seen in the *kyahi antakusuma*, an heirloom jacket worn by the sultans of Yogyakarta to ward off evil and illness. The Indian painted version of this design is embodied in a *dodot*, an over-sized skirt-cloth, expressly designed for Javanese court use. Almost certainly then, this patchwork design was intended to carry these same protective messages.

The vast majority of Indian textiles traded to Southeast Asia were intended for personal attire. A glimpse into the inventory records of the European trading companies makes this clear. Most were in the form of untailored lengths of cloth of uniform dimensions that served as waist-cloth *(kain panjang)* or shoulder cloth *(selengdang)*. However, what distinguishes the majority of the earliest extant trade cloths is that they were intended to serve functions other than dress. Their proportions, scale and disposition of their designs all point to these cloths being better suited to display.

Precisely how these cloths were used in the past remains opaque – we have no pictorial depictions or literary descriptions of how they were intended to be used. Modern ethnographies provide a level of understanding of their use in the recent past, as witnessed by the work of Hetty Nooy-Palm amongst the Sadan Toraja of central Sulawesi, Ruth Barnes in Lamalena and Penelope Graham in eastern Flores.[13] Nooy-Palm identified some trade cloths displayed as architectural décor of communal houses and mounted as banners or standards on tall bamboo poles **(9)**. The single richest area for preserving these early trade cloths appears to be the Sulawesi interior, most notably among the Sa'dan Toraja people, who treasure these *maa'* cloths as heirloom objects. According to the fieldwork of Nooy-Palm these cloths were ascribed spiritual powers and were carefully preserved, only to be displayed for important religious festivals, most notably the annual *merok* thanksgiving ceremony when offerings are made in appreciation of the year past and buffalo sacrifices performed to ensure prosperity in the next.[14] Significantly, this category of foreign textile finds a place in local creation myths,

46

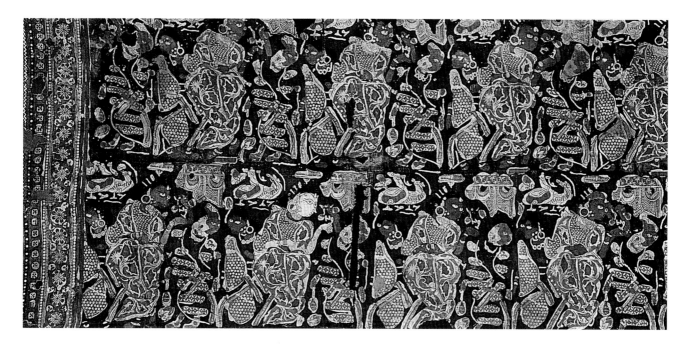

11 Ceremonial banner cloth, with a repeat design of a woman with parrot. Gujarat, for the Indonesian market. Painted mordant-dyed and resist-dyed cotton. Radio-carbon dated 1370 ± 40 years. *(Victoria and Albert Museum, London (IS 95-1993))*

where they are assigned various supernatural roles. *Maa'* cloth are remembered in myth as having arrived in the lands of the Sa'dan Toraja from "across the sea", thus acknowledging their exotic nature.[15] Central Sulawesi in the pre-colonial period was served by the early kingdom of Luwu, on the southern arm of the island, and these cloths were most probably imported through this centre.

Landscape cloths

Amongst the most spectacular trade cloths discovered in Indonesia to date is a Gujarati painted cotton decorated with wonderously stylised wooded landscape (6). A variety of plant-life is depicted: flowering trees, plantains, mango and date palm can be discerned in the landscape, and echo pictorial conventions seen in western Indian manuscript painting of the period (10).[16]

Radiocarbon-14 dating places this textile in the late fourteenth - fifteenth century, contemporary with many of the comparable Gujarati textiles recovered from the Red Sea-Fustat region, including fragmentary examples with closely comparable designs (8). Such a large and weighty cloth was not designed to be worn. Rather, it is a rare survivor of the early trade in display cloths from India to Indonesia. This cloth is large scale – the half section preserved in the Victoria and Albert Museum measures 1 metre in height, by 5 metres in length. It is evident from the continuous design on the upper salvage

that the pattern extended onto another section of the same dimensions, creating an overall design of 2 x 5 metres, far too large to be worn. This was a display cloth of impressive proportions.

The courtesans

Indonesia has yielded a significant number of large display cloths decorated with a frieze of female figures. The earliest examples have the design repeated over two registers; the later versions have a single register of full height figures (cf. 11, 14). These cloths are in a style that can most immediately be linked to the western Indian painting of Gujarat and Rajasthan. The stylisations of human form and costume treatment that characterises this style are the most distinctive feature of this genre of painted cloth. The figures are depicted frontally but with the face in three-quarter profile, with a projecting second eye which extends beyond the silhouette. This convention has a long tradition in Indian painting and does not disappear until Mughal conventions of naturalism become dominant in the sixteenth century.

The oldest group from Indonesia, again radiocarbon-14 dated to the fifteenth century, all have their baseline design laid out by the repeat use of a wood block pattern. This has been used to print the iron-black outline, which has then been hand-coloured with a combination of moranted red and resist-dyed indigo blue, both rather casually applied with only cursory regard for the printed design. The summary and rough style of their execution suggests that these cloths had a secure market in Southeast Asia; it is unlikely that such rough work

12 Ceremonial banner cloth, with a repeat design of a woman with parrot. Gujarat, for the Indonesian market. Painted mordant-dyed and resist-dyed cotton. Radio-carbon dated 1468 ± 45 years.
(Collection H. & H. Neumann, Switzerland)

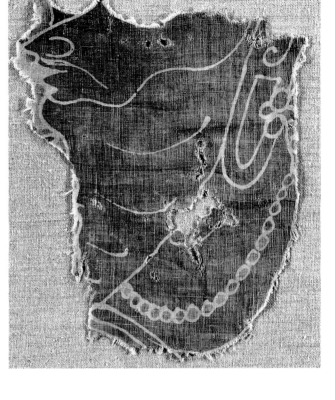

13 Fragment of Gujarati block-cotton with a female face design, recovered at Fostat, Egypt. 14th-15th century.
(Cleveland Museum of Art)

14 Detail of a ceremonial banner cloth, with a repeat design of a woman holding a parrot and stringed instrument. Gujarat, for the Indonesian market, with *devanagari* inscription. Painted mordant-dyed and resist-dyed cotton. *(Jyuraku Collection, City Museum, Kobe)*

would have been accepted in the discerning Indian home market. They are also uniformly painted with a red ground, as are so many of the early trade cloths. This is certainly a factor of technology – the widespread use of madder red – but it nonetheless helped ensure that these cloths found a receptive audience in some societies in Indonesia, where the colour red, through its associations with blood, was understood to evoke powerful life forces.

As with the landscape motif cloth, examples of the figurative designs do survive from the Egyptian finds, including one painting of a female face, presumably a fragment of a full length figure, now lost. **(13)**. This example is dyed in mordanted resist, creating a silhouette line design against a red ground. The face is drawn in three-quarter profile with a sharply pointed nose and wide, tear-shaped eyes. These conventions were waning by the mid-sixteenth century in western Indian painting.

The case for a long period of production of cloth versions, which extends beyond the expiration of the painting style that undoubtedly inspired it, is supported by the appearance of these archaic figure-types on cloths which have other features firmly associating them with the later export trade repertoire, most notably seen in the treatment of border and end-registers **(14)**. The ornamentation of the figures, especially the diadem worn by the women in the Kobe example, has close parallels with the costume worn by women who participate in Jain temple festivals **(16)**. These women perform a stick-dance in celebration of the inauguration of a temple or

the installation of a new Jina image. This is precisely the dance being performed on another Gujarati trade cloth from Indonesia, in which pairs of female performers strike wooden sticks together as part of the dance choreography **(15)**. In a medieval Hindu temple context, such performers would be regarded as *devadasi,* "slaves of god". In the Jain temple, such performers may not have been "professional" dancers but rather lay community, who dressed for the day as celestial dancers from Indra's Heaven.

This category of figurative cloths, with female musicians and dancers, may have been inspired by scenes of "Indra's Heaven" depicted in Jain manuscripts. This subject – a vision of celestial heaven – was popular in Jain arts, and recurs in both illustrated manuscripts and in temple relief depictions. Did medieval Jain temples also have a custom of using large cloth depictions of this subject for display during temple festivals? It is very probable though, to my knowledge, none survive in an Indian context. A future search of Jain temple storerooms and libraries *(bandar)* might perhaps reveal some traces of this practice.

A unique version of this cloth type collected in central Sulawesi and now in the National Gallery of Australia, Canberra, is critical for an understanding of this group of cloths. The cloth depicts a frieze of twelve women in the Gujarati-style, grouped in pairs, variously holding an umbrella, parrot, a stringed instrument, and fly-whisk *(chauri)*. Its importance lies in its stamped

15 Detail of a ceremonial banner cloth, with a repeat design of woman performing a 'stick-dance'. Gujarat, for the Indonesian market. Painted mordant-dyed and resist-dyed cotton. *(Photograph courtesy the Museum for Textiles, Toronto)*

16 Performance of a 'stick-dance' by members of the Jain community on the occasion of the installation ceremony of Jina images, Jain Temple, Potters Bar, London, August 2005. *(Photograph John Guy)*

17 Detail of a ceremonial banner cloth, with a royal hunting scene design. Gujarat, for the Indonesian market. Painted mordant-dyed and resist-dyed cotton, date uncertain, c. late 15th century.
(Abbott Collection, National Gallery of Australia, Canberra (1988))

inscription that bears the numerals '1556' *(vikram samvat)* which equates to 1500. This date corresponds in Gujarat to the reign of Muhamad Shah (1459-1511). This is the earliest Indian trade textile dated by inscription in Southeast Asia.[17]

Hunting scenes

Another textile type obviously intended for ceremonial use is the Gujarati-style hunting scene. The earliest type has the elephant, horsemen and footmen repeated in two registers over the length of the textile, the outline design printed in iron-black, and red and blue mordanted and resist-dyed respectively. The design depicts the ruler – crowned and seated in an umbrella-covered howdah – engaged in a tiger hunt. In the detail illustrated, the scene is animated, with the mahout lancing a tiger that is attacking the royal elephant; foot soldiers and cavalry engage in the hunt (17). The scene fits well with the

description of the late thirteenth century Chinese commentator on international trade, Zhao Rugua:

> *[The ruler of Gujarat possesses] over four hundred war-elephants and about one thousand cavalry horses and when the king goes about he rides an elephant; on his head he wears a cap. His followers ride on horseback and carry swords.[18]*

One can imagine – though we have no evidence whatsoever – such cloths having a place in Gujarati society, for public display on festive occasions; to see how such subject matter resonated with the local inhabitants of eastern Indonesia is less clear, beyond the glorification of martial kingship. Nonetheless, these splendid pictorial cloths form a significant group of the early export class. Fragments of a cloth depicting a horseman hunting boar survive from Egypt.[19]

A rare *patola*-imitation painted cotton version of the hunting scene theme was collected in Indonesia (18).

18 (above) Ceremonial banner cloth, with a royal hunting scene design. Gujarat, for the Indonesian market. Painted mordant-dyed and resist-dyed cotton, date uncertain, c. 17th-18th century.
(Collection H. & H. Neumann, Switzerland)

19 (below) Ceremonial cloth and sacred heirloom *[patolu]* Gujarat, India, traded to Sumatra, Indonesia, 18th century, silk, natural dyes; double ikat. 86.0 x 26.0 cm.
(Collection National Gallery of Australia, Canberra, 1991.1095)

Although the subject depicted on this cloth directly descends from the great pictorial narratives described above, the treatment is inspired by a separate textile tradition, *patola*. The conscious copying of *patola* is seen in every detail, as all motifs are stylised in imitation of the geometricized effect that the cluster-binding of threads creates in *ikat*. An unusual feature is the treatment of the elephants, which have human figures represented on them, a devise seen in later Indian paintings where the animal is a composite, made of a number of figures.[20] This is rarely seen in trade cloths, and principally on *patola* (**19**).[21] Yet, surely this painted cotton version was produced in direct imitation of a *patola*. It may also be assumed that the popular and, I would argue, later, elephant-and-tiger *patola* design, widely seen in Indonesia, evolved out of these more complex hunting scene cloths.[22]

The widespread appearance of painted cotton versions of silk *patola* cloths in Indonesia underscores the nature of the Southeast Asian market for Indian trade textiles. *Patola*-substitutes were widely produced in the seventeenth and eighteenth centuries - as we can judge by the occurrence of the Dutch East India Company's 'VOC' stamp on the salvages of cloths handled by the company – and maybe earlier. The VOC actively sought to restrict the distribution of *patola,* reserving them as high-status gifts of inducement to local rulers, and it may have been these monopolistic measures which curtailed

supply and so stimulated the production of cotton copies. The cotton versions were less expensive, as can be judged from the VOC records, and so they also assumed a place in the market hierarchy as *patola*-substitutes. Modern ethnographic observations suggest that today they are more or less interchangeable in ceremonial contexts, serving the same status-marker role.

Ramayana cloths

A highly distinctive group of cloths depict a battle scene from the Ramayana epic. They are all of a standard design, depicting Rama and Ravanna engaged in combat. The two formidable contestants face each other, releasing arrows armed with magic powers (**21a** & **b**).

It must be assumed that the meaning of the scene depicted was encompassed within the local belief systems in Indonesia, but we have no archaeological or ethnographic evidence to demonstrate what belief systems these were. Followers of concepts of the Big Man/Warrior Chief would undoubtedly have responded to the Vishnu-Rama image of the warrior-hero deity. Certainly there is evidence for the appeal of Vishnu to local rulers in fifth-century west Java in the form of a rock-cut inscription eulogising a local king in the devotional language intended for Vishnu worship. The King Purnavarman inscription (Ciaruten, near Bogor) even employs Vishnu-pada – the holy footprints denoting Vishnu – to evoke the king's presence.

20 Story-teller (*dalang*) seated before a narrative handscroll (*wayang beber*), palace (*kraton*), Yogyakarta. Late 19th century.
(Photograph courtesy the Museum voor Volkenkunde, Leiden)

21a & **b**   Ceremonial banner cloth, a scene from the Ramayana depicting Rama (top) and Ravana (bottom) in battle. Coromandel coast, for the Indonesian market, found in eastern Indonesia. Cotton, painted mordant-dyed and painted cotton. Date uncertain, c. 18th century. *(Victoria and Albert Museum, London (IS 23-1996))*

22 Detail of a painted narrative scroll *(wayang beber)* depicting characters from the Panji story, with projecting eyes.
(Museum voor Volkenkunde, Leiden)

23 Detail of ceremonial banner cloth depicting the face of a female musician, with projecting eye. Gujarat, for the Indonesian market, found in Sulawesi. Cotton, block-printed mordant-dyed and resist-dyed. Photograph AEDTA no. 2610. *(Riboud Collection, Musee Guimet, Paris)*

The popularity of the *Ramayana* legend in Indonesia is further attested in the sculptural relief programmes at Chandi Loro Jonggrang, Prambanan, the late ninth-century Hindu temple complex in Central Java. This Indian epic had been widely assimilated into the local dramatic traditions of Indonesia and therefore the appearance of this subject is less enigmatic than might first appear. A number of these cloths have reportedly been found in Bali, the island which strongly retained elements of the Hinduised culture it inherited from Java. These communities would have readily understood and appreciated the explicitly narrative function of these cloths; both Java and Bali have well established traditions of story-telling **(20)**.

Obscure borrowing

It is interesting to reflect on the fact that the oldest body of Indian textile trade to Indonesia are those decorated with figurative and narrative designs. It is only in the later periods, perhaps around 1600 and beyond, that geometric and floral repeat patterns become the dominant type. Clearly such generalisations are dangerous – perhaps these cloths are only the category that survived because they had special ritual functions which ensured their preservation. Putting this qualification to one side, what impact did these grand, impressive display items have on local textile design traditions? The answer has to be, minimal. There was great impact from silk *patola* and what we understand to later geometric and floral patterned designs, most significantly in regional ikat styles.[23] But given the significant – dare one say – seminal role that early trade cloths appear to have assumed in some Indonesian societies, we would expect to see far greater evidence of the presence of these cloths in local textile design. This is not the case. Rather, this absence of significant influence points, in my view, to the antiquity of these cloths. With few exceptions, any impact this "first wave" of Indian imports had on local textile design was displaced by later waves of influence.

Nonetheless, one can detect what are arguably memories of these early trade cloths in surviving textile and painting traditions in the region. Two examples illustrate the point:

The oldest pictorial story-telling tradition known in Java, but sadly no longer performed, was that of *wayang beber*. This involved the use of painted cloth in which the narrative scenes are depicted in a sequence of scenes on painted cloth in a "landscape" format, which the narrator slowly scrolls past his audience as he recites the story. This is essentially the same story-telling practice widely seen in rural India even today, in the *pata* scrolls of Bengal and the narrative cloth paintings of Maharasthra, western India. It is conceivable that the *Ramayana* cloths were employed in Indonesia in a similar manner, either displayed fully extended or rolled past the audience as a 'moving picture' by the narrator.

The second legacy of early trade cloths is also to be found in *wayang berber* (20). The few that survive all exhibit a very distinctive stylistic feature – the faces of the refined and noble *(halus)* characters are drawn with pronounced, exaggerated features – attenuated nose and chin, and feature that curious convention, the protruding second eye (22). This has no apparent antecedents in earlier pictorial arts outside the *wayang*-shadow theatre tradition. The only other context in which this device occurs is in fact in medieval and later Gujarati trade cloths with figurative designs (23). It is reasonable to suggest this convention in the Javanese *wayang* world may have its origins in these imported Indian painted textiles.

As observed above (11-14), female dancers are a recurring motif on a class of Indian trade cloths, and evolve over several centuries. A recently exhibited cloth from Sarawak, an Iban *pua sungkit,* displays a triple register of dancing figures (24).[24] This motif, as on many others in Iban ikat (and more rarely in *sungkit*), has associations which link it to the earliest group of Indian trade textiles recorded in Indonesia. Those cloths depicting dancers are many and varied, but close parallels can be drawn with a rare surviving type depicting

pairs of female dancers performing the "stick-dance" (15). Cloths of this type were traded upriver to the communities of Borneo and into the hinterland of Sulawesi, where their role in the ritual life of these communities ensured their longevity.

The little we know about the ritual and ceremonial functions of imported trade cloths and their associations with life-cycle rituals and annual festivals is based on modern ethnographic observations. In 1987 the anthropologist Penelope Graham recorded a ceremony to mark the re-inauguration of an ancestral temple in the hill village of Lewotala, eastern Flores.[25] Figure **25** depicts young unmarried women of the community dancing during the celebrations; they wear fine locally woven cotton skirts and local blouses and each has a shoulder cloth *(selendang)* of imported Indian silk *patola*. These cloths are preserved as clan-owned heirloom property, acculturated and appropriated for ancestral worship purposes. How and when the transformation of these cloths took place from status-imbued royal assets to community heirloom objects is unclear, but over time they have acquired sets of meanings and a scale of importance that is very different from when they were first received into the community as bride-wealth or as a part of contractural gift exchanges between communities. A metamorphoses has taken place whereby these exotic cloths have acquired a status beyond being mere commodities. They have become, at some point in the past, embedded in the communities shared understanding of itself.

We can only speculate on the validity of extrapolating from the recent ethnographic record into the distant past. All we can say is that these cloths were "exotic", highly valued status objects and over time were absorbed into local cosmologies and origin-myths. They were to be displayed in the cycle of rituals observed by certain communities, to evoke the authority these belief systems imbued them with. Such cloths resonated with the shared memory of specific communities in which oral history and local legend merged.

Exotic cloths served as potent objects necessary for the performance of key ceremonial functions, particularly those associated with the life transition rituals of birth, marriage and death. As lineage-owned heirlooms they were, and are, retained and valued as community property important for expressing shared beliefs. Both court and village culture shared a belief in the power of cloth, as potent objects embodying on occasion's supernatural properties, including talismanic powers. Beyond that, I have tried to suggest some possible lines of further enquiry, arguing for links and continuities to older art forms and earlier evidence of cross cultural dialogue.

24 Detail of an Iban ceremonial cloth *(pua sungkit)*, with dancing figures design. Sarawak, west Malaysia. Cotton with supplementary weft and weft twining. *(Textile Museum, Washington, gift of The Christensen Fund, (2000.25.18))*

25 Young unmarried women of Lewotala, eastern Flores, Indonesia, dancing during the celebration of the re-inauguration festivities of a renovated ancestral temple. They wear local cotton garments and display heirloom *patola* shoulder cloths *(selendang)*.
(Photograph courtesy Penelope Graham, 1987)

To conclude, one further observation can be made: it is clear that whilst *patola*-inspired designs are a persistent presence in the visual record of Indonesian textile designs, Gujarati figurative designs have left a very modest legacy. I would suggest that this is directly related to their relative antiquity in the trade textile context. The large figurative cloths discussed in this paper had largely disappeared from circulation relatively early in the trade textile story - probably in the course of the sixteenth century or early seventeenth century. The clearest indicator of this is the *absence* of their influence in that most reliable barometer of textile design, *batik,* which resonate with imagery and designs from the later waves of Indian trade textiles to Southeast Asia. But that is another story.

Bibliography

Barnes, R., *The Ikat Textiles of Lamalena,* Leiden, E. J. Brill, 1989.

Barnes, R., 'Indian Trade Textiles', *Hali,* No. 87, 1996: 80-85.

Buhler, A. and Fischer E., *The Patola of Gujarat,* 2 vols., Basel, Krebs A. G., 1979.

Chou Ta-kuan [Zhou Daguan], *Notes on the Customs of Cambodia (1296-97),* Bangkok, 1967.

Del Bonta, R., 'Indian composite painting: a playful art', *Orientations,* January 1996.

Fox, J. J., 'Roti, Ndao and Savu' in M. Kahlenberg (ed.), *Textile Traditions of Indonesia,* Los Angeles County Museum of Art, 1977: 97-104.

Graham, P., 'Vouchsafing fecunity in Eastern Flores: textiles and exchange in the rites of life', in R. W. Hamilton (ed.), *Gift of the Cotton Maiden. Textiles of Flores and the Solor Islands,* Los Angeles, Fowler Museum of Cultural History, 1995.

Gittinger, M., *Master Dyers to the World. Technique and Trade in Early Indian Dyed Cotton Textiles,* Washington DC., The Textile Museum, 1982.

Murray, T., review of M. Gittinger, *Textiles for this World and Beyond: Treasures from Insular Southeast Asia,* Washington, The Textile Museum, 2005, in Hali, no. 141, 2005: 79.

Guy, J., 'Sarasa and *Patola:* Indian Textiles in Indonesia', *Orientations,* vol. 20, no.1, 1989: 48-60.

Guy, J., 'Jain manuscript painting', in P. Pal (ed.), *The Peaceful Liberators. Jain Art from India,* London, Thames & Hudson, 1994: 89-99.

Guy, J. *Woven Cargoes: Indian Textiles in the East,* London, Thames & Hudson, 1998.

Guy, J., 'Tamil Merchant Guilds and the Quanzhou Trade', in A. Schottenhammer (ed.), *The Emporium of the World. Maritime Quanzhou,* 1000-1400, Leiden, Brill, 2001, pp. 283-317.

Guy, J., 'Early ninth-century Chinese export ceramics and the Persian Gulf connection: the Belitung shipwreck evidence', in *Chine-Mediterranee. Routes et echanges de la ceramique avant le XVI siecle,* TAOCI, no. 4, 2005: 9-20.

Hirth, F. and Rockhill, W. W., *Chau Ju-kua: His Work on the Chinese and Arab Trade in the Twelfth and Thirteenth centuries, entitled Chu-fan-chi,* St Petersburg, Imperial Academy of Sciences, 1911, reprinted Taipei 1967.

Holmgren, R. G., and Spertus, A. E., *Early Indonesian Textiles for Three Island Cultures: Sumba, Toraja, and Lampung,* New York, Metropolitan Museum of Art, 1989.

Holmgren, R. J. and Spertus, A. E., 'Is Geringsing Really Balinese?', in G. Volger and K. Welck (eds.), *Indonesian Textiles Symposium 1985,* Cologne, Ethnologica, 1991: 59-86.

Lohuizen de Leeuw, J. E. van, 'An early 16th century link between Gujarat and Java', in Ba Shin et al (eds.), *Essays Offered to G. H. Luce,* Ascona, Artibus Asiae Supplement XXIII, 1966.

Maxwell, R., *From Sari to Sarong,* Canberra, National Gallery of Australia, 2004.

Nooy-Palm, C. H. M., *The Sa'dan Toraja: A Study of their Social Life and Religion. 1. Organization, Symbols and Beliefs,* The Hague, Martinus Nijhoff, 1979.

Pires, Tome, *The Suma Oriental of Tome Pires (1512-15),* translated by A. Contesao, 2 vols, London, Hakluyt Society, 1944.

Footnotes

[1] Pires, 1944: 45, 207.

[2] Guy, 2001.

[3] Hirth and Rockhill, 1911: 218.

[4] Chou Ta-kuan 1967: 23.

[5] Sauvaget, 1948.

[6] Guy 2005.

[7] See van Lohuizen de Leeuw, 1966.

[8] Pires, 1944: 42, 108, 270.

[9] Pires, 1944: 45.

[10] See also Holmgren and Spertus, 1985, 1989.

[11] The earliest example is radiocarbon dated to 895 $\pm$75 years; see Barnes, 1996 and Guy, 1998: fig. 46.

[12] Information courtesy of George Breguet, who witnessed the event on 20 August 2005.

[13] Nooy-Palm,1979; Barnes, 1989; Graham, 1995.

[14] Nooy-Palm, 1979, 220.

[15] Nooy-Palm, 1979: 257, 276.

[16] For a discussion of these conventions, see Guy, 1994.

[17] Published Guy 1998, 112-13, and Maxwell, 2004, 128.

[18] Hirth and Rockhill, 1911: 92.

[19] Gittinger, 1982: fig. 31.

[20] Del Bonta, 1996.

[21] Guy, 1998, fig. 110; Maxwell, 2004, 152.

[22] Illustrated Guy 1998: 88-89.

[23] For the impact of imported trade textiles on Indonesian ikat styles, see Barnes, 1989, and Maxwell, 2004.

[24] Murray, 2005.

[25] Graham, 1995.

Barkcloth Skirts from Southwestern Borneo

Roy W. Hamilton

In 1908 Dr. William Louis Abbott (1860-1936) traveled up the Kendawangan and Membuluh rivers in the southwestern corner of Borneo to collect ethnographic materials for the U.S. National Museum (now the National Museum of Natural History, Smithsonian Institution).[1] Among the items he collected was a group of thirty-one highly unusual barkcloth skirts intended as women's ceremonial wear **(1)**. On some of the skirts, striking patterns were created by appliqué with contrasting colours of barkcloth. Others bear complex patterns executed in a waxy red-brown pigment. How this pigment was applied, Abbott never recorded.

Today these skirts constitute an extremely rare record of a long-abandoned tradition. I have so far been able to locate only three similar skirts, one belonging to the Museum für Völkerkunde in Vienna and two to the Rijksmuseum voor Volkenkunde in Leiden.[2] Using Abbott's hand-drawn map as a guide, in 1993 I spent two weeks in the communities where he collected the skirts.[3] Although I was disappointed to find that there was no longer anyone alive who recognized the specific styles of skirts Abbott had collected, I learned that the unusual procedure for applying the red-brown pigment had continued in use for the making of barkcloth headbands and I was able to document it. I was also able to inquire about the usage of more recent types of ceremonial skirts that are obviously the antecedents of the skirts Abbott collected.

The Abbott Collection and Southwestern Borneo

Abbott trained as a physician at the University of Pennsylvania, but when he received a large inheritance two years after his 1884 graduation, he abandoned any plans to practice medicine. A man with a markedly misanthropic bent, he was eager to get away from the "vile hot unventilated American houses" and travel to the most remote places he could find.[4] "I never voluntarily go near any people, black white or brown, except the jungle people or wild tribes," he once wrote in a letter.[5] He took up a life as a museum collector, working first in East Africa, Madagascar, and South Asia, and finally arriving in Malaya in 1896. In 1899 he had a 65-foot schooner, the *Terrapin,* built for him in Singapore. Using this boat as a home base, he spent the next ten years making excursions ranging from the Andaman Islands to western New Guinea. He periodically returned to Singapore only long enough to ship his collections off to his contact at the U.S. National Museum, curator Otis T. Mason (1838-1908).[6]

Abbott made five trips to Borneo between 1905 and 1909, collecting nearly two thousand items for the Smithsonian. On June 17, 1908, he arrived at Batu Jurong, just south of the mouth of the joint estuary of the Kendawangan and Membuluh Rivers. Although he left no notes that tell how he traveled upriver, he must have anchored his schooner at the coast and proceeded in a smaller craft. The *Terrapin* was equipped with an 18-foot double-ended boat that could be rowed by two men (Kloss 1995: 2), so perhaps that was the vessel he used. Abbott spent more than two months traveling to the headwaters of the Kendawangan and back, then made a

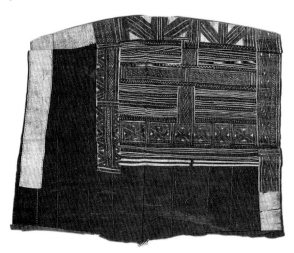

1 Woman's ceremonial barkcloth skirt with barkcloth appliqués *(umbong taping)*, Gerimai[16], Kendawangan River. Collected in 1908 by William Louis Abbott. Anthropology Department, National Museum of Natural History, Smithsonian Institution (NMNH), #254092. *(Photo: RWH, with permission of NMNH)*

two-week trip up the Membuluh. He collected over nine hundred items on these excursions. Heavily represented among them are products of two of the most important technologies of the region: basketry (337 items including plaited mats) and barkcloth (174 items). He also collected fifteen heavy wooden barkcloth beaters to represent the process of beating strips of bark into soft, pliable barkcloth.

The extant information about the objects Abbott collected comes primarily from tags he attached to the items, recording in his own handwriting the details that he thought were most important. In some cases these tags are quite comprehensive, but in others they are rather perfunctory. The National Anthropological Archive at the Smithsonian also maintains a collection of Abbott's papers, including miscellaneous field notes, photographs (mostly head shots of the type once valued for anthropometry), the sketch maps he drew of his collecting locations, and a number of letters he wrote to Mason and others.[7] None of this material is extensive, however, and Abbott consistently resisted any suggestion that he compile a more thorough account of his travels or the items he collected. There is no detailed record of his experiences, of the people or communities he encountered, or of the manner in which the items were used within the social setting. Abbott felt that he was simply the collector, and that it was the job of museum curators to interpret the objects he sent them (Taylor and Hamilton 1993: 313). This meant, according to the ideas of his day, that the curator would classify the items within an evolutionary developmental hierarchy. In deferring to the curators, Abbott failed to realize that the information he had available to him as a field collector would in the future be far more valuable than the now discredited scientific theories that prevailed at the time.

Using Abbott's map of the Kendawangan and Membuluh as a guide, I set out in August 1993 to determine what more could be learned about how the skirts were made and used in the communities in which they originated. In Pontianak, the provincial capital of West Kalimantan, I had the good fortune of meeting Hawad Suryantho, who was born in the region where Abbott collected. I could never had succeeded in obtaining the field documentation presented in this paper without his participation as a guide and research assistant. Because many of the discussions our questions provoked were conducted in the local language, he also translated into standard Indonesian for me. When I use the term "we" in this paper, it refers to the research team the two of us formed.

The southwestern corner of Borneo, though not as remote as the deep interior of the island, is paradoxically even more obscure. While groups such as the Iban, Kayan, Ngaju, and Penan in other parts of the island have drawn intense interest by anthropologists and art historians, virtually nothing has been written about the Kendawangan and Membuluh region in all the time since Abbott visited there. Today access to the region is via the district (kabupaten) capital, the town of Ketapang, which can be reached by plane or boat, but not by road, from Pontianak. From there, we traveled by motorcycle, first down a paved coastal road and then turning inland on a one-lane road with unpaved sections rutted by heavy logging trucks. The countryside stretching for about thirty miles inland from the coast consists of a swampy forest of stunted trees, as uninhabited today as it was in Abbott's time. Only when the land rises slightly and becomes better drained do communities begin to appear. Most of the people are subsistence farmers who grow dry rice and other crops on swidden plots. Wet rice agriculture is limited to a few favorable sites. Some limited additional income is obtained from coffee growing and rubber tapping.

The villages where Abbott collected are today part of the subdistrict (kecamatan) of Marau. In Abbott's time, these communities were all longhouses, but the last longhouses were abandoned in the 1950 or 1960s. Most of the communities we visited in 1993 were of recent construction, consisting of a double row of simple rectangular houses raised slightly off the ground on pilings, with a dirt road running down the center (2). Community life seemed more focused on the thin network of roads than on the rivers, as it had been in Abbott's day. Of the seven communities in which Abbott collected skirts on the

2 Communities of individual family homes have replaced longhouses. Perendaman, Marau Subdistrict, West Kalimantan, 1993. *(Photo: RWH)*

Kendawangan, by name five still exist today, while the inhabitants of the remaining two have moved to join a larger community. Without conducting more extensive field research, however, I could not be sure that the communities that bore these names were still in the same locations, or inhabited by the descendants of the same people, where Abbott had visited them in 1908. Of the six communities on the Membuluh, I was only able to verify the current existence of only two.[8] This is perhaps not surprising, given a residence pattern that always included the periodic relocating of longhouse communities.

The local people do not identify themselves as belonging to any particular named group of people other than using the name of their community or of the river drainage in which they live. If pressed, they will say they are "Dayak," a catch-all term for the indigenous inhabitants of Borneo first used by outsiders but now widely used in Borneo. Thus, when we asked, people would say they were "Dayaks of the Kendawangan" or "Dayaks of the Membuluh." This same absence of a regional group identity has also been remarked by Christine Helliwell (2001), who has conducted the most detailed anthropological research to date in southwestern Borneo. Her research site, however, was along the Semendang River (a tributary of the Simpang River) over a hundred miles north of Marau, with no direct river or road connections.[9] More generally, the complex problems associated with the concept of ethnicity in Borneo have been described by many authors, most recently Peter Metcalf (2002: 77-107). In the region we visited, people told us that the language they spoke differed slightly from community to community. Although we did not systematically gather linguistic data, we judged that the local language belongs to the so-called Malayic Dayak group, which is consistent with the available linguistic maps of Borneo (Wurm and Hattori 1981).

The longhouses that once existed in the area were constructed in an unusual manner, with individual family apartments arranged on both sides of a central walkway. Although the whole structure was elevated high on poles, the walkway was somewhat below the level of the floors of the apartments. Helliwell found this kind of longhouse on the Semandang, some still in use.[10] They contrast rather sharply with the much better known longhouse type of the Iban, in which the walkway is flanked on one side by the apartments but on the other by an open veranda and all of these living areas are on the same level.

The Barkcloth Skirts

Since barkcloth garments are no longer worn on a daily basis anywhere in Indonesia, we were not surprised that everyday dress for women consisted almost entirely of Western-style skirts and dresses or sometimes a Javanese wrap-around batik. Despite seeking out the oldest people to interview, we could find no one who even recalled seeing a decorated barkcloth skirt like the ones Abbott collected. Coarse barkcloth *(kapua)* was still made from time to time, but used mostly as carrying straps for burden baskets **(3)**. The idea of a wrap-around ceremonial skirt, called *umbong* in the villages of the Kendawangan and *rupit* along the Membuluh, was still current, denoting a skirt that would be worn for special events. At the one event we were able to attend, however, women were dressed either in their fanciest party dresses or in Javanese batik **(4)**. We found it instructive to contemplate how something that was clearly culturally important in 1908 could be so thoroughly forgotten only eighty-five years later, especially since Southeast Asian textiles are so often mistakenly interpreted as bearers of unchanging tradition.

Abbott did not record how the skirts were worn or for what occasions. It may be that he witnessed no special events in his short time on the Kendawangan and Membuluh. In the Simpang River drainage, he photographed women wearing skirts of undecorated barkcloth, presumably their every-day wear **(5)**. Catalog records regarding the skirts that belong to the Rijksmuseum voor Volkenkunde state that the garment was brought to a close behind the left thigh and held up with a band of red and black rattan strips, or with a belt made of silver coins in the case of wealthy individuals (Juynboll 1909: 106). Many of the skirts have asymmetrical designs, suggesting that the less decorated portion may have been wrapped under the more elaborate portion.[11]

While barkcloth skirts were worn in many parts of Borneo, the Kendawangan and Membuluh skirts are unique in their patterning and in the techniques used to create those patterns. In twenty-eight of the thirty-one skirts, strips or rectangles of one colour of barkcloth have been appliquéd over a contrasting colour of barkcloth **(6)**. Abbott recorded the term *umbong taping* for these skirts which were found in the Kendawangan drainage, but did not record a special term for those from the Membuluh. In all of these skirts except one, appliqués of cream-coloured barkcloth made from the inner bark of *Aquilaria malaccensis* (known in Malay as

3 A woman pounds a strip of bark to make barkcloth. Perendaman, 1993. *(Photo: RWH)*

4 These women have dressed to attend a wedding, wearing the Javanese style skirt and blouse combination (*kain kebaya*) featuring a wrap-around Javanese batik skirt. Lumpak, Marau Subdistrict, West Kalimantan, 1993. *(Photo: RWH)*

5 Abbott photographed these women in their daily wear of unadorned barkcloth skirts on his 1907 expedition to the Simpang and Semandang Rivers. National Anthropological Archives, Papers of William Louis Abbott, #20373. *(Photo courtesy of the National Anthropological Archives)*

6 Woman's ceremonial barkcloth skirt (*umbong taping*) with appliqués of cream-coloured *kaias* barkcloth on a dark *kraiah* barkcloth ground. Gerimai, Kendawangan River. NMNH #254073. *(Photo: RWH, with permission of NMNH)*

gaharu and on the Kendawangan as *kaias*) are stitched onto a background of dark barkcloth made from a ficus species (*kayu ara* in Malay and *kraiah* locally).[12] The dark barkcloth, naturally a reddish-brown colour, has been further blackened by treating it with iron-rich mud. The one exception is an unfinished skirt with appliqués of dark *kraiah* barkcloth on a white barkcloth ground (made from *Antiaris toxicaria*, discussed further below).

Several additional techniques are used to further embellish these skirts. Simple decorative stitches of plant fiber are found in many of them. In one of the most finely worked examples, this thread has been dyed with indigo **(7, 8)**. Abbott noted that indigo dyeing was used particularly with fibers taken from the leaves of a plant in the lily family, *Curciligo sp.*, probably *C. latifolia* (Burkill 1966: 714). This fiber, known locally as *lemba*, is still processed and used for many purposes. It is the same fiber from which Benuaq women in East Kalimantan make loom-woven cloth.

8 Detail of fig. 7. *(Photo: RWH, with permission of NMNH)*

Small quantities of imported materials have been used for additional decoration on some of the skirts, primarily in the form of coloured commercial cotton thread embroidered in simple designs. In more elaborate examples, strips of imported cotton cloth have been used in place of local barkcloth for some of the appliqués **(9, 10)**.

All of these sewn techniques not only decorate the skirt but also add to its structural integrity. In general, the barkcloth of Borneo is much coarser than the famous *tapa* of Polynesia or even the *fuya* barkcloth of Central Sulawesi, both of which are made from the fine-grained inner bark of the paper mulberry, *Broussonetia papyrifera*. The processing also differs, with fewer steps of retting, fermenting, layering and felting practiced on Borneo. Because of the minimal processing often used, Borneo barkcloth is sometimes prone to separating along the grain of the fiber. This is particularly true of barkcloth made of ficus bark, like the *umbong taping*, or other relatively coarse types of bark. For this reason, various techniques were developed to strengthen the cloth. Kooijman (1963:74) has noted the use of both appliqués and supplementary threads applied across the grain of barkcloth headbands from the Ketapang region. Barkcloth vests in many parts of Borneo are strengthened with heavy plant fibers darned at regular intervals across the grain. The embroidery technique used in cloths like the *umbong taping* decorated with indigo thread may have developed as a refinement based on this strengthening procedure (Kooijman 1963: 74).

The most distinctive *umbong taping*, however, are decorated by an entirely different technique, which creates deep red geometric patterns with a waxy surface on the cream-coloured *kaias* barkcloth appliqués **(11-**

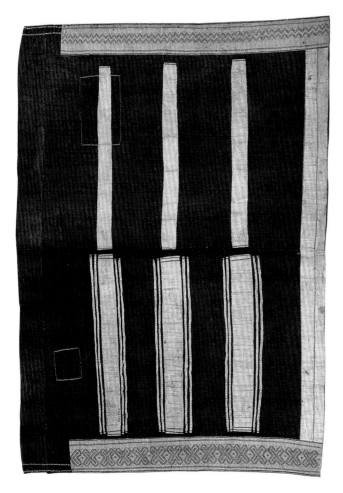

7 Woman's ceremonial barkcloth skirt (*rupit*) with decorative stitching of indigo-dyed *lemba* fiber. Tanah Itam, Membuluh River. NMNH #254069. *(Photo: RWH, with permission of NMNH)*

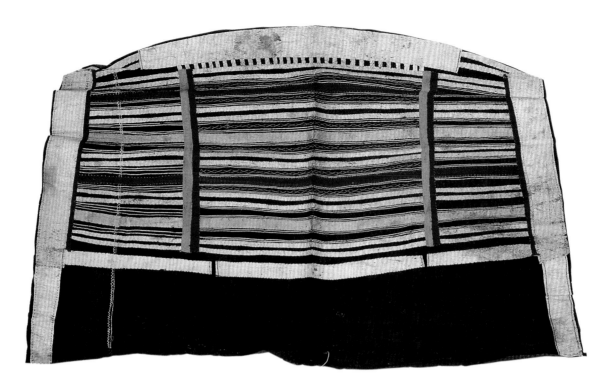

9 Woman's ceremonial barkcloth skirt (*umbong taping*) with appliquéd strips of commercial cotton trade cloth and decorative stitching. Tebing Tinggi, Kendawangan River. NMNH #254065. *(Photo: RWH, with permission of NMNH)*

10 Woman's ceremonial barkcloth skirt *(umbong taping)* with appliquéd strips of commercial printed cotton trade cloth. Gerimai, Kendawangan River. NMNH #254070. *(Photo: RWH, with permission of NMNH)*

15). Abbott left a confused record regarding the source of this distinctive red pigment. In his notes he wrote that the skirts, and also local barkcloth headbands, were coloured with a substance derived from seeds contained in the inch-long conical pods of the *gingam* tree. He is certainly referring here to annatto *(Bixa orellana)*, a plant of American origin that has long been cultivated pan-tropically. On the tags attached to the skirts, he only names the pigment in one case, and there he calls it *jernung,* saying it was derived from the fruit of a rattan. This refers to a famous Borneo forest product sometimes called "dragon's blood," a waxy resin collected from the fruit of the rattan *Daemonorhops draco.*

Not only was the identity of the pigment in question, but Abbott also made no mention anywhere of how it was applied to the cloth. Due to the straight lines and regularity of the patterns, I first thought that some kind of stamping procedure might have been used. While stamped patterns are not common on Borneo, a missionary traveling in the upper reaches of the Pawan River in 1842 observed barkcloth being decorated with carved wooden stamps used to apply the sap of some kind of berry (Veth 1854: 150). The waxy surface on Abbott's skirts, however, did not look like a pigment that could be applied by stamping, and the designs seemed more complicated and less regular than would be produced with a stamp.

11 Woman's ceremonial barkcloth skirt (*umbong taping*) showing added patterning with a waxy red-brown pigment. Belaban, Kendawangan River. NMNH #254077. *(Photo: RWH, with permission of NMNH)*

12 Woman's ceremonial barkcloth skirt *(rupit)* showing added patterning with a waxy red-brown pigment. Simuncong, Membuluh River. NMNH #254077. *(Photo: RWH, with permission of NMNH)*

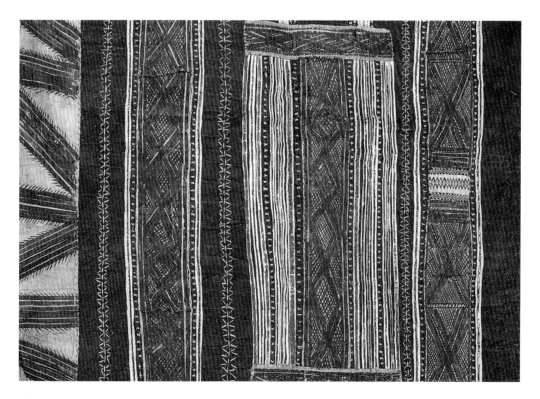

13 Detail of fig. 12, showing a small embroidered detail at the top. *(Photo: RWH, with permission of NMNH)*

14 Woman's ceremonial barkcloth skirt (*umbong taping*). Upper Kendawangan River. NMNH #254077. *(Photo: RWH, with permission of NMNH)*

15 Detail of 14. Even the finest horizontal lines are narrow appliqués of barkcloth. *(Photo: RWH, with permission of NMNH)*

Fortunately, a means of resolving this mystery presented itself in the field. While no one we interviewed recalled any barkcloth skirts resembling Abbott's *umbong taping,* when I showed photographs of barkcloth headbands that he had also collected, there was instant recognition. Some of these were decorated with the same waxy red patterns, and to our delight we were told that this type of headband was still made in the Membuluh River community of Batu Keling **(16)**. The following day we located a middle-aged woman who knew how to make the patterns and was willing to demonstrate. First she cut thin strips of palm leaf rib (known as *lidi* in Malay), about a quarter of a centimetre wide. Then she took a lump of a red waxy substance she called *jerenaung,* which looked like a glob of red crayons that had been melted together, and rubbed it along the surface of the *lidi.* The wax rubbed off, leaving a smooth, even coating on the *lidi.* Next she heated a metal plate in a fire until it was too hot to touch but not yet to the glowing stage. When it was hot, she removed it from the fire and laid it on the ground, covering it with a layer of fresh banana leaf. Next she laid a clean piece of *kaias* barkcloth on top of the warm banana leaf. Finally she took the *lidi,* waxed side down, and pressed it firmly onto the surface of the barkcloth for a moment **(17, 18)**. When she removed the *lidi,* a fresh, straight, waxy, red mark was left on the surface of the barkcloth. The pigment had been transferred from the *lidi* to the barkcloth by the heat from the metal plate. She then demonstrated that complex cross-hatched patterns could be built up by laying down successive marks. This process explained the waxy surface of the pigment and the somewhat irregular geometric patterns. She also created black lines using the same method, with a pigment derived from lampblack

This demonstration confirmed both the technique and the identity of the pigment, for her *jerenaung* is merely a local variant of the term Abbott used, *jernung*. Still another variant, widely used in Borneo is *jernang*. We had actually already encountered this substance and had been looking for more information about it. We had met one man who still made beautiful twined burden baskets *(kindai)* using *jerenaung* to colour the red twining elements. Unlike the skirts, these baskets were being made in a form identical to the examples Abbott collected eighty-five years earlier, although they were only produced by this one elderly man. He told us that along the Kendawangan, people say *jerenaung* can only be collected where the cock's crow cannot be heard – in other words, far from any village site, deep in the forest. He obtained his supply from men who brought it from villages further east, a couple of hour's motorcycle travel by rough track deeper into the interior. There is still a local market for this trade good, however there are also complaints about adulterated supplies.[13]

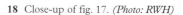

17 The stick *(lidi)* covered with waxy *jerenaung* pigment is pressed face down onto the warmed surface of the barkcloth. The heated metal plate is under the banana leaf. Batu Keling, Membuluh River, 1993. *(Photo: RWH)*

18 Close-up of fig. 17. *(Photo: RWH)*

16 The red-brown patterning on this woman's ceremonial headband (*tekolok rantang*), modeled for the photograph, is created by the same method as that used in the skirts. Air Upas, West Kalimantan, 1993. *(Photo: RWH)*

Abbott must have made a mistake when he wrote in his notes that the skirts were colored with *gingam*. In fact he collected two different types of headcloths, one coloured with *jerenaung* like the one we saw being made in Batu Keling, and the other rather crudely coloured with a more orange-red, dye-like pigment. Surely these are the headcloths coloured with annatto. The annatto plant is still common in the region, though we were told that its local name is *sampang*.

In addition to the twenty-eight skirts of the *umbong taping* type, the collection also includes one unadorned skirt of *kraiah* barkcloth and two examples of a third type of skirt, known on the Kendawangan as *umbong ballit* according to Abbott's tag (*umbong balit* in today's orthography). These use a whitish barkcloth and carry designs that are painted freehand **(19)**. The most elaborate example bears four different colours of pigment. Abbott noted that the green was made from *tarum* (indigo), the orange from *gingam*, and the yellow from turmeric, and the red from *jernang* mixed with lime.[14]

The source of the bark used in these two skirts is the tree *Antiaris toxicaria* (*upas* or *ipoh* in Malay, *katatai* locally). The latex of this tree is used as a poison for blowgun darts and it must be thoroughly removed by washing or the finished barkcloth will irritate the skin (Burkill 1966: 184). Presumably the extra labor was considered worthwhile because this bark produces a particularly desirable result, stronger and more supple than the other types of barkcloth commonly found in Borneo. It also provided a whiter background for the painted designs. Henry C. Raven, who observed *upas* bark being processed, reported that it was yellow-brown until rubbed with the juice of a wild citrus fruit while it was being pounded and then later bleached in the sun (1932: 381). Raven, incidentally, was funded by Abbott to continue collecting in Indonesia after Abbott himself was forced to return to the U.S. in 1909 when a spirochete infection left him partially blind.

Social and Ceremonial Uses of the Skirts

Because no one in the communities we visited could comment on any significance of the patterning of the skirts, many questions remain unanswered. In an Indonesian context, it seems likely that differences in patterning might have served to communicate some information about their wearers, such as their community of origin or their social standing. The relatively small number of skirts in the sample available to us, as well as the variety of the patterning and its seemingly random distribution throughout the range of villages represented, prevent any conclusions along these lines.

Although the barkcloth skirts are no longer remembered, a few elderly women in the area still owned skirts made of commercial cotton cloth, which were clearly the antecedents of the 1908 barkcloth skirts **(20)**. The single example we were able to examine was decorated with embroidery and appliqué in contrasting colours reminiscent of the work on Abbott's skirts. Furthermore these skirts were called by the same names, *umbong* or *rupit*. Although it would take a substantial period of field work to fully document the use and social meanings of these skirts, it seems clear that they must always have been cer-

68

20 For this portrait the woman chose to wear her ceremonial skirt, but nearly covered it in a breast cloth *(timban)* of commercial fabric. The bands of appliqué barely visible at the bottom of her skirt attest to its relationship to its appliquéd barkcloth predecessors of Abbott's time. Singkuang, West Kalimantan, 1993. *(Photo: RWH)*

emonial wear donned specially for significant events in the social life or religious life of the community. Therefore we questioned everyone we talked to about how such skirts might formerly have been used in their communities.

One man of about eighty years of age from the village of Batu Perak immediately mentioned the rice harvest festival, *tikar pati,* as the biggest ritual event of the year, for which such ceremonial dress would be appropriate. *Tikar* means to count and *pati* is a storage box. This festival involved the measuring and totaling up of

the annual rice crop as it was being placed in the granaries. Another word that came up in this discussion was *gendang,* which refers to various types of gongs or drums and is used as both a noun and a verb. The playing of *gendang* accompanies major ceremonial events and thus could be said to mark an appropriate occasion for wearing an *umbong* skirt.

With the exception of this one man, however, everywhere we asked about the use of the skirts the discussion very quickly turned to the subject of *belian.* A *belian* is a shaman, charged with the responsibility of communicating with the spirit world. Shamanism is a complex subject in Borneo and the extensive body of literature about it reveals that shamanist practices differ widely from one culture to another (see Winzler 1993). Without a much more extensive period of research, it is impossible for us to give a thorough account of the significance of shamanism in the Kendawangan and Membuluh area. Even within the local area, there seemed to be differences in shamanist practices. For example, in some communities all *belian* were men, we were told, while in others the most important *belian* were women.

We obtained the most complete information about *belian* and the ceremonies they conduct, known generically as *babelian,* in the community of Air Upas.[15] There, two different types of *belian* ceremonies, called *rayah* and *lalai,* are curing ceremonies led by male *belian.* The only difference between the two is the rhythm with which the accompanying drum is beaten. This drum is of a type known by the onomotopoeic term *ketabung.* The use of musical features in this way to classify and describe various types of ceremonies was an interesting pattern we encountered consistently. In these curing ceremonies, the *belian* may rub a stone over the body of the patient to determine the source of illness. For example, if the rubbing produces a thorn, the sickness is thought to be caused by a spirit disturbed when land was being cleared of brush for a new rice field. Or, if the stone is held to a flame and produces an odor of burning flesh, the cause is a spirit of the dead from the graveyard. These types of *belian* ceremonies take place whenever a need for them is felt. No particular forms of dress are required for the observers, but the male *belian* wears a special form of headband *(ambinarai)* with trailing ends. If the cure is successful, thanksgiving celebrations (called *baraya* and *balalai,* respectively) are given depending on the means of the family involved.

19 Woman's ceremonial barkcloth skirt with hand-painted designs *(umbong balit).* Batu Payong, Kendawangan River. NMNH #254080.1. *(Photo: RWH, with permission of NMNH)*

These relatively simple curing ceremonies, however, paled in significance compared to the major rites called *ganja,* held for the investiture of a new female *belian.* We had been directed to Air Upas because it was there that the last of these great ceremonies was held, in approximately 1980. A new *belian* is installed after a lengthy process involving meditation, visions, spirit possession, apprenticeship to an experienced *belian,* and the memorization of ritual texts. We were told that *ganja* is considered the most important ceremony in the entire social and religious life of the community. The celebration lasts for seven days and seven nights and features musical accompaniment by a *gendang gerantung* (a metal gong), a *gendang belian* (the shaman's drum, with a head made of the skin if a proboscis monkey), and three or four more ordinary *ketabung* drums. Of particular relevance to our story, very specific forms of dress are sanctioned for all participants. Women are required to wear a ceremonial skirt (in recent decades, presumably one made of commercial cotton cloth), a length of red trade cloth as a breast wrap (*timban,* see fig. **20**), a special headband (*tekolok rantang*; see fig. **16**), and a coir belt (*ringgit*). Men wear a loincloth (*cawat*), a shirt (*baju*), a headband (also called *tekolok,* but in recent times a batik cloth), and ankle bells (*gengiring,* another wonderfully onomotopoeic name). *Pantun,* or improivsed poems, are made up to make fun at anyone who is not properly attired. The *belian* herself wears an elaborate headdress made with a branch of young areca nuts and coconut fronds that have been cut into elaborate decorative patterns.

I was struck by the importance placed on this ceremony by the people who described it. While shamanism is widespread in Borneo, I have not found descriptions of other cultures where the initiation of a new shaman would be considered the single most important ceremonial event. The type of female *belian* described is obviously not simply a curer, but rather a broader religious specialist whose command of sacred texts and ability to communicate with spirits gave her a dominating role in vouchsafing the community's welfare. As H. S. Morris has observed regarding major shaman ceremonies among the Melanu of Sarawak, the spirits may raise unexpected issues that involve the entire community: "the occasion is sacred and permeated by a sense of danger, awe, and mystery..." (1993: 111). In neighboring Mindanao, oral histories that trace the origins of kin groups often center around a female shaman who is the defacto temporal leader of the community, guiding her people on a series of journeys in search of a home.

Although Air Upas also has a harvest festival called *nyapat tahun* (new year), which is still celebrated every year, this does not involve the wearing of ceremonial skirts. We did, however, hear a tale, rather playfully related to us, that involves the wearing of such skirts. This story centers on Atu Panji Pauh, a local culture hero of sorts, or perhaps more accurately a ne'er-do-well. While his name suggests a relationship to the famous Panji stories of Java, in character Atu Panji Pauh secms to bear more in common with the Iban comic hero and shaman Apai Aloi (see, for example, Sather 1993). Atu Panji Pauh was a handsome playboy who refused to marry, an unfathomable oddity according to local conception, because he would never be satisfied with just one woman. This made the women of his community furious, so they hatched a plan to seek revenge. They invited Atu Panji Pauh to come visit them, and when he arrived, he found them all gathered together – stark naked. He set to work, doing what he was famous for, but in the end it was too much for him and he became so exhausted that his penis broke. Out of this incident came an agreement among all the women that they would have to celebrate this momentous day annually or else some great natural calamity would befall them. The imagined scope of such a disaster is encapsulated in this rhyme:

Tabu jadi tebarau	Sugar will become bitter cane.
Padi jadi rumbut	Rice will become grass.
Keribang jadi batu	Yams will become stones.

This folktale provides the basis for a lighthearted celebration that is apparently still held in Air Upas once every three years. Its main points are that the women have to give seven fistfuls of rice to the men, seven cups of rice wine are to be at hand, the women must wear their ceremonial skirts, and they must stand in front of the men and "swish" these skirts in a particular way. The word that was used to describe to us this motion (*kibas*) can mean to "swish" or "wag" or "flap," so amid much laughter, room was left for a certain amount of ambiguity. While this may just be a playful festival, in the Southeast Asian context it also suggests a fertility festival that may once have involved a prescribed period of sexual license. As with the *belian* rituals, these issues were somewhat sensitive and more prolonged research would be required to confirm them. Nevertheless, we may have erringly stumbled upon the most culturally significant "use" of the ceremonial skirts of southwestern Borneo.

References

Boruchoff, Judith
1986   *Register of the Papers of William Louis Abbott.* Washington: National Anthropological Archives.

Burkhill, Isaac Henry
1935   *A Dictionary of the Economic Products of the Malay Peninsula* London: Crown Agents for the Colonies.

Helliwell, Christine
2001   "Never Stand Alone" *A Study of Borneo Sociality.* Borneo Research Council Monograph Series, Vol. 5. Phillips, ME: Borneo Research Council.

Juynboll, H. H.
1909   *Borneo.* Katalog des Ethnographischen Reichsmuseums, Bd. 1-2. Leiden: E. J. Brill.

Kloss, Cecil Boden
1995 [1903] *In the Andamans and Nicobars.* Bangkok: White Lotus.

Kooijman, Simon
1963   *Ornamented Bark-Cloth in Indonesia.* Mededelingen van het Rijksmuseum voor Volkenkunde, Leiden, no. 16. Leiden: E. J. Brill.

Leigh-Theisen, Heide
1995   *Textilien in Indonesia.* Vienna: Museum für Völkerkunde.

Metcalf, Peter
2002   *They Lie, We Lie: Getting on with Anthropology.* London and New York: Routledge.

Morris, H. S.
1993   "Shamanism among the Oya Melanau." In Winzeler 1993, p. 101-130.

Raven, Henry Cushier
1932   "Barkcloth Making in Central Celebes". Natural History 32 (4): 372-383.

Sather, Clifford
1993   "Shaman and Fool: Representation of the Shaman in Iban Comic Fables." In Winzeler 1993, p. 281-319.

Taylor, Paul Michael
1985   "The Indonesian Collections of William Louis Abbott (1860-1936): Invitation to a Research Resource at the Smithsonian Institution." Council for Musuem Anthropology Newsletter 9 (2): 5-13.

Taylor, Paul Michael
2002   "A Collector and His Museum: William Louis Abbott (1860-1936) and the Smithsonian" In Reimar Schefold and Han F. Vermeulen (eds.), *Treasure Hunting? Collectors and Collections of Indonesian Artefacts,* Mededelingen van het Rijksmuseum voor Volkenkunde No. 30, Leiden: Research School of Asian, African, and Amerindian Studies (CNWS), University of Leiden.

Taylor, Paul Michael and Roy W. Hamilton
1993   "The Borneo Collections of W. L. Abbott (1860-1936) at the Smithsonian." In Vinson H. Sutlive, Jr., ed., *Change and Development in Borneo.* Selected Papers from the First Extraordinary Conference of The Borneo Research Council, August 4-9, 1990. Williamsburg, VA: Borneo Research Council.

Veth, Pieter Johannes
1854   *Borneo's Wester-afdeeling, Geographisch, Statistisch, Historisch, Voorafgegaan door eene Algemeene Schets des Ganschen Eilands.* Zaltbommel (Netherlands): J. Norman en zoon.

Winzeler, Robert L., ed.
1993   *The Seen and the Unseen: Shamanism, Mediumship and Possession in Borneo.* Borneo Research Council Monograph Series, Volume Two. Williamsburg, VA: Borneo Research Council.

Wurm, Stephen A. and Shiro Hattori
1981   *Language Atlas of the Pacific Area.* Canberra: Australian Academy of the Humanities.

Footnotes

[1] My work with the Abbott Collection in Washington from 1990 to 1992 was arranged and supervised by Dr. Paul Michael Taylor, Curator of Asian Ethnology, and funded by the Smithsonian's Scholarly Studies Program.

[2] The skirt in Vienna has been published (Leigh-Theisen 1995: 226). The museum in Leiden also has a couple of painted skirts that somewhat resemble one of Abbott's painted skirts.

[3] My travel to Borneo was partly supported by a grant from the Southeast Asia Council of the Association for Asian Studies. In Indonesia, the late Basrul Akram of the Directorat of Museums kindly made arrangements for my study.

[4] Quotation from a letter to his mother dated Dec. 22, 1898; Smithsonian Institution Archives, Personal Correspondence of William Louis Abbott, Box 2, Folder 12, Document 17.

[5] Quotation from a letter to Otis T. Mason dated March 30, 1904; National Anthropological Archives, Papers of William Louis Abbott, Box 1, Folder 2, Document 5.

[6] For more thorough treatments of Abbott and his collection, see Taylor (1985), Taylor and Hamilton (1993), and Taylor (2002).

[7] The National Anthropological Archives has published a finding aid for the collection, Boruchoff 1986.

[8] I would be remiss if I did not make brief mention of the deplorable political and environmental situation we encountered in 1993, five years before the end of the Suharto regime. Vast tracks of the land scape through which we traveled, including in the swamp forest zone, were literally on fire. While swidden farmers traditionally clear their plots by burning and a pall of smoke covers Borneo in the dry season months of July and August, it was clear that devas tation on a much more catastrophic scale was taking place. Through the collusion of corrupt local officials, large areas were being turned over to palm oil corporations. These were lands that under the traditional system were owned by the entire community, with temporary use rights granted to those who cleared and farmed the land. Without modern legal deeds of ownership, the state chose to interpret these lands as un-owned, and villagers soon found their supply of farm lands occupied by palm oil corporations. To me the scale of the burning seemed diabolical – far beyond any reasonable plan to clear land for oil palm plantations – and the local people felt that it was a deliberate campaign being waged to force them off their land by rendering it unusable.

[9] Abbott also collected along the Simpang and Semandang Rivers, in 1907, but he found no decorated barkcloth skirts there.

[10] Pers. com, 1992.

[11] If this is the case, they appear to have been wrapped to close over the right thigh rather than the left, as the more highly decorated portion of all of the asymmetrical designs is always on the left as the viewer faces the skirt (it seems unlikely that the main design was intended to appear at the back of the skirt rather than the front). Abbott's photo of women wearing barkcloth skirts in the Simpang River drainage and shows undecorated skirts wrapped to close – barely – at the wearer's left side.

[12] All of these details about the types of bark are from Abbott's hand written tags, as are the local names for the skirts.

[13] To an inexperienced eye, mine included, it would be hard to tell genuine jerenaung from coloured wax. Although we tried to pursue this fabled pigment to its local source, we could never really be sure of what was being offered to us.

[14] Actually, the tag is partially illegible, and only jer[...]g is certain, but this could hardly be anything other than his *jernang.* He goes on to say, however, that this is mixed with lime. I have not been able to locate full descriptions of dyeing technology using "dragon's blood," but the waxy substance we saw in use would not seem to be readily soluble in water. It is possible that the same names were applied to different materials as long as they produced the desired deep red colour.

[15] This community name was not mentioned by Abbott; it may not have existed in his time, or perhaps he simply did not go there. Due to the lack of an accurate local map with current place names, I can not place it with certainty, although we may have crossed over from the drainage of the Membuluh River into the drainage of the neigh boring Air Hitam.

[16] I have attempted to render the village names, as recorded by Abbott, into contemporary Indonesian orthography; thus his Greemai becomes Gerimai, Tebbing Tinggi becomes Tebing Tingi, etc.

Piety and Protection
Talismanic Textiles in Islamic Southeast Asia[1]

Robyn J. Maxwell

Many of the most sumptuous textiles in Southeast Asia are closely associated with the Islamic courts of the region. The rulers of the region's principalities, which were strategically located along the seemingly endless coasts and riverine reaches of insular and peninsular Southeast Asia, drew on a wide range of sources to create a courtly presence entirely appropriate to their role as conduits between the older worlds of local ancestral traditions and the lively sphere of international maritime trade. In fact at receptions for allies and enemies alike, displays of finery confirmed the political and economic importance of a principality, while for the more overtly religious, such opulence demonstrated the righteousness of the reign.

While the textiles used in the Southeast Asian courts included cloth imported, often at great expense, from neighbouring and distant shores, many of the most spectacular were locally made. The techniques and tools by which these fine cloths were created were largely indigenous to the Southeast Asian region, although the silk and gold threads were also luxury trade items. Sources for the motifs which appear on the textiles are many, and the complex designs reveal the skills of local textile-makers in selecting and interpreting the visual offerings of past and present. Today the most popular designs reveal the gamut of the region's history – from Southeast Asia's ancestral and Hindu-Buddhist pasts, and the region's location at the cross roads of maritime trade.

Thus although Islam has been an important feature of Southeast Asian culture since at least the thirteenth century, many of region's textiles do not exhibit specifically Islamic designs. In fact much of the discussion of Southeast Asian textiles has ignored the input of Islam, including the impact of the great empires of Persia, Mughal India, and Ottoman Turkey as powerful influences on the arts of the wider international realm of Islam and beyond. Even the popular stylized floral and tendril motifs and geometric patterns are often drawn from the repertoire of the international Islamic orna-ment. The courts of Islamic Southeast Asia played a key role in mediating the transformation of international forms to local textiles.

This paper focuses, however, on a small number of rare types of Southeast Asian textiles which display overtly Islamic motifs and designs inspired by international models[2] (1). It argues that, while such apparently Islamic textiles can be understood in terms of the internationally recognizable symbols they display, the functions and meaning closely parallels other local Southeast Asian textiles of similar form. With few exceptions, the textiles with specifically Islamic motifs are strongly imbedded in local textile traditions in terms of style, form, decorative technique and meaning. Many can only be understood within Southeast Asian contexts and in terms of pre existing and coexisting textile practice. This meaning derives precisely from the fact that Islam was relatively readily absorbed into many Southeast Asian cultures. A combination of the syncretic disposition of Southeast Asian cultures to exotic ideas and objects, and the forms of Islam, especially Sufism, that were attractive to local adherents, led to quite subtle shifts in the meanings of preexisting arts – and conversely to the oft-remarked appearance that Islam had little impact on the arts that survive.

In Southeast Asia these common traditions and indigenous origins are evident not only in the techniques, loom technology and dress forms but, most importantly, in the central role of women in the production of both fine court and village fabric. Unlike the royal workshops of Persia, Turkey and Mughal India, where the fabrics worn by rulers and presented as regal gifts were created by men, textile creation continued to be the art practised by women throughout Islamic Southeast Asia, both in the village and in the palace, and in both cotton and silk. This is, perhaps, not surprising where respect for older ancestral practices continues and time-held rites were adapted to the new ideas which came with Islam. Enduring beliefs in the complemen-tarities of male and female elements for the prosperity

1 Cirebon, west Java, Indonesia, exported to south Sulawesi. Ceremonial drape or covering for bier, 19th century, handspun cotton, stamped batik, 228.0 x 106.0 cm. *(National Gallery of Australia, Canberra 2005.156)*

and fertility of family and realm continue to pervade all parts of Southeast Asia. Textiles, from the hands of women, thus comprise a crucial element in all rituals: their presence at key ceremonies in the life cycle of both peasant and aristocrat ensures harmony and abundance. Throughout Islamic Southeast Asia the ceremonial wedding dais and bridal bed are swathed in fine textiles produced by female relatives.

The arrival of Islam in Southeast Asia also resulted in the slow development of overtly Islamic designs and motifs on some of the region's textiles. The role of the international trade in these significant innovations in textile design is unclear. Distinctly Islamic designs, especially calligraphic motifs, appear rarely on Indian textiles, and few Persian cloths displaying cartouches in Arabic script have survived in Southeast Asia. The treasuries of the rulers of the region often do contain fine textiles, largely acquired during the pilgrimage to Mecca, but these are invariably decorative, like the popular Egyptian flat ribbon embroidered netting. However, a fine vest from Malaysia tailored from eighteenth-century century Ottoman silk lampas indicates the type of textiles also circulating in the Islamic world, although extant examples in Southeast Asia are very rare (2). Turkish fabrics with calligraphic designs of this type were used to cover tombs and cenotaphs. The chevron designs combine bands of a Quranic verse in the smaller inscriptions, with the *Shahadah* (There is no god but

Allah and Muhammad is His prophet) in the bold broad bands. Like many textiles and garments inscribed with Quranic verses and pious invocations such as the *Shahadah*, the garment is both decorative and protective, the revelation of the sacred Word providing talismanic protection for the aristocratic owner of the vest.

A number of specifically Islamic motifs and designs, including Arabic inscriptions, and drawn from a variety of sources appear on textiles made in Southeast Asia (3, 4). While the designs are recognizably international and pan-Islamic, the textile forms on which they are displayed are usually versions of traditional textiles, little modified in layout and size to accommodate the important motifs. In fact, the meaning and function of Southeast Asian textiles with clear Islamic content, such as Arabic inscriptions, appear to be consistent with older cloth usage: the textiles clearly signal the identity of the owner (and maker) to an audience who appreciates the vocabulary of local cloth, while the cloths fulfill the ancient protective role of enveloping and sheltering the wearer. In such instances, the religious identification with Islam in no way negates older indigenous beliefs in the properties of cloth as symbols of status and safeguards against the unknown and the uncertain; rather, the incorporation of the Islamic motifs adds another layer of meanings to cloth whose origins lie in a distant and different past.[3]

2 Malaysia, Talismanic vest, early 20th century, imported Turkish silk lampas fabric, European printed cotton lining, embroidery, 51.0 x 49.0 cm. (*Department of Museums and Antiquities, Kuala Lumpur*)

4 Aceh, Sumatra, Indonesia, Shoulder cloth or ceremonial drape *[ija tobuléë kasab bungong kalimah]*, 19th century, silk, metallic thread, supplementary weft weaving, 149.0 x 84.0 cm. (*Museum of Asian Art, University of Malaya , Kuala Lumpur, um80.108*)

3 Kelantan, Malaysia, Ceremonial drape or covering in the form of a shoulder cloth *[kain lemar bersurat]*, late 19th century, silk, weft ikat, 216.0 x 83.0 cm. (*Department of Museums and Antiquities, Kuala Lumpur*)

The image of the bouraq, the fabulous creature on which the Prophet Muhammad ascended to Heaven, is popular in the arts of Southeast Asia, appearing in wood, glass painting, and, of course, textiles. Like the hand of Fatima in other parts of the Islamic world, the bouraq became an attractive and decorative motif for ceremonial objects, particularly throughout coastal Sumatran communities where a love of composite creatures has a long history.[4] With its human face, equine body and the wings and tail of a peacock, the bouraq was embroidered in gold onto many of the ornate hangings that surround the formal dais or throne at weddings and other festive ceremonies (5). On these textiles, the fantastic creature is often displayed in a paradisiacal setting, with flowering trees on mirror mounds.

The lion is another recurring Islamic motif on textiles, frequently combined with the image of the double-bladed sword; both of these are symbolic of the Caliph Ali, the son-in law of the Prophet. At its most spectacular, the lion of God was formed from Arabic calligraphy in the style of Central Asia and Turkey. On a charming head cloth from Cirebon in West Java, a calligraphic lion appears in each corner (6). Head cloths with Islamic designs – in batik, *songket* brocade, embroidery and even gold leaf *perada* – were popular in the nineteenth and early twentieth centuries, and occasionally Islamic motifs were also incorporated into other forms of head wear. They were believed to afford the wearer protection, and their use in covering the most sacred part of the human body was especially auspicious. Lions, often in conjunction with an inscription of the name of Allah, also appeared in the gold embroidered velvet coverings for gifts offered at Malay ceremonies throughout Sumatra.

On a very rare and imposing banner from the court of Cirebon in west Java, calligraphic lions formed from the *Basmalah*, In the name of God the Compassionate, the Merciful, are positioned around a dominating cen-

5 Aceh, Sumatra, Indonesia, Ceremonial hanging, early 20th century, cotton, wool, silk, gold thread, sequins, beads, mica, appliqué, lace, couching, embroidery, 64.0 x 208.0 cm. *(National Gallery of Australia, Canberra 1984.1986)*

6 Cirebon, west Java, Indonesia, Man's headcloth *[ikat kepala]*, 19th century, handspun cotton, natural dyes, batik, 86.0 x 84.0 cm. *(Jakarta Textile Museum, Jakarta. 025.1)*

tral image of the sword, an appropriate image for marshalling troops (7). This very early Javanese batik on fine handspun cotton was created through the masterful display of calligraphy. This raises a number of questions about the role and background of the maker. Most of strokes and swirls on the blue and white batik cloths produced in Java in the late nineteenth and early twentieth centuries are merely suggestive of Arabic calligraphy, but in fact largely illegible. Although the script form the shapes of stars and birds, it is often impossible to decipher, with only a simple rendition of the name of

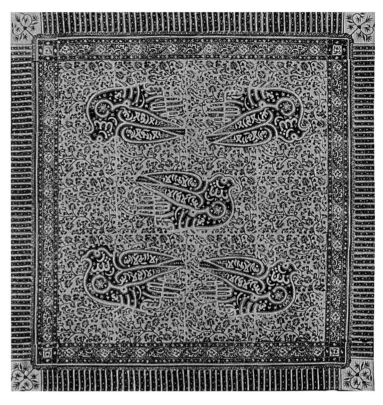

8 Java, Indonesia, Man's headcloth *[ikat kepala]*, early 20th century, cotton, indigo, stamped batik, 90.0 x 91.0 cm. (*Powerhouse Museum, Sydney A10014*)

7 Cirebon, west Java, Indonesia, Royal banner, late 18th century, handspun cotton, indigo, handdrawn batik, Indian mordant painted trade cloth border. (*Jakarta Textile Museum, Jakarta 017*)

Allah can be discerned from the sweep of the *canting* waxing pen (8). This is not surprising, since the women who made these commercial products for trade across Java and Sumatra were illiterate – in Javanese (or Sundanese) and in Arabic. The purchasers of the rectangular textiles were probably also unable to read Arabic, yet this was irrelevant. The value of the cloth was in the clear and unambiguous message it sent to viewers – that the owner was Muslim. The calligraphic cloths largely served as coverings – for the dead as shrouds and for the living as shawls and head covers (9). The clear and stylish calligraphy on the Cirebon banner was unlikely to have been drawn by a Javanese peasant, but rather by a highly literate and learned Muslim. It was undoubtedly made in the royal palace of Cirebon and probably not penned by a woman: Cirebon alone has a history of men involved in the actual production of hand-drawn batik and this was, in all probability, in the very early days in the history of the development of batik. (The accessibility of fine commercially woven cotton cloth in the nineteenth century would see the batik industry burgeon).

However, this banner was not an aberration. Within a short period of time, it appears that the export of batik throughout insular Southeast Asia expanded. Another rare handspun indigo and white batik from Cirebon, part of a noble collection in south Sulawesi, also displays the same bands of the inscription, There is no God but Allah, as the banner, along with clear and legible verses from the Qur'an (10). It is said to have functioned as a shroud, temporarily displayed over a funeral bier or tomb, a popular function of the later cruder calligraphic batiks. The ancestral practice of burying textiles and other items of wealth with the dead no longer applied at Islamic funerals. In fact, while the honouring of the dead remains an obligation to the descendants, the ceremonial shift to the celebration of life rather than death still marks distinct differences in the function of textiles in Islamic and animist Southeast Asia.

10 Cirebon, west Java, Indonesia, exported to south Sulawesi. Ceremonial drape and covering for bier, 19th century, handspun cotton, stamped batik, 228.0 x 106.0 cm. (detail). Note the central cartouche with the name of Allah is read from the reverse side of the cloth. *(National Gallery of Australia, Canberra 2005.156)*

This development of calligraphic imagery made an important contribution to Southeast Asian textile arts.[5] The protective role of textiles in life cycle ceremonies encouraged the incorporation of calligraphy into cloth **(11)**. In this way, the Kelantan *kain limar* bearing calligraphic motifs was formed into tent to cover a young prince at his circumcision rites[6] **(12)**. An embroidered hanging with calligraphic designs was also hung during the meeting of district heads in west Sumatra. In some instances, the Islamic inscription took the form of a magic grid, a secret combination of auspicious numbers, a practice widely adopted throughout the Islamic world. A combination of beliefs in the Divine origin of numbers and a confidence in the display of talismans for protection encouraged the placement of squares and diagrams containing Arabic numerals on a variety of textiles. The magic grid appears on head cloths, ornamental buckles for the bride, golden discs for attaching to sword belts and on charm containers to ward off evil **(13)**. Magic grids also appear on the great batik banner. It is a subtle motif embroidered on a rich velvet cushion for the royal baby's first hair cutting in Palembang[7] and the dominant design on a crude talismanic cloth from Sarawak **(14)**. The magic grid is found across the entire Islamic world, yet its meaning on Southeast Asian textiles resonates with beliefs about the talismanic properties of many textile designs from previous eras.

9 North Java, Indonesia, overdyed in Aceh, Sumatra, Head or shoulder cover or shroud for bier *[kain batik tulisan Arab]*, late 19th century, cotton, natural dyes, handdrawn batik, 220.0 x 87.4 cm. *(National Gallery of Australia, Canberra 1987.347)*

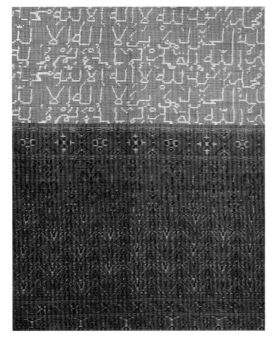

11 Sasak, Lombok, Indonesia, Sacred cloth *[usap or subah nalé]*, 19th century, handspun cotton, natural dyes, supplementary weft weaving, 54.0 x 54.0 cm. Note the calligraphy reads correctly from the reverse side of the cloth. (*National Gallery of Australia, Canberra 2005.275*)

12 (Detail) Kelantan, Malaysia, Ceremonial drape or covering in the form of a shoulder cloth *[kain lemar bersurat]*, late 19th century, silk, weft ikat. (*Department of Museums and Antiquities, Kuala Lumpur*)

13 Buginese, south Sumatra, Indonesia, Man's ceremonial sword belt, late 19th century, cotton, natural dyes, tablet weaving, 12.0 x 380.0 cm. (*National Gallery of Australia, Canberra 1984.1989*)

In some parts of Southeast Asia, it is not only the application of Arabic inscriptions that evokes protection. Other older scripts are also applied to textiles to act as charms and talismans. A poignant prayer in the form of a poem inscribed in batik in Javanese *kawi* script on the ends of a central Javanese baby carrier demonstrates belief in the power of protective cloth and of talismanic inscriptions which, in this instance, appeal to both Allah and the ancestors for the recovery of a sick child (15). The textile design of the broken sword *parang rusak* reveals the noble connections of the family willing the child's recovery through traditional means. Another talismanic cloth, said to be appropriate for wedding ceremonies, combines Arabic calligraphy with inscriptions in old Buginese, the designs symbolically protected by a pair of *naga* serpents, creatures that, like the textiles, appear to have survived the changes of religious orientation (16).

Growing tensions, especially in Indonesia and the Philippines, between local polities and colonial government authorities encouraged the repeated use of a number of interesting textile designs and the creation of others. The widespread use of calligraphic designs on the brocades of the Acehnese nobility can be seen as a response to increasing Dutch military incursions in the longest of their colonial wars[8] (17). The gold and silver inscriptions were not only of talismanic significance, but a visual rallying point in the face of the European invasions. Talismanic jackets with Islamic calligraphy in supplementary cotton were also produced by the Sasak on

14 Malay, Malaysia, Talisman and man's headcloth *[kain kalimah]*, cotton, ink drawing, 82.0 x 80.0 cm. (*Sarawak Museum Department, Kuching 91/48*)

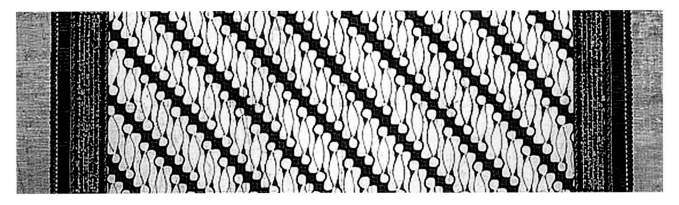

15 Jogjakarta, Java, Indonesia, Baby carrier *[kain gendongan]*, cotton, natural dyes, handdrawn batik, early 20th century, 278.0 x 75.0 cm. *(National Gallery of Australia, Canberra 1987.344)*

17 Aceh, Sumatra, Indonesia, Ceremonial shouldercloth *[ija tobulëë kasab bungong kalimah]*, 19th century, silk, metallic thread, supplementary weft weaving, 240.0 x 92.0 cm. *(Rijksmuseum voor Volkenkunde, Leiden 1599-140)*

16 Buginese, south Sulawesi, Indonesia, Talismanic cloth, 19th-early 20th century, cotton, pigments, drawing, 66.0 x 46.0 cm. Given by Jonathan Hope to remember Yamin Makawaru. *(National Gallery of Australia, Canberra 2005.154)*

the island of Lombok, another arena of colonial war-fare.[9] Yet the textiles often known as the 'Lombok Wars' batiks were made on the north coast of Java in Eurasian ateliers (18). Their quaint scenes of Dutch and Indonesian figures within a landscape of nineteenth-century military apparatus seem to have appealed to both indigenous and colonial audiences alike, and a con-siderable number of the hand-drawn batiks appear to have been produced in the early years of the twentieth century. The eventual market for another batik design from the same region of Java, showing a caravan of laden camels and a row of tents with robed figures holding flags which read *Bendera Radja Mekkah* (the Flag of the Ruler of Mecca) in Roman script, is unknown (19). Similar imagery is found on a baby carrier depicting the nineteenth-century resistance leader, Prince Dipo-negoro, turbaned as he was depicted in contemporary images, on horseback holding a flag aloft (20). This tex-tile is particularly fascinating, since baby carriers in the style were largely used by local Chinese communities which were also actively involved in the production of north-coast batiks.

18 Batavia, west Java, Indonesia, Skirt *[kain sarong]*, late 19th-early 20th century, cotton, dyes, hand-drawn batik, 104.0 x 199.0 cm. (*National Gallery of Australia, Canberra 1984.616*)

19 Pekalongan, north Java, Indonesia, Skirt *[kain sarong]*, early 20th century, cotton, batik, 107.2 x 88.9 cm. (*Asian Civilisations Museum, Singapore 2000.5573*)

81

20 Lasem, north Java, Indonesia, Baby carrier [*kain gendongan*], late 19th century, cotton, natural dyes, handdrawn batik, 296.0 x 98.5 cm. (*National Gallery of Australia, Canberra 1984.3151*)

Southeast Asian textiles remain symbols of both innovation and resistance to change. Over centuries they have been key items in trade, and yet are also the interesting outcome of such exchanges. Although the most luxurious fabrics are extravagant symbols of wealth and high status, some of the most powerful textiles are modest products of simple looms. The textiles of Islamic Southeast Asia serve as a metaphor for a mercantile era in which the cultural and commercial centres of the region played a vital role. Those principalities provided a link between the international outside world and the indigenous interiors of the realm. Their textiles absorbed many elements of that internationalism, while remaining firmly grounded – in form, function and techniques – in the older indigenous belief systems and traditions. Textile remained a symbol of the finest of regional skills, while their makers looked to the wider world for inspiration. Thus the Islamic nature of such textiles, their motifs and meaning is often subtle and multivalent, even when the designs incorporate such quintessentially Islamic imagery as Arabic calligraphy.

Bibliography:

Baker, Patricia L., *Islamic Textiles*, British Museum Press, London,. 1995.

Bennett, James (ed.), *Crescent Moon: Islamic Art & Civilisation in Southeast Asia*. Art Gallery of South Australia, Adelaide/National Gallery of Australia, Canberra, 2005.

van Brakel, Koos (ed.), *Budaya Indonesia, Art and Crafts in Indonesia*, Royal Tropical Institute, Amsterdam, 1987.

van Brakel, Koos (ed.), *A passion for Indonesian art: The Georg Tillmann (1882-1941) Collection at the Tropenmuseum, Amsterdam*, Royal Tropical Institute, Amsterdam, 1996.

Fischer, Joseph, *The Folk Art of Java*. Oxford University Press, Kuala Lumpur & New York, 1994.

Gittinger, Mattiebelle, *Splendid Symbols: Textiles and Tradition in Indonesia*, Oxford University Press, Singapore, 1985.

Gittinger, Mattiebelle, *Textiles for this world and beyond: Treasures from insular Southeast Asia*, Scala Publishers, London/The Textile Museum, Washington DC, 2005.

Gittinger, Mattiebelle (ed), *To Speak with Cloth: Studies in Indonesian Textiles*, Museum of Cultural History, University of California, Los Angeles, 1989.

Guy, John, *Woven Cargoes: Indian Textiles in the East*, Thames & Hudson, London, 1998.

Hamilton, Roy (ed), *From the Rainbow's Varied Hue: Textiles of the Southern Philippines*, UCLA Fowler Museum of Cultural History, Los Angeles, 1998.

Kerlogue, Fiona, 'Islamic Talismans: the Calligraphy Batiks' in *Batik: Drawn in Wax*, ed. Itie van Hout, Royal Tropical Institute, Amsterdam, 2001.

Laarhoven, Ruudje, 'A Passion for Plaids: A Historical Consideration of Maguindanao' in *From the Rainbow's Hue: Textiles of the Southern Philippines* (Roy W. Hamilton ed). Los Angeles: UCLA Fowler Museum of Cultural History, 1998.

Leigh, Barbara, *Tangan-tangan Trampilan: Hands of Time: the Visual Arts of Aceh*. Jambatan: Jakarta, 1988.

Maxwell, Robyn, 'De rituele weefsels van Oost-Indonesie' in *Indigo: leven in een kleur* (L. Oei ed). Fibula-Van Dishoeck , 1985.

Maxwell, Robyn, 'The Tree of Life in Indonesian Textiles', in G. Völger and K. Welck (eds), *Indonesian Textiles: Symposium 1985*, Rautenstrauch-Joest-Museum, Cologne, 1991.

Maxwell, Robyn, 'Faith, Hope and Charity: The Use of Calligraphic Motifs in Southeast Asia', in Songsak Prangwatthanakun (ed.), *Textiles of Asia: A Common Heritage*, Center for the Promotion of Arts and Culture, Chiangmai University, Chiang Mai, 1993.

Maxwell, Robyn, *Textiles of Southeast Asia: Tradition, Trade and Transformation*, rev. edn, Periplus, Singapore, 2003.

Maxwell, Robyn, *Sari to Sarong: 500 Years of Indian and Indonesian Textile Exchange*, National Gallery of Australia, Canberra. 2003.

Maxwell, Robyn, 'Tradition and Innovation in the Islamic Textiles of Southeast Asia' in *Crescent Moon: Islamic Art & Civilisation in Southeast Asia* (James Bennett ed). Adelaide: Art Gallery of South Australia; Canberra: National Gallery of Australia, 2005.

Mohd. Kassim B. Hj Ali, *Gold Jewelry and Ornaments of Malaysia*, Muzium Negara, Kuala Lumpur, 1988.

Mohd. Kassim B. Hj Ali, *Barang Kemas Melayu Tradisi*, Dewan Bahasa dan Pustaka. Kuala Lumpur, 1990.

Muzium Negara, *Gold Jewelry and Ornaments of Malaysia*, Muzium Negara, Kuala Lumpur, 1988.

Othman Mohd. Yatim, *Batu Aceh: Early Islamic Gravestones in Peninsular Malaysia*, Museum Association of Malaysai, Kuala Lumpur, 1988.

H. Santosa Doellah, *Batik: The Impact of Time and Environment*, Danar Hadi, Surakarta, 2002.

Selvanayagam, Grace, *Songket: Malaysia's Woven Treasure*. Singapore: Oxford University Press, 1990.

Sheppard, Mubin, *Taman Indera, Malay Decorative Arts and Pastimes*, Oxford University Press, Kuala Lumpur, 1972.

Siti Zainon Ismail, *Tekstil Tenunan Melayu: Keindahan Budaya Tradisional Nusantara*, Dewan Bahasa dan Pustaka, Kuala Lumpur, 1994.

Summerfield, Anne and John Summerfield (ed), *Walk in Splendour: Ceremonial Dress and the Minangkabau*, UCLA Fowler Museum of Cultural History, Los Angeles, 1999.

Taylor, Paul Michael & Lorraine V. Aragon, *Beyond the Java Sea: Art of Indonesia's Outer Islands*, National Museum of Natural History, Smithsonian Institution, Washington DC., Harry N. Abrams, New York, 1991.

Van Hout, Itie (ed.), *Batik: Drawn in Wax*, Royal Tropical Institute, Amsterdam, 2001.

Zubaidah Shawal, *Busana Melayu*, Jabatan Muzium dan Antikulti Malaysia, Kuala Lumpur, 1994.

Footnotes

1 This paper forms part of a longer essay, "Tradition and innovation in the textiles of Islamic Southeast Asia" in James Bennett (ed.), *Crescent Moon: Islamic Art & Civilisation in Southeast Asia (Bulan Sabit: Seni dan Peradaban Islam di Asia Tenggara)*, Art Gallery of South Australia, Adelaide/National Gallery of Australia, Canberra, 2005.

2 While this discussion does not include the southern Philippines, many of the observations may well also apply to those textiles also. While the interest in Islamic aspects of Malaysian and Indonesian textiles has been minimal, there has been even less research and documentation of the traditional textile traditions of the Islamic communities of the Philippines.

3 Fiona Kerlogue, 'Islamic Talismans: the Calligraphy Batiks' in Itie van Hout (ed.), *Batik: Drawn in Wax*, Royal Tropical Institute, Amsterdam, 2001; Robyn Maxwell, 'Faith, Hope and Charity: The Use of Calligraphic Motifs in Southeast Asia', in Songsak Prangwatthanakun (ed.), *Textiles of Asia: A Common Heritage*, Center for the Promotion of Arts and Culture, Chiang Mai University, Chiang Mai, 1993.

4 Barbara Leigh, *Tangan-tangan Trampilan: Hands of Time: the Visual Arts of Aceh*. Jambatan: Jakarta, 1988; Joseph Fischer, *The Folk Art of Java*. Oxford University Press, Kuala Lumpur & New York, 1994.

5 Fiona Kerlogue, 'Islamic Talismans: the Calligraphy Batiks' in Itie van Hout (ed.), *Batik: Drawn in Wax*, Royal Tropical Institute, Amsterdam, 2001.

6 Robyn Maxwell, *Textiles of Southeast Asia: Tradition, Trade and Transformation*, rev. edn, Periplus, Singapore, 2003.

7 Robyn Maxwell, *Textiles of Southeast Asia: Tradition, Trade and Transformation*, rev. edn, Periplus, Singapore, 2003; Robyn Maxwell, 'Faith, Hope and Charity: The Use of Calligraphic Motifs in Southeast Asia', in Songsak Prangwatthanakun (ed.), *Textiles of Asia: A Common Heritage*, Center for the Promotion of Arts and Culture, Chiang Mai University, Chiang Mai, 1993.

8 Robyn Maxwell, *Textiles of Southeast Asia: Tradition, Trade and Transformation*, rev. edn, Periplus, Singapore, 2003.

9 Paul Michael Taylor & Lorraine V. Aragon, *Beyond the Java Sea: Art of Indonesia's Outer Islands*, National Museum of Natural History, Smithsonian Institution, Washington DC., Harry N. Abrams, New York, 1991, pp. 296-301.

Shan Expressions of Power and Protection

Susan Conway

Shan shamans were recognised throughout inland Southeast Asia as particularly powerful. Their skills were expressed in the form of tattoos, textiles, charms, mystical chanting, dance and trance. This paper examines what is generally termed "body decoration", namely tattoos, textiles and charms, considered in a historical context and in comparison with contemporary equivalents in the Shan state of Keng Tung. The focus here is on a male practitioner although shamanism has never been confined to men. In fact Sir George Scott claimed in the nineteenth century that the majority were women.[1] There are many powerful Shan women now as in the past, who are particularly known for their skill as fortune-tellers and their ability to call the spirits through dance and trance. In some cases skills were passed down through shaman families although, as this paper will indicate, that was not always the case.

The Shan are Theravada Buddhists but have a strong belief in spirit religion (generally described as animism), which teaches the existence of supernatural spirits. Spirits exist in many forms. They inhabit the fields and forests; they live in villages, in houses and in a host of natural objects within the village boundary. They can be ghosts of the dead, demons, witches or wandering astral spirits. They may enter the body and cause symptoms that require the specialist skills of a shaman who is an exorcist. They have an ability to cause suffering unless they are suitably propitiated. The function of the shaman is to communicate with spirits and to perform appropriate rituals to placate them. The terms used by the Shan for spirits are *phii* (a word of Tai origin) and *nat* (a Burmese word).

At village level most male and female shaman are farmers who practise intermittently. In the towns they may be full-time practitioners. If they have high status in the hierarchy of shaman, they attend all important spirit festivals, particularly the annual ceremony to appease city spirits. Most personal consultations are conducted at the shaman's house where manuscripts and other important ritual paraphernalia are kept on a special altar.

The shaman may recommend a ceremony is held to appease the spirits and he may select magic formulae for protection, administered as a potion, as tattoos, as charms or as talismanic textiles. In the Shan States Buddhist monks add their blessings to magic formulae created by shaman, and it was a belief widely held that magic was not effective unless such a blessing was given. The Yuan sect of Theravada Buddhism, as practiced in the Shan States, was particularly accepting of synchretic rituals.[2]

Induction in the shamanic arts involves an apprenticeship with the study of meditation and mysticism, supervised by a recognised expert. A period of fasting while wearing white clothing is included in the process.[3] Although it is no longer common practise, male apprentices were extensively tattooed with protective images that were considered particularly potent. Many drank water in which the ashes of scrolls, drawn with magic formulae had been dissolved[4] **(1)**.

Shaman used palm leaf manuscripts, and folding paper manuscripts as reference books **(9)**. They were inscribed with geometric diagrams *(ingwet)*, shamanic iconography and text *(yantra)* written in indigenous Shan script and in Burmese script. Shan script was

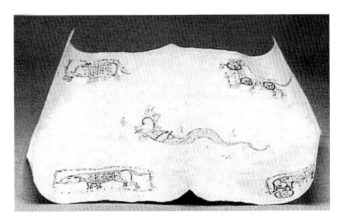

1 Paper scroll with mythical animals and magic formulae. Paper scrolls were often burnt, dissolved in water, and drunk as part of induction ceremonies for apprentice shaman. *(Fowler Museum of Cultural History, University of Los Angeles, X86.2748)*

considered to be particularly potent and was used in magic formulae prepared by shaman in Lan Na (north Thailand), Sipsong Pan Na (Xishuang Banna Province, southwest China) and Lan Xang (western Laos).[5]

Body decoration is an important element of male Shan dress, expressed in the form of tattoos, in charms inserted under the skin, in talismanic textiles and clothing, and in amulets. Until about fifty years ago, extensive tattooing was common practice among valley and hill tribe groups in the Shan States (2). Correctly formulated, tattoos acted like armour, warding off evil spirits, protecting the body against injury and imbuing the wearer with magical skills to defeat an enemy in war. Contrary to many societies where tattooing was common, there were no special marks or signs to denote senior rank, leading to the comment "beggar and king were equal in the hands of the professional tattoo artist".[6] However, the Shan authorities used small tattoo marks to brand prisoners of war, criminals and slaves.

Some Shan shaman were tattoo specialists and they were considered throughout inland Southeast Asia to be particularly accomplished. The technique involved first drawing the patterns freehand with a brush or imprinting them on the skin with a tattoo stamp. Using a special needle with longitudinal grooves to hold the pigment, the designs were pricked below the surface of the skin. Border patterns were applied with a sharp serrated plate resembling a comb. In the nineteenth century the pigment was a concoction of burnt animal fat, soot or lamp-black mixed with bile from a pig, a bear or a bull and with water added to achieve the correct consistency.[7] Opium was administered to ease the pain caused by the needles and the subsequent swelling and irritation on the surface of the skin. Not all men endured the tattooing process and gave up before the tattoos were finished.

Master copies of tattoo designs and patterns were inscribed on palm leaf or drawn on paper made from mulberry bark. The designs include legendary humans, particularly a cannibal king called Bawdithada, mythical animals and birds, and hideous monsters. The tiger (singha) and the water dragon (naga), and the monkey god Hanuman were popular figures. Some animals were selected in the belief that their natural instincts could be transferred in the tattoo image. Soldiers and professional thieves had a preference for tigers because they believed they would gain the strength and speed of the tiger.[8] The monkey Hanuman was thought to bring longevity while cats were associated with stealth. Men tattooed with an image of the cannibal king Bawditha believed that their bodies would be able to resist bullets, sword cuts and physical beating, and that they would be capable of outstanding feats of athleticism.

Tattoo designs also included mystical diagrams with complex ingwet grids, and yantra circles with numbers, letters and symbols. The numbers and letters represented stars, suns and planets or their mythical gods and goddesses, and were selected according to the horoscope of the person for whom the tattoos designs were created. A shaman interpreted yantra contained in the circles and squares as incantations (gatha), a Pali word for magical chanting. Although mythical characters, animals and mystical diagrams were common, thigh tattoos were often dominated by repeat abstract patterns that imitated dragon scales or waves on water.

The most impressive tattoos covered the legs from thigh to ankle and were known as shan baung-bi. During an audience in the 1870s with the Prince of Muong Li, a Shan state tributary to Keng Tung, the French explorer Louis de Carné noted the extent of the prince's tattoos:

At last he [the Prince of Muong Li] presented himself in great pomp, dressed in striped yellow and black

2   A man with tattooed thighs. *(Photo: Susan Conway, 1989)*

silk [trousers]...a large white calico dressing gown reaching below his knees, half hiding his thin calves which were tattooed all over..... . [9]

Some men also had their stomachs and buttocks tattooed, but until the recent past, most were tattooed on the thighs and legs as far as the knee, a widespread practice among men in Lan Na (north Thailand) and Lan Xang (western Laos). To create an impressive display they wore their sarongs *(pah-soe)* folded, twisted and tucked between the legs so that their thighs were clearly visible.

Tattoos applied to the upper body, to the chest, shoulders and arms, and to the back were less common but were believed to be particularly effective in rendering a person invisible. Red pigment was often used for tattoos on the upper body, concocted from vermilion dye mixed with animal fat. Although dramatic in appearance, red pigment was less permanent than black pigment.

Fierce images enhanced the potency of tattoos but the ability to tolerate excessive levels of pain during the tattooing process, added to their potency, winning admiration among fellow villagers. Tattooing was a symbol of maturity and young men were considered "unripe" or "not cooked" and certainly not ready for marriage until they had been tattooed.[10] Tattoos were also a symbol of sexual potency and many women would not marry a man without at least a set of thigh tattoos.

An additional way of protecting oneself against evil spirits was to wear a talismanic textile, in the form of a turban, a sash, an apron, a vest or a jacket. A talismanic textile provided the wearer with protection against physical injury, particularly on the battlefield and when undertaking a dangerous journey. To be tattooed, and to wear a talismanic textile, was seen as a particularly powerful protective force. Un-dyed plain weave cotton, unbleached mill cotton, and imported Chinese silk were used as a background for the magic formulae that were drawn freehand with a stylus using black ink. Images in frequent use were printed in outline with a wooden block, and filled in with coloured pigment. The iconography was similar to that produced for tattoos. The cannibal king Bawdithada, and other monsters and mythical animals were common, and as with tattoos, certain animals were selected for their special attributes **(3)**. *Yantra* were added within the outlines of human and animal figures, and *ingwet* grids were illustrated around them. In some cases Buddhist iconography, particularly guardian figures *(deva)* and Buddhist monks in meditation were included. They appeared as individual figures or were included in mandala designs.

3 The cannibal king Bawdithada, mythical animals and *yantra* and ingwet drawn on a cotton vest. *(The Oriental and India Office Collections, The British Library)*

Talismanic cloths about the size of handkerchiefs were kept on house altars, with other spirit offerings. Some were buried or hidden close to the entrance of the house to deter malignant spirits from entering. Smaller versions were added to bamboo trays containing rice, flowers and other offerings that were positioned at a special location in a village or in a field, or on the edge of the forest, where a particular spirit was to be propitiated.

The Shan used a wide range of amulets and charms to ward off evil spirits and bring good luck. Small balls of mercury, iron and orpiment were inserted through incisions in the skin, creating hard bumps on the skin's surface[11] **(4)**. The wealthy might choose precious stones such as rubies, fine gold wire and small gold and silver discs. The British surveyor Holt Hallett wrote:

It is not at all uncommon to meet a Shan with several knobs on his chest, concealing the talismans that he has inserted as charms to render him proof against bullet and sword. [12]

4 A Shan man tattooed with *yantra* and *ingwet*. The raised area on his right shoulder is where a metal charm has been inserted under the skin. *(The Green Centre for Non-Western Art, Brighton, P0073)*

Many Shan chose less invasive practices by wearing amulets on chains round their necks or on bracelets, or in small pouches tucked into a belt or sash. Some were engraved with animals whose form the Buddha had assumed in previous lives before taking the appearance of a man. They were considered particularly intelligent and wise and wearing their representations endowed a person with their attributes.[13] Some charms had tiny versions of *yantra* and *ingwet* incised on them. There were also complex sets attached to long cotton cords or chains that were tied around the waist and passed around the upper arms and the neck and behind the ears. If they were to be effective against bullet wounds, cuts from swords and fatal blows, a shaman had to put them through special tests to ensure their effectiveness.

Shaman also administered magic potions for bravery and endurance. They were given to soldiers to drink before going into battle and to villagers before they embarked on dangerous journeys. Soldiers could also have their skin massaged with magic ointments made from local plant oils, mixed with the ashes of magic scrolls.[14] Shaman also issued potions to protect against, or to drive out evil spirits from the body, a condition that presented as a physical or mental illness. Not all potions were taken internally or applied to the skin; some were distributed in sealed vials intended as special talismans.

The practises described above are based on nineteenth and early twentieth century accounts, and the textiles, charms and manuscripts used as illustrations in this article are from a similar time frame. Today people continue to consult shaman and take part in rituals to appease ancestor spirits and to ward off evil spirits of all kinds. Dance and trance remain at the centre of many shaman rituals, and performance has changed little since the nineteenth century. However, many shamanic manuscripts, textiles and talismans have been sold to antique dealers who in turn sell them on to foreign collectors. Modern versions have been made to replace them. Today, most shaman combine ancient performance rituals with contemporary artefacts. The following account demonstrates how one particular shaman approaches this phenomenon.

In the Keng Tung valley there is a particularly charismatic shaman who practises from a typical wooden Shan house, built on piles and situated in a village lane among other similar houses. He sees clients in the living room which is reached by ascending a wooden staircase. There are mats on the floor for clients to sit on, and the walls are decorated with photographs of his family, Chinese landscapes cut from magazines, photographs of revered Buddhist monks, and in a prominent position, a photograph of the King of Thailand. The floor is stacked with piles of small plastic bags and cardboard boxes, containing glass vials and jars. In the corner of the room on a table are a number of folded mulberry paper manuscripts. Paper scrolls, tied with red string are piled close by.

The shaman has agreed to perform a ceremony of protection on a middle-aged woman who arrives with a small entourage. This type of ceremony has been defined elsewhere as a simple propitiation ritual.[15] The client and the shaman have agreed a price for the ceremony, to be paid in cash. He asks her age, her state of health, where she lives and her occupation. He then gives some information about himself. As a boy he had witnessed a gang brutally attacking his father and it deeply affected him. He vowed to become a powerful shaman so that no one could inflict such cruelty again on him or his family, and so that he could give protection to others. As a young man he had consulted experienced shaman and had been accepted as an apprentice. During the period of initiation he had fasted on a vegetarian diet and wore white robes, a process aimed at cleansing his body.

When the woman who had requested the ceremony and her party arrived, the shaman was dressed in a white vest and an ankle length sarong. Following the initial introductions he left the room to prepare himself for the ceremony. He returned a few minutes later dressed only in a plaid sarong, tucked high on his thighs. His body was completely covered in tattoos so that his skin appeared to be totally black, except his face, the palms of his hands and the soles of his feet. When he showed the palms of his hands they were tattooed with images of water serpents *(naga)* **(5)**. He informed the group that thirty-two tattoo masters had worked on his body. They tattooed layer upon layer of legendary figures, *ingwet* and *yantra*. He stresses to the assembled group that his tattoos are potent body armour and nothing harmful can penetrate his skin. He demonstrates by pushing large sharp needles into his arms but they did not pierce the

6   A shaman demonstrates that his skin cannot be penetrated by sharp objects. *(Photo: SC, 2004)*

skin **(6)**. He then performs a type of sword dance that includes running the sword blades up and down his body to show that they will not penetrate the skin. By this stage the client and her party are convinced of his great strength and resilience.

The shaman puts the swords to one side and sits down on a mat facing the client. His mother-in-law enters the room and sits next to her to offer assurance. The shaman chants a series of *gatha* over her. He then prepares the potions and talismans that she will take away with her **(7)**. He opens a series of plastic bags to select small glass vials. He examines them and reserves two, which he lays on a tray. He places inside them pieces of red cord, some grains of rice, some plant seeds and a small lump of earth. He adds a small silver-coloured rod to one vial. He then selects from another plastic bag, one amulet with a red cord and two with white cords, and a separate length of white cord. Searching in other plastic bags, he chooses three small sealed containers of yellow paste, and finally a thin cotton square the size of a hand-

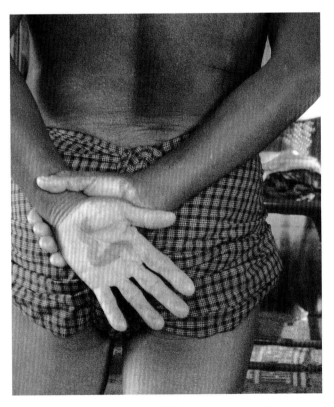

5   A shaman reveals the palms of his hands, tattooed with water serpents *(naga)*. *(Photo: SC, 2004)*

7 A shaman selects a set of talismans for a client. (*Photo: SC, 2004*)

kerchief, stamped with six images, each contained within frames of Shan script. The images include a naked couple embracing, a woman holding a set of scales, a tiger suckling a mouse, a *naga* coiled around a woman's body, a bird embracing a woman and a woman having sex with a horse.

These selected talismans represent the sacred and the profane, opposite elements used by shaman to control evil spirits.[16] The sacred is the small lump of earth in the glass vial, gathered from a religious site, often the grounds of a temple or the land around a stupa. The profane is the cotton cloth with its un-natural sexual images. Parallels can be drawn with earlier talismanic cloths with profane spirit images of monsters and animals positioned alongside Buddhist iconography of guardian figures *(deva)* and monks in meditation. The shaman places these selected items on a tray and chants over them. He passes the tray to the client and she accepts it. He tells her that these talismans are powerful and must

be kept together in a position that will be above the level of the head, for example on a high shelf.[17]

It is interesting to compare the quality and type of talismans distributed at this village ceremony with those made in the past. The glass vials filled with magic ingredients have been recycled from a hospital and previously contained liquid for intravenous injection. One had the words "for intramuscular use only" stamped in red ink on the side. The writing underneath is in Thai and includes a date stamp. The imitation silver rod is a modern replacement for the hand-stamped silver, the inscribed balls of metal, and the incised silver discs that were previously distributed in small leather, or cotton pouches. The red and white cord used at this ceremony was made from synthetic yarn whereas shaman cords in the past were made from un-dyed hand-spun indigenous cotton. The small talismanic cloth was thin mill cotton whereas in the past, village shaman used hand-spun, hand-woven cotton. At this ceremony the cloth was already printed with figures and animals, and *ingwet* and *yantra*. Formally, the magical figures, the *yantra* and *ingwet* were selected to suit individual clients and drawn on the cloth at the time of the consultation.

When the ceremony was concluded the shaman offered to show the assembled group a range of talismanic cloths. They were made of mill cotton and the large figures had been silk-screened using bright pigments (**8**). The *yantra* and *ingwet,* and smaller images had been block printed. The shaman kept a variety of these ready-prepared cloths so that he could find one to suit individual clients.

In conclusion, the production of talismans and talismanic cloths has changed with the introduction of modern technology in the Shan States. The shaman, who previously would have prepared talismans and cloths on a one-off basis, now keeps a store of products and distributes them in a way that mirrors modern patterns of consumption. However this shaman retains an aura of invincibility and charisma that has been the hallmark of Shan shaman for many centuries. Of particular note is his spectacularly tattooed body, an outward symbol of inner strength, and a sign of immense physical and mental power to tolerate pain, a phenomena that is rarely seen in inland Southeast Asia today.

8 A contemporary talismanic cloth. *(Photo: SC, 2004)*

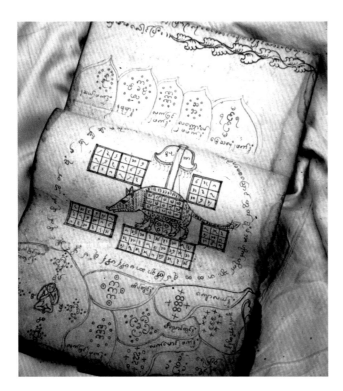

9 A reference manuscript used by shaman, red and black ink on mulberry paper. *(Collection of Barbie-Campbell-Cole)*

Footnotes

1 Scott, Sir George, Burma, *A Handbook of Practical Information*, 1906, Reprint Orchid Press, Bangkok, 1999.

2 Keyes, Charles, *Buddhism and National Integration in Thailand, in Visakha Puja*, B.E. 1514, Bangkok, 1971, pp. 22-34.

3 Oral communication, Keng Tung 2004.

4 An example are the paper scrolls in the Fowler Museum of Cultural History, University of Los Angeles. They are printed with mythical animals and inset with letters and diagrams.

5 Oral communication, with monks in Keng Tung, November 2004.

6 Bock, Carl, *Temples and Elephants* 1884, reprint. 1986, pp. 170-174.

7 ibid.

8 Scott J. G. and Hardiman, J. P., *Gazeteer of Upper Burma and The Shan States*, Vol. II. (Rangoon: Superintendent of Government Printing, 1900, 1901, pp. 79-83.

9 De Carné, Louis, *Voyage en Indo-Chine et dans l'Empire Chinois*, 1872, reprint White Lotus, Bangkok, 2000 p. 180.

10 Similar rules apply to young men who enter the monastery as novice monks. Until they have completed this obligation, they are considered immature members of society.

11 Milne and Cochrane, *Shans at Home*, 1910, reprint Paragon, New York, 1970, pp. 66-67, Le May, Reginald, An Asian Arcady, 1926 reprint, White Lotus, Bangkok, 1986, pp. 120-121.

12 Hallett, Holt, A *Thousand Miles on an Elephant in the Shan States*, 1890, reprint White Lotus, Bangkok, 1988.

13 Milne and Cochrane, 1910, pp. 66-67, Le May, 1986, pp.120-121, Hallett, 1988, p. 138.

14 Scott and Hardiman, Vol II, pp. 79-83.

15 Spiro, Melford, *Burmese Supernaturalism*, Prentice-Hall, New Jersey, 1967.

16 ibid

17 These instructions parallel those that apply to Buddha images kept in the home.

Bibliography

Bock, Carl, *Temples and Elephants* 1884, reprint. 1986

De Carné, Louis, *Voyage en Indo-Chine et dans l'Empire Chinois*, 1872, reprint White Lotus, Bangkok, 2000.

Hallett, Holt, *A Thousand Miles on An Elephant in the Shan States*, 1890, reprint White Lotus, Bangkok, 1988.

Keyes, Charles, *Buddhism and National Integration in Thailand, in Visakha Puja*, B. E. 1514, Bangkok, 1971.

Le May, Reginald, *An Asian Arcady*, 1926 reprint White Lotus, Bangkok, 1986

Milne & Cochrane, *Shans at Home*, 1910, reprint Paragon, New York, 1970.

Scott, Sir George, *Burma: A Handbook of Practical Information*, 1906, Reprint Orchid Press, Bangkok, 1999.

Scott J. G. and Hardiman, J. P., *Gazeteer of Upper Burma and The Shan States, Vol. II* (Rangoon: Superintendent of Government Printing, 1900, 1901.

Spiro, Melford, *Burmese Supernaturalism*, Prentice-Hall, New Jersey, 1967.

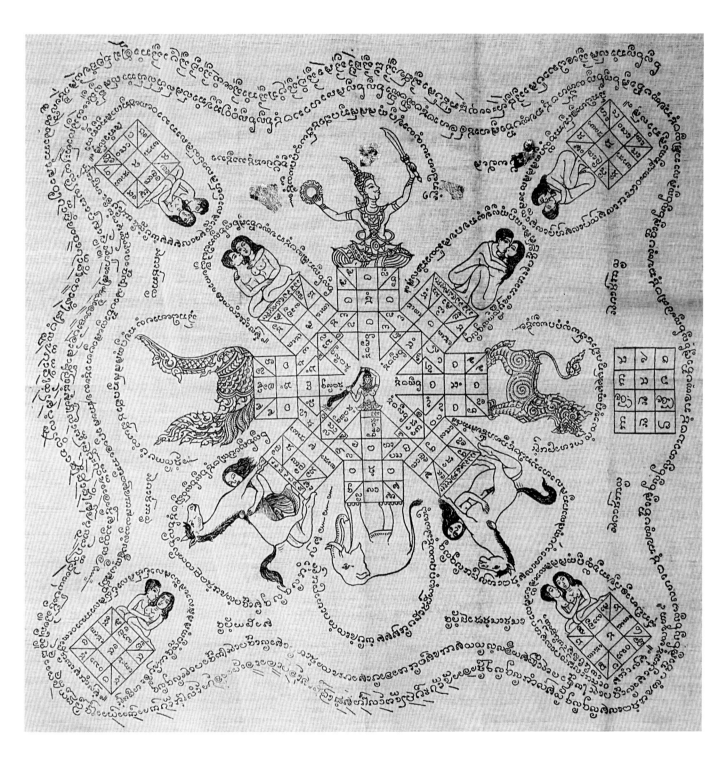

10 *Yantra* cloth produced in Chiang Rai by a monk well-known for his skills in this field. The cloth is drawn with mythical and profane imagery of humans and animals, mystical diagrams (*ingwet*) and texts (*yantra*) generally interpreted as incantations (*gatha*). *(Collection of Bhujjong Chandavij, photo by Paisarn Piammattawat)*

Hidden Threads
Structure and Status in Chin Textiles

Barbara G. Fraser and David W. Fraser

Introduction

As with many traditional Southeast Asian ethnic groups, status plays an important role in the social organization of the Chin (also known as the Zo, Lai or Kuki).[1] Complimenting the role of status is wealth, which is essential to maintaining and increasing status within the community. Status may be connected to one's stage in life (age or marital), one's gender or one's role in the community (e.g., headman, religious leader). Traditionally, high status might be attained from success in warfare, which led to greater wealth in the form of land and people controlled and loot acquired. It may be attained from the ability to pay or demand a high bride price, thereby forming marriage alliances with high status members of the community. And, it may be attained by hosting Feasts of Merit at which high status is validated in this life and, through sacrifice, the next.[2]

In traditional Chin material culture, status was reflected in the ownership of certain prestige goods, which generally were obtained from outside the Chin culture through raids or trade. These goods included brass gongs and pots, beads, silver for belts or jewelry and iron for spears or other uses. The only prestige goods that were fully local in material and manufacture were cotton, hemp or flax heirloom textiles dyed with local plants. Among all Chin groups, these textiles were an important reflection of the status of the owner (1). The number and quality of textiles constituting the bride price reflected the status of the families of the bride and groom. Certain blankets and skirts indicated that one had performed a particular Feast of Merit or celebrated the successful hunting of a wild animal. Without exception, these cloths were woven on a back tension loom by women, often using weaving techniques or structures that by hiding either the warp or the weft enhanced the beauty of the textile. Invariably, these methods are perceived by Chin weavers as requiring exceptional skill. This paper focuses on four of these methods, two that hide some or all of the weft and two that hide portions of the warp.

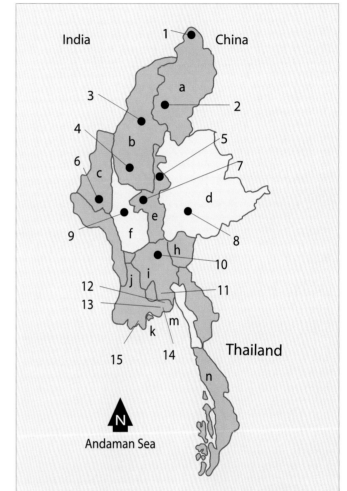

1. Khakaborazi national park
2. Indawgyi lake wildlife sanctuary
3. Chatthin wildlife sanctuary
4. Alaungdaw Kathapa national park
5. Maymyo botanical garden
6. Nat Ma Taung (Mt. Victoria) national park
7. Popa mountain park
8. Inle lake werland sanctuary
9. Shwesettaw wildife sanctuary
10. Sein Ye forest camp
11. Moneyingyi wetland wildlife sanctuary
12. Myaing Hay Wun elephant camp
13. Hlwaga park
14. Yangon zoological garden
15. Meinmahla (island) wildlife sanctuary

States and divisions
a = Kachin state
b = Sagaing division
c = Chin state
d = Shan state
e = Mandalay division
f = Magwe division
g = Rakhine state
h = Kayah state
i = Bago division
j = Ayeyarwaddy division
k = Yangon division
l = Kayin state
m = Mon state
n = Thaninthayi division

1 Haka chiefs standing with attendants sitting. Chiefs wear high status *can-lo puan* and *cong-nok puan* and *lung pawng* head wrappers. Attendants wear lower status blankets including plaids. Circa 1910. *(Courtesy American Baptist Historical Society, JHC)*

2a Reverse of 1-faced supplementary weft patterning of thin white warp stripe. Supplementary weft essentially invisible.

2b Obverse of 1-faced supplementary weft patterning of thin white warp stripe, with free ends of supplementary wefts visible.

One-Faced Supplementary Weft Designs on White Warp Stripes

A distinctive motif of the highest status textiles, especially blankets, of a number of the Chin groups in the northern Chin Hills, Manipur and Mizoram is a narrow white warp stripe decorated on the obverse only with a supplementary weft in up to three different colours, floating in different patterns.[3] When not floating on the obverse, the supplementary weft rides in the shed with the structural weft so on the reverse of the blanket, the supplementary weft is hidden. Even the ends of this weft do not show on the reverse **(2a)**, although they may hang free on the obverse **(2b)**. In some Chin textiles these stripes are the only pattern **(3)**; in others these stripes are combined with warp stripes of other colours, which may be decorated with patterns that appear on both the obverse and reverse. Among the Chin groups that use this motif, creating patterned white stripes decorated only on the obverse is thought to be the most difficult form of weaving, of which only an experience and talented weaver is said to be capable **(4)**.[4] The quality of such a blanket is judged solely by the execution of these stripes. Accordingly, blankets decorated with them are greatly prized and are worn generally only by those of high status or on the most important occasions. These stripes are the prominent feature of the most ceremonially important blanket of the Zahau (*puandum* or *vai puan*) **(5)**; Mizo (*thangchhuah puan*); Paite (*thangsuaphuan*)[5]; Sukte[6] and Yo[7] (*puandum*); Haka (*vai puan*); Tiddim (*dap zal* and *tawnok*); and Hmar (*thangsapuan*)[8]. They are also an important design element of Tiddim[9] and

3 Blanket with *vai puan* stripes worn by man in Mara(?) family. Circa 1930. *(British Library MSS Eur F 185/199 no. 40. Photo: Rev. Reginald Lorrain)*

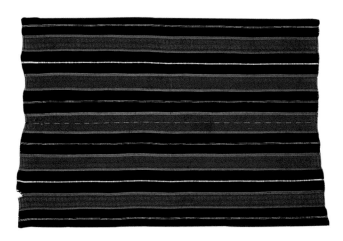

5 Blanket, Zahau *(vai puan or puandum)*. Reportedly 1945-1955. l = 175 cm; w = 117 cm. 2 loom widths, joined with 2-colour cross-knit looping. 21 warps/cm, 10 wefts/cm. Warps are black, red, green and white cotton. Structural wefts are black cotton. Supplementary wefts are black and red cotton. 1-faced supplementary weft patterning. Z-twining. *(Photo: Jeff Crespi)*

4 Zahau weaver, Hlawn Kil, in Yangon weaving stripes in a blanket with both discontinuous 1-faced supplementary weft patterning and discontinuous 2-faced supplementary weft patterning.

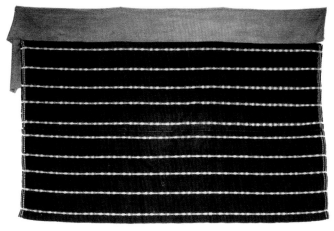

6 Woman's wrap skirt, Tiddim. Estimated 1930-1960. l = 126 cm (excluding Burmese-style top panel); w = 72 cm. 2 loom widths (+ Burmese-style top panel), joined simply. 28 warps/cm, 14 wefts/cm. Warps are black, green, purple and white cotton. Structural wefts are black cotton. Supplementary wefts are red, green, black and yellow cotton. Discontinuous 1-faced supplementary weft patterning. Checkerboard. End finish is running overhand knots. Burmese-style panel is commercial cloth. *(Collection of Digna and Neil Ryan. Photo: Neil Ryan)*

Mizo jackets, Tiddim **(6)** and Bawm **(7)** ceremonial skirts and some high status shoulder bags.[10]

White warp stripes decorated only on the obverse appear also in textiles of some of the Chin living south of those described above. Two of the oldest examples from "Arracan" (Rakhine State) were accessioned by the Victoria & Albert Museum (V&A) in 1855. They appear to be hanging panels *(hondiat)* worn by Laytu women as their lower body garment, one in front and one in back. The examples from the V&A are dark blue;[11] other examples are red **(8)**. Reportedly, dark blue or black panels are worn more commonly by women in the plains

and red ones more commonly by women in the hills. The white stripes on the V&A examples are broader than those on the textiles from the northern hills and on more recent *hondiat*. Unlike the white stripes on the textiles from the northern hills that are patterned only with a supplementary weft that shows only on the obverse, the stripes on Laytu textiles may also include patterning created by a supplementary weft that floats on the reverse as well as the obverse and by false embroidery. While these white stripes continue to pattern red *hondiat,* the white stripes of older dark blue or black *hondiat* are replaced by dark stripes in more recent examples. The

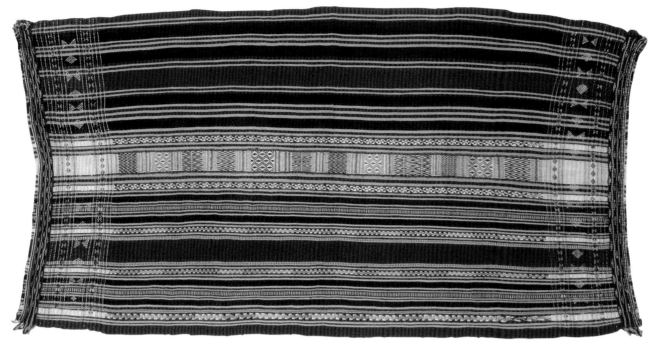

7 Woman's wrap skirt, Bawm. Estimated 1930-1960. l = 96 cm; w = 49 cm. 1 loom width. 28 warps/cm, 7 wefts/cm. Warps are homespun red, black, yellow, white and green cotton. Structural wefts are homespun black cotton. Supplementary wefts are homespun white, red, yellow, black and white cotton. Discontinuous and continuous 1-faced supplementary weft patterning. Checkerboard variant with 6 (3+3) supplementary wefts per row. Twined tapestry. Eccentric twining. *(Photo: JC)*

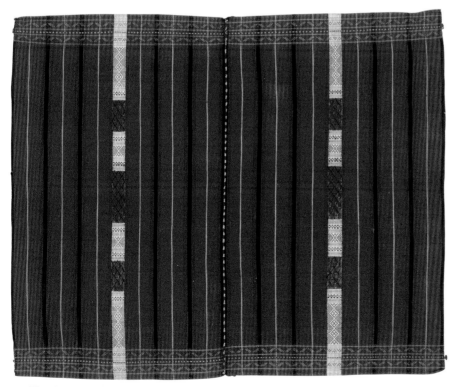

8 Hanging panel, Laytu *(hondiat)*. Estimated 1910-1950. l = 39 cm; w = 48 cm. 2 loom widths, joined with running half hitches. 31 warps/cm, 14 wefts/cm. Warps are red, white, black and olive cotton. Structural wefts are red and olive cotton and pink silk. Supplementary and twining wefts are olive cotton and pink silk. False embroidery yarns are black cotton and pink silk. 1-faced supplementary weft patterning. False embroidery. Checkerboard. Countered weft twining. *(Photo: JC)*

Laytu may also weave narrow white stripes on their woman's tunics[12] and at the ends of head covers for both men *(yan lupaung)*[13] and women *(lukhu)*.[14]

A third group, the Kaung Su, have a distinctive style of breast cloth, skirt and head cover that is red or green on black, decorated with thin white warp stripes patterned on the obverse only with supplementary weft figures much like those used in the northern Chin Hills.[15]

The source from which the Chin may have acquired this important design element and the manner in which it spread among the Chin are unknown. The earliest known examples come from the Laytu in Rakhine State where they had been collected by Europeans by the mid-nineteenth century. From this fact, it might be inferred that the Laytu were the first Chin to use this patterning. On the other hand, the use of this patterning is most widespread in the northern Chin Hills and among the peoples who migrated out of this area into India and Bangladesh. Europeans did not occupy the northern Chin Hills until late in the nineteenth century and may not have had access to textiles from this area until that time. The Bawm, who use this patterning in their traditional textiles, migrated from the northern Chin Hills and are reported to have been living in eastern Bangladesh by the mid-nineteenth century.[16] If they brought this structure with them from the northern Chin Hills, as it appears they may have done with many of their weaving structures, the structure would have had to been used there before they began their movement west.

Use of Structural Weft to Accentuate Colour or Create Stripes

Most Chin textiles, like other back-tension loom-woven textiles, are warp-faced. In some of the most culturally important of these textiles, Chin weavers choose a colour for the weft that, though hidden or almost hidden by the warps, heightens the appearance of the colour in the warps or creates a subtle weft patterning. One such ceremonially important textile is a man's warp-striped blanket *(puandum)* ("black cloth"). This blanket also is used widely by groups living in the northern hills of the Chin area including, among others, the Mizo, Zahau, Tashon and Kamhau, as well as the Paite and Gangte in Manipur. The blanket gets its name from the fact that this warp-faced textile is woven with black structural wefts,[17] which in the hands of a skilled weaver are invisible. The dark weft, however, deepens the colour of the warp stripes, which among the Mizo are usually red, blue, yellow, green and pink **(9)**. This simply patterned but beautiful blanket serves many purposes. A gift of a

puandum indicates friendship. A bride should weave one to bring to her husband's home on her wedding day to serve one day as his shroud. If given as a token of affection or to establish a marital or other family relationship, a blanket is called a *zawlpuan*.[18] If a bride brings a *puandum* as the *zawlpuan*, she need bring only one blanket. If not, she must bring two blankets. A girl's family may show acceptance of a suitor by spreading a *puandum* in their house for their daughter and the suitor to sleep on. A *puandum* may also be worn by mourners.

Two Chin textiles use a red or pink weft to heighten colour. The Mizo married woman's blanket, which is also worn as a wrap skirt *(puan laisen; puanchei,* in Mizoram) **(10)**, is made of three loom widths with either a pink or red structural weft in the centre panel to heighten the colour of the red warp stripes in this panel. The structural weft in the side panels is white, however, resulting in paler red stripes in these panels than in that of the centre panel. The Tiddim man's ceremonial blanket *(dap zal)* also is made in three loom widths **(11)**. As with the Mizo *puan laisen,* the weft in the central panel is pink, deepening the magenta and green colour of the warp stripes patterning this panel thereby creating a clear contrast with the side panels in which the warp and all but a few of the structural wefts at the ends are white.

Chin weavers may also choose a weft colour to create subtle weft stripes that are almost hidden in a warp-faced textile. These wefts may be structural or supplementary and may extend only a short distance[19] or across the entire textile. In addition to the white weft described above, the side panels of most *puan laisen* **(10)**, and all panels on a blanket worn by Mizo adolescents of both sexes while courting and by men *(ngo te kherh puan or puanhruih)*,[20] are frequently decorated with subtle black weft stripes created by black structural wefts that are barely visible through the white, red, green or yellow warp stripes. A Tiddim weaver may add several red structural wefts at each end of a *dap zal* to create subtle narrow red weft stripes just visible through the white warps **(11)**. A Khamau weaver may lay in several supplementary yellow or white wefts at the end of a shoulder cloth.[21] Some weavers may alternate pairs of contrasting coloured wefts to create subtle stripes over an entire textile **(12)**.[22] The beautiful patterning created by this technique gives lie to Emery's statement that "obviously, with a warp-faced ground weave, 'laid in' patterning would not be effective."[23]

The use of wefts on a warp-faced textile to saturate colour or to create subtle weft stripes is shared by the Chin's northern neighbours, the Naga, who make four

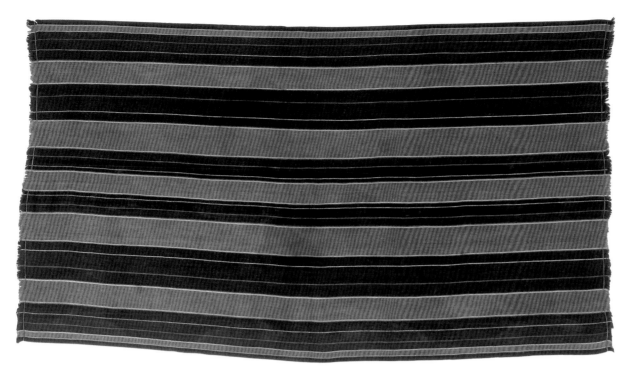

9 Blanket, Mizo or Kuki (?) *(puandum)*. Estimated 1900-1930. l = 162 cm; w = 89 cm. 2 loom widths, joined simply. 24 warps/cm, 8 wefts/cm. Warps are homespun blue, red, olive, gray, white and lavender cotton. Structural wefts are homespun dark blue cotton. Twining wefts are homespun red cotton. Countered weft twining. *(Photo: JC)*

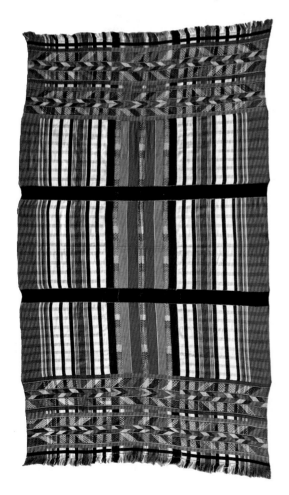

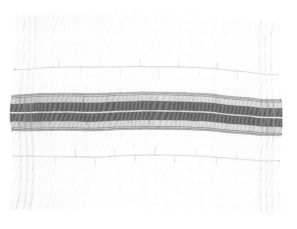

11 Man's wedding blanket, Tiddim *(dap zal)*. Made by Pi Ning Saw in Tiddim township in 1946. The Textile Museum, Washington, D.C., 1996.7.9, Ruth Lincoln Fisher Memorial Fund. l = 180 cm; w = 123 cm. 3 loom widths joined by cross-knit looping. 41 warps/cm; 11 wefts/cm. Warps are white and red cotton and magenta and green silk. Structural wefts are white cotton in the side panels and pink cotton in the central panel. Supplementary wefts are purple, black and green silk. Discontinuous 1-faced supplementary weft patterning. *(Photo: JC)*

10 Woman's blanket, Hualngo *(puan laisen)*. Reportedly 1955-1965. l = 175 cm; w = 98 cm. 3 loom widths, joined simply. 44 warps/cm, 17 wefts/cm (black weft-faced bands: 11 warps/cm, ~80 wefts/cm). Warps are red, green, white, black, yellow, pink and blue commercial cotton. Structural wefts are white, black, yellow and red cotton and pink, green and blue mercerized cotton. Supplementary wefts are yellow cotton, purple, pink, blue, green and red mercerized cotton and red wool (or wooly synthetic). Weft-faced plain weave. Tapestry. 2-faced continuous and discontinuous supplementary weft patterning. Laid-in wefts.

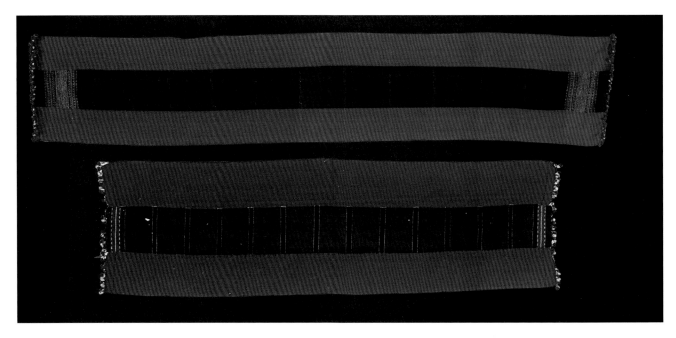

12 Man's dress headband, Lauktu. Myebon township, reportedly c. 1917. l = 196 cm; w = 35 cm. Single 1 loom width. 42 warps/cm, 13 wefts/cm. Warps are red and two shades of black cotton. Structural wefts are red, black, green and yellow cotton. Supplementary wefts are white cotton. Pom-poms. Alternating warps. Alternating wefts. 1-faced supplementary weft patterning. Checkerboard. *(Photo: JC)*

loom-width blankets and lower body wraps on which the outer dark panels have dark wefts and the light-coloured central panels have white wefts, like those on the outer panels on the *dap zal* and *puan laisen*. Both blankets also have laid-in wefts of contrasting colour that create subtle weft stripes at the ends. Such Naga (probably Angami) pieces collected in 1912-13[24] are as early as any of the known Mizo or Tiddim pieces. Therefore, it is uncertain in which group these structures were used earlier or whether they pre-date the time when the Naga and the Chin diverged.

Weft-faced Panels

As described above, most Chin textiles are warp-faced. In textiles made on a back-tension loom the absence of a reed (used both to keep warps spaced and to pack wefts tightly) and the difficulty in maintaining high warp tension contribute to a higher density of warps than wefts.[25] Among those from the northern Chin Hills and culturally related emigrants from that area, however, selected ceremonial textiles have panels that regularly are weft faced. A weaver able to create a weft-faced textile under such circumstances is to be respected for her skill.

The simplest example of a weft-faced panel in Chin textiles is a black weft-wise stripe that crosses an otherwise all-white blanket or head wrapper. The blanket (Haka: *puan rang;* Mara: *chiarakua;* Matu: *va tang*) with two of these stripes **(13)** is of second-level status **(1)**, a cut below the *can-lo puan* discussed below, while the head wrapper (Haka: *pawng pi;* Mara: *khuthang*) is of the highest status. Both are used by a wide range of groups from the northern Chin Hills. In both cases closely packed black wefts pass over and under groups of white warps in order to create the weft-faced stripe.

The Mizo and Hualngo, in particular, employ a similar pair of black weft-faced stripes in a variety of traditional blankets with more complex patterning. These include the *ngo te kherh puan and puan laisen* **(10)** described previously. Occasional blankets have a single black stripe, although the significance of that variant is unknown.[26] The skill of the Mizo weaver is judged in large part by her success in compacting the weft so tightly that the underlying warp stripes are invisible through the black weft stripe. An additional challenge is to maintain constant weft tension so as to avoid blousing of the warp-faced areas. The Mizo also weave a skirt *(tawlh lo)* with weft-faced white and red stripes across a warp-faced black field.[27] This skirt is said to be worn only by members of a village leader's family.

The favored high status man's blanket of the Haka, Mara and other culturally related groups from the northern Chin Hills is the *can-lo puan* (Mara: *cheulopang;*

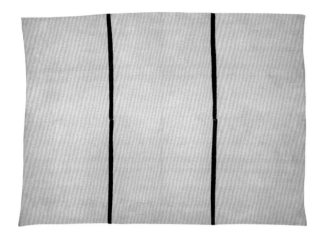

13 Blanket, Matupi *(va tang)*. Chan Phyan village, estimated 1920-1950. l = 162 cm; w = 117 cm. 2 loom widths, with simple overlapping join. Warp-faced: 16 warps/cm, 6 wefts/cm. Weft-faced: 5 warps/cm, 48 wefts/cm. Warps are homespun white cotton. Structural wefts are homespun white and black cotton. Weft-faced plain weave. Alternating wefts. *(Photo: JC)*

14 Blanket, Zotung or Zophei *(can-lo puan)*. Haka township, close to Matupi, estimated 1920-1935. l = 188 cm; w = 120 cm. 2 loom widths, joined with 3-colour cross-knit looping. 10.5 warps/cm; 56 wefts/cm. Warps are homespun white cotton. Structural wefts are homespun black, white and red cotton. Supplementary wefts are homespun red, yellow, blue, green and white cotton. Discontinuous 2-faced supplementary weft patterning. Weft-faced plain weave. *(Photo: JC)*

Zahau: *tawn-lo puan*) **(14)**. Its dark, figured field is crossed with four white weft-wise stripes. Uniquely, the *can-lo puan* is entirely weft-faced (although the figured field – though not the white weft-wise stripes – of its counterpart for women is warp-faced[28]). It tends particularly to be preferred by conservative men, despite the fact that, being made of cotton, it was generally less expensive through much of the 20th century than the *cong-nak puan,* an all-silk, twill-decorated ceremonial blanket **(1)**.[29] Traditionally, weaving a *can-lo puan* was said to be the only labour for the wives of chiefs and other high-status men.[30] The *can-lo puan,* and it alone, plays a prominent role in the *boi-te* feast, during which it is used to wrap the sacrificial head of the mithan[31] and, in one other village at least, in the *khaung tsawi* feast when the mithan fetus is wrapped in it before burial.[32] The oldest known *can-lo puan,* which may date to the 19th century, are made of such fine homespun cotton that they are thin and supple despite the fact that they are remarkably tightly woven.[33] These old *can-lo puan* tend to have open, unpatterned areas (and often to be dark blue), in contrast to the dense patterning on a black field typical of the best recent *can-lo puan*. In 20th century examples the colouring of the supplementary weft patterning may offer a clue to their origin, with orange figures typical of the Mara and yellow ones typical of the Zotung and Zophei **(14)**. Throughout, high quality is demonstrated by the tightness of the weave (which should completely hide the white warps) and the careful burying of loose ends of the supplementary wefts.

Traditionally worn with the *can-lo puan* is a broad loincloth (Haka: *biar pi;* Mara: *dua ah*) with dark blue or black, figured, weft-faced end-panels contrasting with a white, slightly warp-faced central length **(15)**. This is the highest status loincloth of the Haka cultural area, although loincloths of any sort have been worn rarely there in the last 40 years. Some observers have concluded that the black ends and white central portion are separate pieces of cloth, but in fact the same white warp is regularly used throughout. At the transition from warp-faced to weft-faced weave, the warps are grouped so as to permit tight packing of the black wefts **(17)**; in some examples some of the warps are excluded from the weaving of the weft-faced panels and are later cut off at the transition point.

The women's textiles of these groups may also have weft-faced panels. The dress tunic *(kor)* of women of Falam and Haka often illustrates their finest weaving and the widest range of structures. The *kor* consists of two loom widths of cloth, folded and sewn together along the back and side seams, with openings left for the arms. Each loom width is organized with a central, figured, warp-faced panel that covers the upper torso and shoulder **(18)**. In back and in front, that panel is flanked below first by a complex band of diamond twill and then by a band of weft-faced plain weave (with or without tapestry) at the bottom edge. The weft-faced and twill bands of the Haka *kor* are broader than those of the Falam *kor*.[34] Given the prominence of warp stripes in many of these *kor,* fine workmanship is needed to hide those

16 Detail of transition from (white) warp-faced to (black) weft-faced weave in the loincloth in (15).

15 Man's loincloth, Northern Chin *(biar pi)*. Estimated 1880-1920. l = 744 cm; w = 39 cm. End panels are 81 cm and 84 cm long. 1 loom width. End panels: 9.5 warps/cm, 66 wefts/cm. Central field: 30 warps/cm, 14 wefts/cm. Warps are homespun white cotton. Structural wefts are homespun white, black and red cotton. Supplementary wefts are gold, white, olive, light blue and red silk. Discontinuous 2-faced supplementary weft patterning. Weft-faced plain weave. Cut warps (1 in 3). *(Photo: JC)*

17 Woman's tunic, Thlantlang (*kor*). Lunghrei village, Thlantlang township, estimated 1925-1945. l = 41 cm (x2); w = 57 cm. 2 loom widths, joined simply. Warp-faced: 36 warps/cm, 15.5 wefts/cm. Weft-faced: 12 warps/cm, ~84 wefts/cm. Warps are red and light blue silk and black cotton. Structural wefts are black, red, white, yellow, green and orange silk and black cotton. Supplementary wefts are orange, gray, white, black and red silk. Discontinuous 2-faced supplementary weft patterning. Diamond twill. Cut warps. Alternated wefts. Tapestry. Weft-faced plain weave. Finish of running overhand knots. *(Photo: JC)*

18 Woman's skirt, Khualshim. Falam township, reportedly 1923-1933. l = 130 cm; w = 73 cm. 2 loom widths, joined simply. 35 warps/cm, 8.5 wefts/cm. Warps are homespun brick, green, black, gold and white cotton. Structural wefts are homespun black cotton. Supplementary wefts are homespun red, gold, blue, white, yellow and orange cotton. Twining wefts are homespun red, black, white, green and yellow cotton. Continuous 1-faced supplementary weft patterning. Discontinuous 2-faced supplementary weft patterning. Checkerboard variant with 6 (3+3) supplementary wefts. Weft-twined tapestry. Eccentric twining. Weft-faced plain weave. Finish of running overhand knots. *(Photo: JC)*

stripes in the weft-faced band, particularly in the Haka *kor,* in which silk is the preferred fiber in the best pieces. The transition between the twill and weft-faced bands is often marked by a short fringe hanging on the obverse, where one-third or so of the warps have been excluded from the weaving of the weft-faced band and later cut off, much as is done with the *biar pi.*

Weft-faced bands may also be found on the women's skirts and headbands from these groups. The wrapped skirts *(hni or nik)* are worn with the warps horizontal. Weavers typically insert a band of supplementary weft patterning at either end of these skirts and of similarly constructed headbands. In Falam a band of weft-faced plain weave is commonly placed between the supplementary weft-patterned band and the end of the warps. Regularly decorating this weft-faced band is one or more rows of eccentric weft twining (or, more recently, supplementary weft patterning), which creates a dotted design complex also seen in the lower border of Falam *kor* and the mouths of women's tobacco bags and men's shoulder bags.[35] Skirts from Haka and Tiddim generally lack these weft-faced woven bands.

One might reasonably seek to learn from what source weavers in (or from) the northern Chin Hills acquired the practice of weft-faced weaving on a back-tension loom. Other Chin groups do not share this practice, except for occasional neighbours, like some Khumi and Kaung Su, whom they have culturally influenced.[36] Of other hill-dwelling groups in the countries where the Chin live, weft-faced panels are prominent primarily among the Kachin peoples, largely Tibeto-Burman speakers who reside to the northeast of the Chin. Skirts of the Kachin have panels of weft-faced plain weave at either end, and their 19th century tunics may have similar panels at the lower border. In pattern, materials and layout, however, Kachin and Chin textiles have little in common. This is no surprise, as in their migration from the north these groups are thought to have separated more than 700 years ago.[37]

Several pieces of evidence suggest that what in the 20th century weavers from the northern Chin Hills did in weft-faced plain weave their predecessors had done in weft twining. Rare fine Falam skirts have end panels completely done in twined tapestry and eccentric weft twining **(18)**. Even the Bawm, who migrated to the Chittagong Hills in present-day Bangladesh from Falam some 200 years ago, may twine the ends of their wrapped skirts **(7)**. A rare 19th century Thlantlang skirt has end bands done in twined tapestry **(19)**, while an unusual early Haka wrapped skirt *(thi hni)* has end bands in weft-wrapped tapestry,[38] a structure that on one face closely resembles twined tapestry.

19 Woman's skirt, Thlantlang. Ranlua village, estimated 19th century (based on yarn, structure). l = 124 cm; w = 90 cm. 2 loom widths, joined simply. 34 warps/cm, 11 wefts/cm. Warps are homespun dark blue cotton. Structural wefts are homespun dark blue cotton. Supplementary wefts are gold, blue and red silk and homespun white, blue and gray cotton. Twining wefts are red and gold silk and homespun green, blue and black cotton. Continuous 1-faced supplementary weft patterning. Discontinuous 2-faced supplementary weft patterning. Checkerboard variant with 6 (3+3) supplementary wefts. Twined tapestry (mostly countered). 2-colour weft twining (Z). Finish of running overhand knots. *(Photo: JC)*

20 "Chin girl from hills of lower country", probably Thayetmyo area, 1888-1896. This Khamau woman has a intricately decorated *phyang*, including 1-faced supplementary weft patterning and ikat. *(Courtesy American Baptist Historical Society, ALC)*

Weft-faced bands done by these groups in twining instead of weaving are not confined to skirts. An exceptional white blanket *(khuah pon)* made circa 1961 by a woman of the Khualshim clan of Falam has its two black weft-wise stripes done in countered weft twining.[39] A Mizo blanket collected by Emil Riebeck in 1882 in the Chittagong Hills also has two weft-wise stripes of weft twining – countered and eccentric – crossing its white field.[40] Another Mizo textile collected by Riebeck has panels of red, white and black weft-twined tapestry on a black field;[41] whether this enigmatic textile is related to the present-day Mizo *tawlh lo* is unknown.

Weft twining is a laborious technique, as heddles are of no use in manipulating twining wefts.[42] However, it is excellent for covering warps and so would have been a logical choice for early back-tension loom weavers who wanted to create weft-faced bands. Indeed, textiles made entirely of weft twining (like the war jackets of the Austronesian-speaking Ndora region of Flores)[43] are immensely sturdy, as the twisted twining wefts firmly protect the underlying warps.

Weft twined panels have been combined with warp-faced plain weave in several well-documented circumstances in Southeast Asia. In ceremonial blankets *(selimut)* and aprons *(pilu saluf)* in Timor Austronesian-speaking Atoni weavers alternate weft-twined panels and warp-faced panels.[44] In men's war jackets *(kalambi)* of the Iban (Austronesian speakers) in Sarawak the panel at the lower edge is typically done in weft-twined tapestry, while the rest of the jacket is done in warp-faced interlacing (although some of the decoration of the warp-faced plain weave ground may be done in supplementary weft twining).[45] Dress loincloths of the Austro-Asiatic speaking Katu, Jeh, Trieng, Sedang and others in central Vietnam highlands and southeastern Laos have end panels in which bands of countered weft twining and warp-faced plain weave alternate.[46] In each of these circumstances weft twining, despite the extra time needed to make it, has been retained for making culturally freighted textiles. This persistence of practices that seem inefficient in modern terms suggests that they arise from deep traditions.

Taking the argument a step further, the fragmentary evidence in Southeast Asia seems to suggest that weft-facedness in back-tension loom-woven textiles may have begun as weft twining. Given the widespread, if spotty, persistence into the 20th century of pockets of weft twining, either this practice arose independently in many locations or it antedated the dispersal of the Austronesian, Austro-Asiatic and Tibeto-Burman peoples throughout the region. Austronesian speakers are thought to have reached the Lesser Sunda islands of Indonesia (which include Flores and Timor) by about 2500 BCE,[47] whereas Tibeto-Burman speakers are thought to have entered Southeast Asia in the first millennium of the Common Era. Just when the transition occurred from weft twining to weft-faced plain weave no doubt varied greatly from group to group. For those from the northern Chin Hills the transition seems not to have been completed before the 20th century, leaving open the possibility that further research could identify weft-faced textiles like the *biar pi* and *can-lo puan* in earlier, weft-twined forms. Similarly, it would be of great interest to identify early Kachin textiles with weft-twined end panels.

Warp ikat

Resist dyeing of warp threads prior to weaving (called warp ikat, after the Indonesian term) is common in many parts of Southeast Asia, but unusual in Chin textiles. Indeed, Howard opines that no Baric-speaking people (including the Chin) use resist dyeing.[48] In the making of warp ikat warp threads are temporarily wrapped with cornhusk or cotton thread prior to dyeing to hide portions of the warp threads from the dye and thus create a pattern in the resulting warp-faced textile. As it is, among the Chin ikat is done only by selected subgroups of the Ashö and in a way that is largely sex-specific.

Khamau weavers used ikat frequently in the 19th century to decorate the field of women's long, dark blue tunics **(20)**. Simple zigzag patterning was typical and contrasted strikingly with the detailed supplementary weft patterning across the breast (and symmetrically across the back) **(21)**. Few tunics of this style from the 20th century have ikat patterning, but those that do are also women's. The other major traditional style of Khamau tunic has broad red warp stripes on a blue field, but no supplementary weft patterning.[49] In the 19th century it was used by both sexes but now only men who are animist religious leaders wear it. A single example is known that is decorated with warp ikat **(22)**. It, too, is a woman's tunic.

21 Woman's tunic, Khamau *(phyang)*. Probably Paduang township, Bago Division. Estimated 1870-1920. l = 90 cm (x2); w = 101 cm. 2 loom widths, joined simply (side seams) and with *abrung* embroidery (center seam). 24 warps/cm, 9 wefts/cm. Warps are homespun blue, yellow, red and white cotton. Structural wefts are homespun blue and red cotton and yellow silk. Supplementary wefts are yellow silk. Resist dyeing. Discontinuous complementary weft patterning. Discontinuous 1-faced supplementary weft patterning. Overlapping tapestry. *(Photo: JC)*

The Het Tui are a small, previously undocumented Ashö group who live in Upper Budha Kamma on Maw Creek, a tributary of the Lemro River north of Mrauk-U.[50] Their language is reported to be closely related to those of the Laytu, Lauktu and Utbu. Their textiles most closely resemble those of the Laytu, near whom they live and of which they may be a sub-group **(23)**.[51] Men and women wear blankets that are laid out similarly, but differ primarily in the means of decorating their warp-wise stripes. The man's blanket *(bawbulung)* has blue stripes decorated with warp ikat **(24)**, while the warp stripes on the woman's blanket *(hyawh lay; hyawh = "blanket, lay = "black")* are white and decorated with supplementary weft patterning **(25)**.

One might speculate that these Ashö groups may have learned the technique of warp ikat from the Karen, who live to the east of the Ashö. Warp ikat patterning of women's skirts is well known among the Karen, whereas warp ikat is not prominent among other groups neighbouring the Chin.

22 Woman's tunic, Khamau *(phyang)*. Thandwe township. Reportedly 100-150 years old. l = 104 cm (x2); w = 108 cm. 2 loom widths, joined with *guzu* embroidery. 26 warps/cm, 9 wefts/cm. Warps are homespun blue, red, yellow, green and white cotton. Structural wefts are homespun blue cotton. Embroidery yarns are white, yellow and red cotton. Warp ikat. Embroidery. *(Photo: JC)*

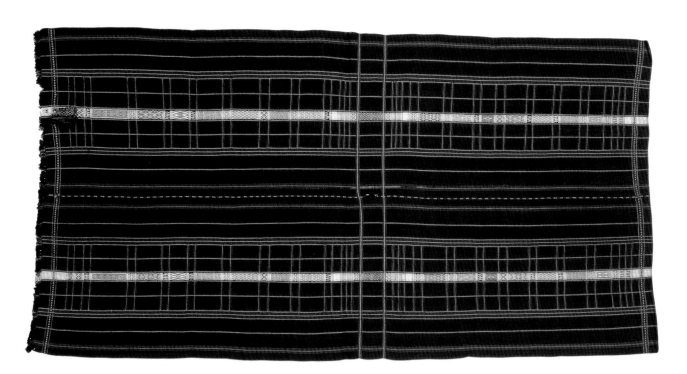

23 Woman's tunic, Het Tui. Lemro River, north of Mrauk-U. Estimated 1930-1960. l = 49 cm (x2); w = 45 cm. 2 loom widths, joined with running overhand knots. 22 warps/cm, 9 wefts/cm. Warps are homespun black, rust, orange and yellow cotton. Structural wefts are homespun black cotton. Supplementary wefts are homespun rust, yellow and green cotton. False embroidery yarns are homespun rust, orange and yellow cotton. 1-faced and 2-faced supplementary weft patterning. Mixed-faced supplementary weft patterning. False embroidery. Laddered warp stripes. *(Photo: JC)*

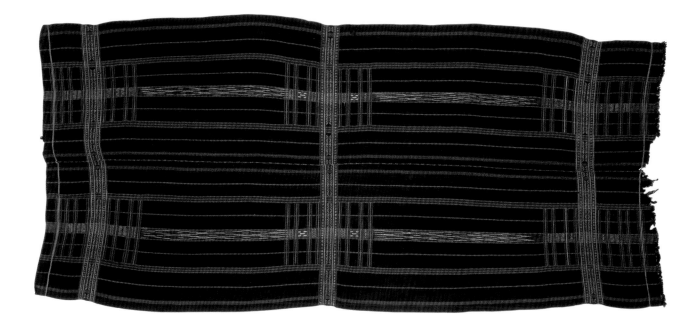

24 Man's blanket, Het Tui. Lemro River, north of Mrauk-U. Est. 1930-1960. l = 169 cm; w = 73 cm. 2 loom widths, joined with 2-colour running overhand knots. 38 warps/cm, 8 wefts/cm. Warps are black, red, orange and (resist dyed) blue and white cotton. Structural wefts are black cotton. Supplementary wefts are red, orange and chartreuse cotton. Twining wefts are red and orange cotton. 2-faced supplementary weft patterning. Checkerboard. Warp ikat. Countered weft twining. False embroidery. *(Photo: JC)*

Conclusion

Status and weaving prowess are intertwined in complicated ways, some of which are illustrated by the preceding four examples. Special clothing – as distinguished by materials, pattern or fine workmanship, singly or in combination – may serve as a badge of status. Weavers whose work is prized may gain status thereby. And women of high rank may be sufficiently freed of other responsibilities to enable them to master the art of sophisticated weaving. All pertain in Chin society.

Textile structures that require certain threads to be hidden pose challenges to the weaver, in terms of both time and skill. Those challenges may contribute to the designation of textiles with such structures as indicia of status. As a mark of skill, the thin white warp stripe decorated only on the obverse stands out in this regard for those from the northern Chin Hills and culturally related Chin groups, as it is considered by them to be the most difficult of weaving and is used nearly exclusively in textiles of high status. Whether the 1-faced supplementary weft patterning of that stripe is as difficult to create as the false embroidery of the Khumi, Khami, Mro and Laytu is hard to judge – and irrelevant, as the importance of status is largely a matter within one's group, not across groups. In contrast to the decorated

thin white stripe, the dark weft of the *puandum* is a subtle indication of skill. Using a dark weft hardly requires more time, nor is it more difficult to insert. But the richness of colour that the largely hidden weft provides to the finished blanket enhances its beauty and, with that, the blanket's status. Hiding the warps in weft-faced panels and wrapping warps before dyeing are further examples of the extra thought and work that status is thought to merit.

The hidden threads that contribute to a textile's status are not all physical. The metaphorical threads of technological evolution, migration and movement of ideas across groups all appear to play roles in some status-bearing Chin textiles. Our attempts to explore here those metaphorical threads are necessarily tentative and preliminary. More evidence would need to be mustered to confirm or refute our hypotheses about the development of the decorated white warp stripe, weft twining as the predecessor of weft-faced interlacing and the spread across groups of contrasting weft colours and warp ikat. However, the paucity of both Chin textiles from the mid-19th century or earlier and documentation of clothing worn then may make impossible the definitive testing of these hypotheses.

25 Woman's blanket, Het Tui. Lemro River, north of Mrauk-U. Est.
1930-1960. l = 148 cm; w = 76 cm. 2 loom widths, joined with 2-
colour running overhand knots. 22 warps/cm, 8.5 wefts/cm. Warps are
black, red, white and yellow cotton. Structural wefts are black cotton.
Supplementary wefts are black, red and yellow cotton. Twining wefts
are red and yellow cotton. 1-faced and 2-faced supplementary weft
patterning. Checkerboard. Countered weft twining. *(Photo: JC)*

Acknowledgements

The authors thank the following for lending their photographs: American Baptist Historical Society, American Baptist Archives Center, Valley Forge, PA, USA; The Textile Museum, Washington, DC, USA; The British Library; Neil Ryan. Photographs not taken by the authors were taken by Arthur and Laura Carson (ALC), Jeff Crespi (JC), Rev. Reginald Lorrain (RL), Neil Ryan (NR).

Bibliography

Bahadur, Mutua
    2000   *Tribal Hand Woven Fabrics of Manipur.* Imphal: Mutua Museum.

Bellwood, Peter
    1985   *The Pre-History of the Indo-Malayan Archipelago.* Sydney: Academic Press.

Bolland, Rita
    1979   "Advice to advisors" in Mattiebelle Gittinger (editor), *Indonesian Textiles. Irene Emery Roundtable on Museum Textiles 1979 Proceedings.* Washington: The Textile Museum, pp. 303-304.

Carey, B. S. and H. N. Tuck
    1896   *The Chin Hills: A History of the People, British Dealings with Them, their Customs and Manners, and a Gazetteer of their Country.* 2 volumes. Reprinted 1983. Delhi: Cultural Publishing House.

Chatterji, N.
    1972   *Puan – the Pride of Mizoram.* Mizoram: Tribal Research Institute. Second edition.

Emery, Irene
    1980   *The Primary Structures of Fabrics.* Washington: The Textile Museum. 2nd edition.

Fraser, David W.
    1989   *A Guide to Weft Twining and Related Structures with Interacting Wefts.* Philadelphia: University of Pennsylvania Press.

Fraser, David W. and Barbara G. Fraser
    2005   *Mantles of Merit: Chin Textiles from Myanmar, India and Bangladesh.* Bangkok: River Books.

Gittinger, Mattiebelle
    2005   *Textiles for This World and Beyond: Treasures from Insular Southeast Asia.* London: Scala.

Hamilton, Roy W., editor
    1994   *Gift of the Cotton Maiden: Textiles of Flores and the Solor Islands.* Los Angeles: Fowler Museum of Cultural History and University of California, Los Angeles.

Hill, L. G.
    1962   *An Ethnographic Survey of the Kuki-Chin-speaking Peoples of the Assam-Burma Border.* Oxford: University of Oxford.

Howard, Michael C.
    2005   *Textiles of the Highland Peoples of Burma: Volume I: The Naga, Chin, Jingpho, and Other Baric-speaking Groups.* Bangkok: White Lotus.

Howard, Michael C. and Kim Be Howard
    2002   *Textiles of the Central Highlands of Vietnam.* Bangkok: White Lotus.

Lehman, F. K.
    1958   "Preliminary field catalogue, Burma-Chin collection, F. K. Lehman, Chin Hills Burma, 1957-1958". Typescript deposited at the American Museum of Natural History, New York.
    1963   *The Structure of Chin Society: A Tribal People of Burma Adapted to a Non-Western Civilization.* Illinois Studies in Anthropology No. 3. Urbana: The University of Illinois Press.

Lowis, C. C.
    1959   *The Tribes of Burma.* Rangoon: Government Press.

Sakhong, Lian H.
    2003   *In Search Of Chin Identity: A Study in Religion, Politics and Ethnic Identity in Burma.* Copenhagen: NIAS Press.

Shaw, William
    1928   "Notes on the Thadou Kukis". *Journal and Proceedings of the Asiatic Society of Bengal* 24: 1-175.

Footnotes

[1] For a fuller analysis of the various Chin groups, see Fraser & Fraser 2005, Chapter 1.

[2] Lehman 1963, pp. 177-182; Shaw 1928, p. 75.

[3] For a more extensive technical description and diagrams of the textile structures discussed in this paper, see Fraser and Fraser 2005, Chapter 3.

[4] Lehman 1958, p. 15.

[5] Bahadur 2000, figure 90.

[6] Bahadur 2000, figure 122.

[7] Bahadur 2000, figure 146.

[8] The authors have not examined a Mizo *thangchhuah puan, Paite thangsuaphuan,* Sukte or Yo puandum, or Hmar *thangsapuan.* It would appear, however, from the figures cited from Bahardur (who does not include images of the reverse of any of these textiles), the descriptions accompanying those figures and the cultural relation ships between these groups and those whose textiles have been examined that it is likely that the narrow white stripes in these textiles are decorated only on the obverse.

[9] Fraser & Fraser 2005, figure 211.

[10] Fraser & Fraser 2005, figure 197.

[11] Fraser & Fraser 2005, figure 507.

[12] Fraser & Fraser 2005, figure 417.

[13] Fraser & Fraser 2005, figure 477.

[14] Fraser & Fraser 2005, figure 478.

[15] Fraser & Fraser 2005, figures 339 and 342.

[16] Hill 1962, p. 9.

[17] Chatterji 1972, p. 33.

[18] Chatterji 1972, pp. 33-34.

[19] Fraser & Fraser 2005, figures 291 and figure 64 (detail).

[20] Fraser & Fraser 2005, figure 165.

[21] Fraser & Fraser 2005, figure 540.

[22] Fraser & Fraser 2005, figure 71 (detail).

[23] Emery 1980, p. 141.

[24] Peabody Museum, Cambridge 13-24-60/85020 and 85021. See also 54-33-60/10215 for black weft in 2 side panels and white weft in center 2 panels.

[25] Bolland 1979.

[26] Fraser & Fraser 2005, figure 146.

[27] Fraser & Fraser 2005, figure 246.

[28] Fraser & Fraser 2005, figure 141.

[29] Lehman 1958, p. 14.

[30] Carey & Tuck 1896, p. 171.

[31] Lehman 1958, p. 14.

[32] Sakhong 2003, p. 70.

[33] Fraser & Fraser 2005, figure 111.

[34] Fraser & Fraser 2005, p. 112.

[35] Fraser & Fraser 2005, figures 197, 198, 202 and 252; Howard (2005; p. 87) calls this dotted pattern "*pseudo*-ikat."

[36] Fraser & Fraser 2005, pp. 203-204.

[37] Lowis 1919, p. 7; Lehman 1963, p. 18.

[38] Fraser & Fraser 2005, figure 225.

[39] Fraser & Fraser 2005, figure 176.

[40] Fraser & Fraser 2005, figure 175.

[41] Fraser & Fraser 2005, figure 94.

[42] Fraser 1989.

[43] Hamilton 1994, pp. 114-117.

[44] Fraser 1989, pp. 10-11.

[45] Gittinger 2005, p. 123.

[46] Pictured in Howard & Howard 2002, figures 77, 78, 86, 101, 114 and 115, although twining is not mentioned.

[47] Bellwood 1985, p. 233.

[48] Howard 2005, p. 21.

[49] Fraser & Fraser 2005, p. 219.

[50] U Cin Lamh Mang, personal communication.

[51] Compare to Fraser & Fraser 2005, figure 507.

Redefinining Status and Identity
Naga Textiles[1]

Vibha Joshi

The paper discusses the role of Naga textiles in the past and their continuing importance with regard to the contemporary socio-cultural and political issues of Naga identity. More than 20 groups of Naga living in northeast India and Myanmar have a unique set of textile traditions which portray the social status, gender and sometimes, within a single group, the clan affiliation of the person.

During the last hundred years the Naga in India and Myanmar have been subject to political changes and a majority have converted to Christianity. The paper will examine how these developments have affected the production and designing of cloth and have imparted new meanings and symbolism to textiles that were in the past associated with headhunting and providers of feasts, and with the indigenous animistic religion.

Naga nationalism draws on indigenous animism but also on distinctive Naga expressions of Christianity, in contrast to the otherwise dominant religion of Hinduism in India and Buddhism in Myanmar. This has given rise to interesting juxtapositions with regards to design and symbolism in Naga textiles. At a practical and secular level Naga textiles may be used for the manufacture of furnishing items. But at a level concerning questions of hallowed and ancestral representation, their use in ways that are not sanctioned by guardians of Naga cultural values is regarded as symbolic and ritual desecration. The paper will address these issues with examples of old and contemporary textiles from museum and private collections.

In October 2004, Naga organisations in Nagaland, India representing their students union, the mothers association, Nagaland Baptist Council of Churches, Naga People's Movement for Human Rights and its indigenous anthropologists objected to the use of a Naga cloth to adorn the idol of the Hindu goddess Durga in Kolkata as being inappropriate. This occurred during the Durga Puja celebrations when one of the dioramas depicting Naga culture used a red and black body cloth, possibly Ao, which traditionally could only have been worn by a person of high status. The diorama committee was obliged as a result of the protest to change the attire of Durga in favour of a more appropriate form, namely a sari. Draping a Hindu goddess in an indigenously significant Naga textile was seen as an affront to Naga religious beliefs and a form of desecration. Interestingly, it was Naga Christianity as well as their indigenous animistic beliefs that were regarded as having been violated, for neither is seen as compatible with Hinduism. The criticism was made that Naga symbolism can only be used to represent Naga culture[2].

Naga nationalism draws on indigenous animism but also on distinctive Naga expressions of Christianity, in contrast to the otherwise dominant religion of Hinduism in India and Buddhism in Myanmar. This has given rise to interesting juxtapositions with regards to design and symbolism in Naga textiles. At a practical and secular level Naga textiles may be used for the manufacture of furnishing items. But at a level concerning questions of hallowed and ancestral representation, their use in ways that are not sanctioned by guardians of Naga cultural values is regarded as symbolic and ritual desecration.

In this paper I discuss the role of Naga textiles in the past and their continuing importance with regard to the contemporary socio-cultural and political issues of Naga identity. More than 20 groups of Naga, who speak Tibeto-Burman languages, live in northeast India and north-west Myanmar. The political boundary between India and Myanmar runs through some Naga villages belonging to Konyak, Khiamungan, Yimchungrü and Tangkhul Naga which straddle the hills of the Eastern Himalayas. In India the Naga cultural distinctiveness is paralleled by the special terrain of Nagaland. It covers an area of 16,527 sq. km. and is one of a number of small northeastern states which are regarded by inhabitants and by many outsiders as standing apart from the rest of India **(1a, b)**. In India the Naga are identified as Scheduled Tribes in the Sixth Schedule of the Indian Constitution. They themselves use the term 'tribe' to identify each of their various groupings. Although known

Map 1: Location of Nagaland

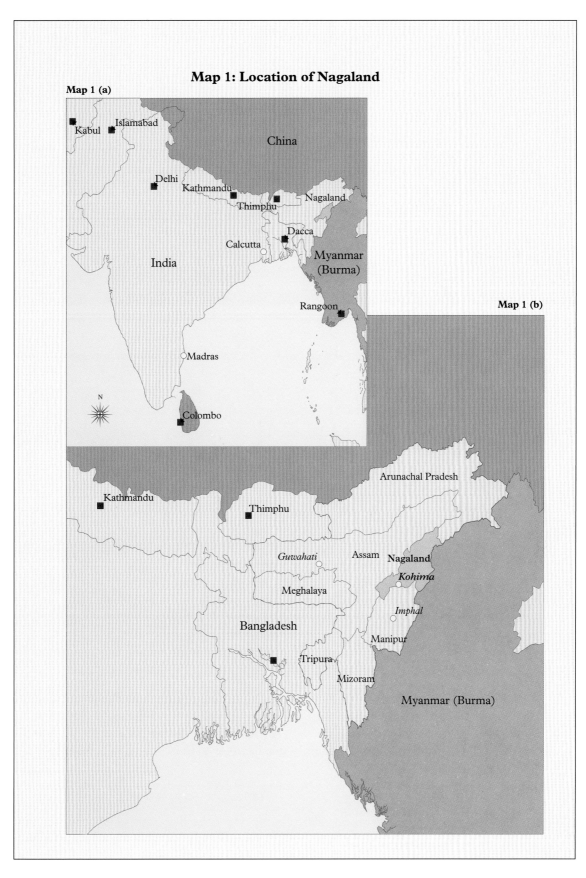

1 Map a and b showing location of Nagaland.

as Nagas to outsiders, each tribe uses a specific name, such as Angami, Sema, Ao, Tangkhul, Konyak to identify itself. It is however a common practice these days to use the word Naga as a suffix to the specific tribe name. Each tribe has a distinct dialect/language and differs in cultural features such as handicraft, house style and dress. The Naga in Myanmar are categorised as one of several hill tribes in Kachin and Sagaing divisions.

Traditional and the modern

"Nagas are westernised" and "Nagas are the head-hunters": these are two different statements about the Naga peoples that one often encounters and which reflect outsiders' perception of a largely Christian people with an 'exotic' past. 'Traditional' and 'modern' aspects permeate the way of living of the Naga especially those living in India. They no longer belong to a headhunting past but who are still partly identified with it. Yet the practice disappeared after the annexation of their region in nineteenth century by the British and with the introduction of Christianity. Almost ninety percent of Nagas in India are now Christian, mainly Baptist and Catholic and those living in Myanmar were introduce to Christianity by the Naga Baptist evangelists and the 'underground' Indian Naga nationalists[3] who use Christianity for the political expression of Naga distinctiveness.

The earlier conversions were accompanied by religious sanctions against participation in any activity that could qualify as being linked to traditional religious practices. The crafts connected with various traditional ritual activities were thus subject to the sanctions. These had a direct effect on costume, as some cloths and accompanying accessories could be worn only by those who had acquired status by showing prowess in war or headhunting, or by giving feasts of merit, all associated with the 'heathen' way of life that required performance of non-Christian rituals. The American Baptist Mission discouraged students in mission run schools from wearing traditional clothing.

However, British administration and Christian missionaries did introduce the Naga to formal education[iv], the legacy of which has vitally influenced people's worldview. Through colonialism and Christianity educated Naga increasingly took on what they regarded as aspects of a western life style, including clothing.

On one hand the educated Naga are in touch with recent developments in the world (including the latest fashions) while on the other are those living in the villages in a largely subsistence economy. In such a situation it is handicrafts that straddle the modern and traditional spheres of Naga life. A hand woven cloth may be an item of daily wear for a Naga while the same cloth, bearing a designer's distinctive touch, may adorn windows of prestigious furnishing shops in Delhi or, in the West, may be sold as 'tribal exotica'. As well as being seen as part of a creative movement where new designs are created and fashion statements made, textiles are enmeshed in Nagaland in major issues of 'Naga identity'.

Issues of 'identity'

What was a limited contact with outside world preceding British annexation and introduction of Christianity by the American Baptist Mission reached a full exposure with the fighting of the battle of Kohima in the World War II between Allied troops and the Japanese Army. With the Independence of India in 1947, Naga Hills became a district in the state of Assam, gaining statehood later in 1963 as a result of negotiations between the Government of India and Naga political leaders. English is the state language of Nagaland and Christianity is the dominant religion (2). The 50 years old Naga secessionist movement has raised issues of identity, for Naga stress their physical, socio-cultural and linguistic distinctiveness from most other Indians. They are after all speakers of a Tibeto-Burman language, are of Southeast Asian phenotype and were religiously animist and never Hindu, Muslim or Buddhist. Even internally among Naga themselves, tribal, clan and village affiliations have taken on new meanings in the new competition for political and economic autonomy.

2 A view of Khiamungan Naga village of Noklak, Tuensang district, Nagaland, near Indo-Myanmar border. Note the prominent structure of the Baptist church building and Pastor's residence. Almost 90% of Naga on the Indian side are Christian. Naga evangelists from the India are actively involved in proselytisation across the border in Myanmar. (Photo: Vibha Joshi)

The question one may ask is how these changes in the social and cultural milieu of the Naga are reflected in their textile tradition?

Textiles in everyday life

Taking a stroll in a Naga village on a sunny day, especially after the harvest, it is not unusual to find women weaving cloth on back-strap looms in front of their houses.

The Naga have been traditionally cultivators as well as warriors. These two activities have been responsible for the development of a stratified textile tradition. Cultivation is at the core of everyday social life and crafts/cloth is are produced to meet the needs of that life; at the same time, warriorhood is the institutional expression of relations external to the village and tribe and is denoted by the honorific bestowal of craft and cloth items.

Although nowadays Naga clothing is influenced by the west (among urban Naga women the north-Indian salwaar kameez is also popular), most Naga women wear the traditional wrap-around skirt cloth while only a few men wear the kilt. Both men and women wear the traditional shawls or upper body cloths or drapes. With hand-woven cloth still being the preferred apparel for most Naga, and with increased demand for it externally, weaving has become a foremost cottage industry in Nagaland supplementing the income of the households from cultivation[5]. Weaving has customarily been the preserve of women among Naga **(3, 4)**. The skill is learnt as part of the normal socialisation process in which young girls are taught to weave on toy looms. It will not be wrong to say that in villages almost all Naga women possess the skills to weave. Women of the household weave the traditional

4 An Angami woman of Zhadima village (Kohima district, Nagaland) weaving panels for Angami *Lohe* cloth. *(Photo: VJ)*

cloths required for both daily wear and festive occasions. In the town centres, however, weaving is not as popular among women (for most are employed in government offices or work as teachers) who therefore tend to rely for their supply of traditional dress on women entrepreneurs operating between rural areas and town. Urban Naga women thus form the main clientele of women weavers by providing them with a ready domestic market. In addition, hand-woven textiles are an intrinsic aspect of gift-giving among Naga generally at such rites of passage as marriage, birth and funerals, and for presentation to a dignitary or as a gesture of welcoming a guest. Gifting textiles is also part of the process of courtship; women gift their lovers finely woven waist belts at special community festivals (for example the festivals of Moatsu and Tsungremong of the Ao).

It is rare to come across older samples of Naga textiles. The tradition among the Naga to bury personal items including textiles and to also display the textiles on the graves **(5a, 5b)** of the deceased means that very few older textiles have survived to present time. Moreover, given the humid climate of the region, it is difficult to preserve textile, which, as other commentators have noted, is a commodity susceptible to early wear and disappearance compared with crafts made of more durable material. Indeed it is not easy to find textiles that have been manufactured before the 1940s, except in museum and private collections that were compiled before 1947.

Traditionally the Naga used home-grown cotton and nettle fibre for weaving. Cloth made of nettle fibre was (and still is) used for making coarse cloth and bedding while cotton was used for personal apparel and other forms of domestic use, such as bags. However nowadays

3 A Chakhasang Naga women weaving on the back strap loom outside her house in the winter sunshine. Due to its easy transportability, back strap loom is more popular for domestic production of cloth. Weaving in recent year has grown into a foremost cottage industry supplementing income from cultivation. *(Photo: VJ)*

5a A man's grave with cloth display (*shiatsa*) in Angami Naga village of Visewema (Kohima disrict, Nagaland). In the past displaying of the personal belongings of the deceased was widely practised among the Naga. This also explains the absence of heirloom textiles among the Naga. Older textiles dating before 1940s are now found only in Museum and some private collections. *(Photo: VJ)*

5b The grave of the chief of Kuthur, a Yimchungrü Naga village in Tuensang district of Nagaland. Notice the elaborate display of status cloths and skulls of sacrificial animals along with other personal belongings. Photo taken in 1960s by Milada Ganguli.

home-grown cotton spinning is in decline and the fine cotton cloth that is used for gift giving is woven from imported mill-made cotton yarn. Even as early as the 1920s and 30s the Naga had already started using yarn which was imported from the Assam plains and from Burma. J. H. Hutton mentions the use of Burmese yarn and wool in the manufacture of some of the textiles which he collected for the Pitt Rivers Museum. Today the most favoured yarn of weavers is acrylic and a wool blend known as cashmilon.

Traditionally, Naga textiles denote both group affiliation and individual status, such as age group, social status in terms of bravery, prosperity and shows of hospitality within the community. Motifs on the cloth are generally group-specific, although Naga groups that live in close proximity and share myths of migration and/or origin, have similar cloths. Thus the headtaker's black cloth with beige or blue stripes, small red squares in weft and cowry shell embellishments (**6**) is common to the Khianmungan, Yimchungrü, Chang, Sangtam and Sema Naga. An everyday blue cloth with deeper blue stripes, with no status connotation is common to the Ao, Sangtam and Khiamungan Nagas. Furthermore, certain kinds of cloth (as well as ceremonial ornaments) were in the past traded among different Naga communities; e.g. a men's red body cloth with black stripes (**7, 8**) and a median white band with painted motifs, is used by the Ao, Rengma and Lotha; the Rengma Naga supplying the white hand woven cotton strip the Ao and Lotha. neighbours.

There is a generic set of textiles for everyday use (**9, 10**) which are supplemented by special textiles that bear elaborate designs in accordance with the status achieved

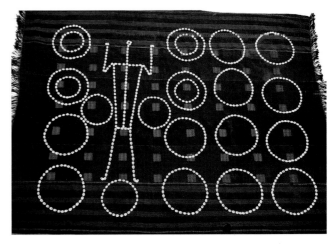

6 Chang Naga men's cloth with red squares of dog's wool and cowry decorations symbolising both wealth and valour in war. Such cloth is common to Chang, Sangtam, Sema, Khiamungan and Yimchungrü Naga. Museum der Kulturen, Basel, #IIa 10115. *(Photo: Wibke Lobo)*

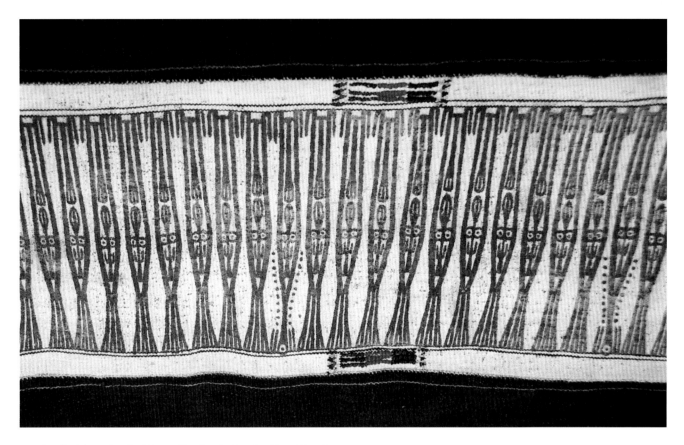

7a Detail of the painted white median band of an Ao Naga *Tsungkotepsü* cloth collected in 1890s. Ethnologisches Museum, Berlin, # IC 28373a. *(Photo:VJ)*

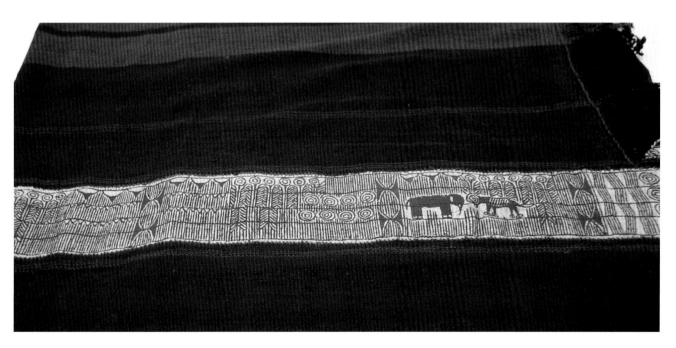

7b Detail of the painted median band of a Rengma Naga *Teri Phiketsü* cloth worn by successful warriors. *(Courtesy Museum der Kulturen, Basel, #IIb 1494)*

by a person through giving of feasts to clansfolk from one's own and neighbouring villages and/or show of bravery in war. These special textiles are worn during festivals and at the time of performance of rituals (11, 12, 13). During a Naga festival the costume of the person reflects the social status he/she holds in the community. While some Naga communities have an elaborate range of cloths depicting status such as married/unmarried, rich man, wife/daughter/son of a rich man and wife of a warrior/headtaker (14a, 14b, 15, 16, 17), certain others like the Angami have only a few such distinctive cloths. Patterns for some men's and women's cloths are similar among the Angami, but differ considerably in other Naga groups.

10 Chakhesang Naga men enjoying a drink (Losami, Kohima district, Nagaland). Men often drape a traditional cloth specific of their group (tribe) affiliation over their everyday Western clothes. The elderly man in the middle is wearing the red cloth symbolic of his status of a *gaonburra*, literally, village elder. The office of Gaonburra, a government appointed headship of the village *khel* or clan ward, was introduced by the Brtish during the colonial period and has continued to present times. *(Photo: VJ)*

8 Ao Naga men of Ungma village (Mokokchung district, Nagaland) in traditional attire celebrating Tsungremamung festival. They are wearing two kinds of shawls: *Tsungkotepsü* with median white band with embroidered motifs which was worn in the past by men of valour and the *Tabensa sü* cloth which could be worn only by wealthy men in the past. *(Photo: VJ)*

9 Konyak Naga women and men working in the jhum/swidden fields of Shangnyu village (Mon district, Nagaland). For everyday purpose the Naga wear a combination of market bought clothes and home woven cloth. *(Photo: VJ)*

12 Yimchungrü Naga men in full dance costume during the ritual dancing at the festival of Metemneo at Kuthur village (Tuensang district, Nagaland). *(Photo: VJ)*

114

11 Ao Naga men and women of Longsa village (Mokokochung district, Nagaland) dressed in traditional costume to welcome the chief guest (late) Mr I. M. Jamir during the celebration of Tsungremamung. Festivals are the time when people who work in townships return to their villages to celebrate with their clans people. *(Photo:VJ)*

13 Angami girls and boys of Khonoma village (Kohima district, Nagaland) in full dance costume during the celebration of Thekreni festival. White cloth with terracotta coloured stripes are particular to the Western group of Angami Naga. *(Photo:VJ)*

14a Wrap around skirt worn by Sema Naga unmarried girl belonging to a wealthy family. The cloth is decorated with green iridescent beetle elytra. Courtesy Pitt Rivers Museum, Oxford. J. P. Mills collection # 1928.69.1393. *(Photo: Suzy Prior)*

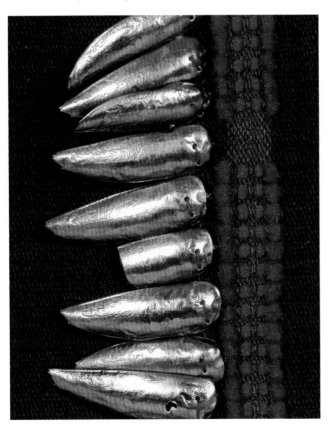

14b Detail of the cloth. Courtesy Pitt Rivers Museum, Oxford. J. P. Mills collection # 1928.69.1393. *(Photo: Suzy Prior)*

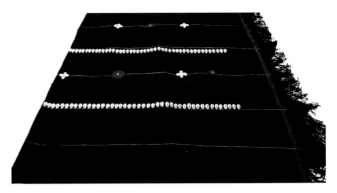

15 Rengma Naga woman's cowry cloth or *Tesükeka nya* which is worn only by a woman belonging to a wealthy family i.e., the wife or a daughter of a man who had performed the feasts of merit rituals. It is decorated with rows of cowry shells and cowry shells arranged in groups of four representing the stars alternating with a tuft of red dog's wool. Ethnologisches Museum, Berlin, # R.N.2. *(Photo: VJ)*

16 An elderly Angami man of Visewema village (Kohima district, Nagaland) wearing the white *Zathopfe* cloth. The right to wear this white cloth can be earned only by completing a series of rituals associated with the feasts of merit. *(Photo: VJ)*

17 Ao Naga women of Longsa village (Mokokchung district, Nagaland) wearing the rich women's cloth during celebration of Tsungremamung festival. Longsa village borders the Sangtam area; the influence of this proximity is reflected in their textile motifs. *(Photo: VJ)*

18a and **18b** (detail) The Ao Naga *Rongsusü* cloth with bunches of dog's hair wool dyed red in the middle of the cloth. The edges of the cloth are decorated with long red and black goat's hair tassels embellished with cowry shells. Such cloth could only be worn by a man

whose father, grandfather and himself had completed the series of feasts of merit, which was a rare feat to accomplish (J.P. Mills 1926: 35). Museum fur Volkerkunde, Vienna, # 126436. *(Photo:VJ)*

In the past specially designed cloth, some with cowry shell decorations, denoted the status of a headhunter, the warrior par excellence (see **6**). Another elaborately designed cloth with squares of tufts of dog's hair wool dyed red on the body of the cloth decorated with elaborate tassels made of red dyed goat's hair embellished with cowry shells on one end **(18)** could only be worn only by those who had earned the social status and the right to wear them after having given the complete series of feasts to fellow villagers. They were thus rarely given items of production. It is interesting to note that the first ethnographers of the Naga, J. H. Hutton and J. P. Mills, noticed that even in the early 1920s there were Naga villages in which this special status cloth had not been woven due to the fact that no-one was eligible to wear it. It is not surprising then that examples of some of these special cloths are now seen only in museum collections which were made almost a century ago!

While the right to wear a rich person or feast givers cloth was passed on to the children of the feast giver, the right to wear a warrior's cloth was restricted to those having participated in a headtaking raid, there being different kinds of cloth denoting the extent of the participation of the wearer. Strict rules for eligibility to wear such distinguishing cloths were followed. However, the Pax Britanica in late nineteenth century with its order prohibiting headtaking practices, made the eligibility criteria an impossibility. Interestingly, J. P. Mills, a British political officer and amateur anthropologist posted in Naga Hills noticed that some Naga communities such as the Ao, had worked around the obstacle by relaxing the rules and introducing 'buying' of the right to wear by making certain payments to the village council made of elders. While other communities such as the Konyak and

Pochuri (or Eastern Rengma as they were previously known) who had not relaxed this rules and were keen to send men to accompany the British officers on punitive expedition as load carriers and thus indirectly gain the status of warrior[6].

Early decades of Christian conversion led to complications when the Christian Nagas in some tribes disregard the traditional rules of eligibility. In his official tour diary of June 1934, J. H. Hutton, who was the District Commissioner of Naga Hills at that time, mentions such a conflict and his suggestions for settling, "The question of the patterns of cloths is giving trouble. Certain patterns are worn by householders who have performed certain social ceremonies and by their unmarried sons, when the boy marries he ceases to wear the cloth until he

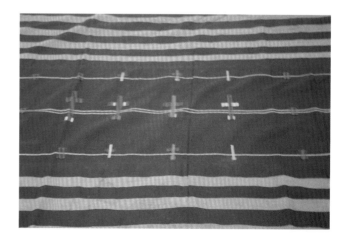

19 Detail of the cloth of a Sema Naga pastor of the American Baptist Mission at Lumitsami village, Naga Hills, collected by J. P. Mills in 1937. The cloth has extra supplementary weft motifs in the form of Christian cross to distinguish the cloth from that worn traditionally by wealthy Sema men who earned the right to wear it by performing feasts of merit. Pitt Rivers Museum, J. P. Mills Collection #1934.82.120. *(Photo:VJ)*

has qualified for it. The pattern is very popular and Christians have started wearing it without qualification which has scandalized the ancients. Both sides came to me about it. I ruled that Ancient had the right to it, but that provided some recognisable alteration was made in the pattern no exception would be taken to Christians wearing similar ones. I suggested a red cross in the middle of the black ground which was accepted without demur by those present."[7] An example of such a cloth with extra weft motifs of the cross which was used by Sema Christian pastors was bought by J. P. Mills for the Pitt Rivers Museum (19)[8].

New designs and patterns

Within the parameters of a notion of the 'traditional', Naga weavers have improvised on old designs and introduced new motifs. Women of the household as wife, mother or sister, are responsible for producing the cloth and, while she would follow a conventional pattern, there was always a possibility of some small degree of innovation, having the effect of making each cloth slightly distinctive. In fact this tradition was recorded in the 1920s by J. P. Mills[9], who deposited an example of a Rengma Naga cloth in the Pitt Rivers Museum, in Oxford, UK (20).[10] In addition to the usual single white band with painted design depicting a row of bodies without heads interspersed with the figures of headtakers, the new style of headtaker's cloth had a second band which depicted the ceremonial 'tail' worn by the leading warrior, tiger's eyes, and animals such as elephant, tiger, mithun, deer and python.

Furthermore, colours and designs used for cloths are continually changing. Such innovation, however, is not new: 'traditional' cloths evolved in the past as well, so that the definition of 'traditional' is open to question.

A Sema Naga rich woman's cloth, for example, was purchased by myself and was stated by its maker to be 'traditional'. However, the entry for a very similar cloth collected by J. P. Mills in 1932 and now in the Pitt Rivers Museum, reads:

Woman's cloth with pale blue bands between narrow strips of red, orange-yellow + black with double cross bands of red + yellow worked on one side of the cloth forming a check pattern. A recently invented pattern growing in popularity.[11]

The Naga textile tradition is not static but has been innovative and ready to experiment with new material, and is keen to introduce new designs and colour combinations. Individual weavers have been influential in setting trends and devising new methods. For example Khrieu Sekhose, an Angami 'master weaver' from Kohima village is credited with the introduction of the strip of embroidery along one end of the black Lohe cloth. She is also credited with developing new designs for the float motifs that are inserted in weft in the white ceremonial *Lohramhoshü* and *Pfhemhou* cloth (21, 22a & 22b, 23).[12] Last few years, a number of Naga villages have been celebrating centenary of Christianity to mark the event special Christian centenary cloths have been designed using traditional and Christian motifs (24).

In recent years, on one hand, new design patterns have been created by fusion of designs from different tribes and neighbouring non-Naga communities, while on the other there is a growing trend to revive older textile designs – a kind of revival of 'antique' fashion. An example is of the women's textile of the Lotha Naga

20 Rengma Naga *Arrhi hü pi* warrior's cloth collected by J. P. Mills in 1931 from Tesophenyu village. The two white median bands are painted with motifs of warriors, decapitated men, warrior's tail, tiger's eyes, elephants, *mithun* bull, deer and python. Pitt Rivers Museum, J. P. Mills Collection #1928.69.1553. *(Photo: Heini Schneebeli)*

21 Detail of the Angami Naga *Loramhoshü* cloth worn by the people of Kohima. V. Joshi Collection. *(Photo: VJ)*

22a An Angami Naga priest wearing the *Loramhoshü* cloth draped on his shoulder, an essential part ceremonial costume, at Sekrenyi festival in Viswema village (Kohima district). *(Photo: VJ)*

22b Men wearing *Loramhoshü* and *Lohe* cloth during the Catholic church Sunday service and the annual harvest feast, Kohima village (Kohima district). *(Photo: VJ)*

24 Tsilie Sakhrie, president of the Western Angami Public Organisation, wearing *Krie Khwe*, the Khonoma village centenary cloth woven by his wife Sieno. It was designed to commemorate 100 years of Baptist Christianity in Khonoma village (Kohima district). *(Photo: VJ)*

23 Young unmarried girls dressed in ceremonial costume wearing *Pfhemhou* cloth on the final day of Sekrenyi festival passing through the wooden gate of T. Khel or ward of Kohima village (Kohima district). *(Photo: VJ)*

119

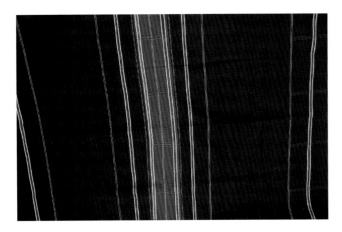

25 Lotha Naga woman's traditional wrap skirt cloth called *Kyong sürüm* woven on fly-shuttle loom. Mrs Lochumlo Yanthan's private collection. *(Photo: VJ)*

26 Contemporary version of the older *Kyong sürüm* cloth with complex weft motifs. The cloth was designed in the 1960s by the Lotha Naga Women's Committee. Mrs Lochumlo Yanthan's private collection. *(Photo: VJ)*

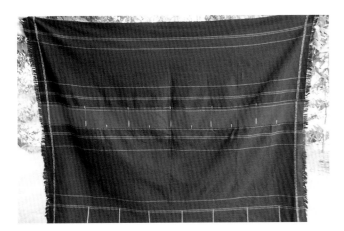

27 Lotha Naga unmarried girl's blue skirt cloth called *Liyoe Sürüm*. The old pattern has seen a revival in recent times, and has become a popular choice for formal wear among young Lotha women. Ms. Narisen Ovung's private collection. *(Photo: VJ)*

28 The Chakhesang Naga 'graduate cloth'. The design is based on the older pattern of warrior's cloth called *Erira*. Courtesy Belho weaving, Kohima. *(Photo: VJ)*

community. The Lotha women's 'traditional' cloth *Kyong sürüm*, (25) has been redesigned using a multi-coloured motif (26), which is an elaboration of the older motif embroidered in weft inserts, on a black base cloth with red and green colour combination. But since the late 1990s, for formal occasion like weddings, Lotha women (especially young girls) have begun to favour wearing sarongs with an older design using a dark blue base cloth with minute weft inserts in red and yellow (27).

The alterations of life-styles and social circumstances have been accompanied by changes in the symbolism of textiles. For instance, the cloth associated with head-hunting has been given new meaning. That which was in the past worn by the successful Chakhesang warrior is now known as the 'educated' person's cloth and worn by those who are university graduates (28). Achievement in education has replaced valour in the war. Similarly, a

special black cloth with broad red band, which was the preserve of Angami Naga women who held high status in the community is now also worn by women graduates. The improvised cloth called *Mhasi nei* or educated woman's cloth, is black with a broad deep yellow band with green and yellow weft float motifs (29).

Although the meaning and importance of certain textiles have undergone change in last few decades, they continue to occupy a prominent place in the socio-cultural identity of the Naga. Be it an occasion of an mistic or Christian festival, marriage or the celebration (in the late twentieth century, continuing to present year) of the centenary of the arrival of the first Christian missionaries in various villages, the appropriate hand-woven cloths in different hues and designs are worn by the participants.

In recent years the new competition for political and economic autonomy **(30)**, tribal, clan and village affiliations have taken on new meanings among Naga themselves. Cloth had always been one of the markers of old status, gender and other differences but has since the political changes had to adapt to the redrawing of such community and individual affiliations. Textiles, then, continue to play a vital role in reflecting the new meanings of such identities. Reviving old motifs and even designing new tribal cloth based on older motifs is part of the process in which Christian and other Naga identities are forged in new combinations.

29 (left) Floret Sekhose, secretary of the Kewhima Zhavipfüko Krotho (or KZK, the organisation of educated women of Kohima) wearing the black and yellow *Mhasi nei* or educated woman's cloth (Kohima village, Kohima district). Designed by members of the KZK, the cloth is worn on formal occasions by women who have at least completed matriculation. Her sister, Ms Mary Sekhose, wears the 'Jubilee church choir' cloth designed for the Catholic church choir to mark 50 years of the Catholic church in Kohima. *(Photo:VJ)*

30 (right) A stone tablet in Merhüma khel/ward of Khonoma village (Kohima district) with names of martyred Naga nationalists. A constant reminder to the people of the ongoing issue of Naga sovereignty and the more than half a century old separatist movement which was begun by Zapuo Phizo of Khonoma. *(Photo:VJ)*

Acknowledgements

I wish to thank Country Eastern for funding fieldwork in India in 2001, and the British Academy for funding research visit to the Ethnologisches Museum in Berlin in 2005.

Footnotes

1   Parts of this paper have appeared previously in Joshi 2001, 2003 and 2004.

2   'Outrage over Hindu deities in Naga attire', Assam Tribune, 22 October 2004, http://www.assamtribune.com/oct2204/ne1.html; 'Nagaland: Durga's attire in Kolkata irk Nagas' *The Sangai Express*, 21 October 2004, http://www.thesangaiexpress.com/

3   See also, Jacobs, 1991, pp 177.

4   Christian missions were welcomed into Naga villages for their educational (and medical) work. In India Nagaland as a matter of fact has a higher literacy rate compared to the national average of India. Poor educational facilities in the Naga villages of Myanmar have forced the Nagas to seek education in Naga villages across border in India.

5   Of the three types of looms used in the cottage industry of weaving, namely fly shuttle loom, power loom, and back strap or loin loom, it is the latter which has remained by far the most popular and most convenient because of its easy transportability from one location to another. It is used for weaving the fabric for shawls, sarongs, kilts, sashes, waist belts and shoulder bags. There are very few fly shuttle looms, while a small number of power looms have been installed by soe weaving cooperatives and are used for producing furnishing cloth and low cost shawls and sarongs.

6   Mills, 1926, The Ao Naga, pp 41.

7   Hutton, J. H., 14 June 1934.

8   J. P. Mills Collection 1934.82.120, Pitt Rivers Museum, University of Oxford.

9   See also Mills, J. P. 1937, Rengma Nagas, pp 22.

10 J. P. Mills Collection: 1928.69.1553. Pitt Rivers Museum, University of Oxford.

11 J. P. Mills Collection: 1928.69.1543, Pitt Rivers Museum, University of Oxford.

12 See also, Ganguli, 1993, pp 63-4.

Bibliography

Ao, Alemchiba, 1968. *Art and Crafts of Nagaland,*. Kohima: Department of Art and Culture, Government of Nagaland.

Ganguli, Milada. 1993. *Naga art*. New York: International Science Publisher.

Hutton, John Henry. 1921. *Sema Nagas*. London: Macmillan & Co.

_____ 1921. *Angami Nagas*. London: Macmillan & Co.

_____ 1934. 'Tour diaries of district Commissioner Naga Hills, Assam, June-July 1934', mansript, J. H. Hutton Box 3. Pitt Rivers Museum Archives, University of Oxford.

Jacobs, Julian. 1990. *The Nagas: Hill Peoples of Northeast India*. London, New York: Thames and Hudson.

Joshi, Vibha. 1995. The handicrafts of Nagaland. Unpublished project report. New Delhi: Development Commissioner for Handicrafts, Ministry of Textiles.

_____.2000. Naga Textiles – Today. *Oxford Asian Textile Group*, 15, February, pp. 7-10.

_____. 2003. 'Naga textiles' in *Textiles from Burma*, eds. E. Dell and S. Dudley. London: Philip Wilson Publishers.pp 83-86.

_____. 2003. 'Design, meaning and identity in Naga textiles: continuity and change' in *Textiles from Burma*, eds. E. Dell and S. Dudley. London: Philip Wilson Publishers, London. pp 115-124.

_____& Aditya Arya. 2004 *The Land of the Nagas*. Mapin Publishing Pvt. Ltd. Ahmedabad and Grantha Corporation, New York.

Mills, James Philip. 1922. *Lhota Nagas*. London: Macmillan & Co.

_____ 1926. *Ao Nagas*. Bombay: Oxford University Press.

Mon Ancestral Textiles

Piriya Krairiksh

Until now the subject of Mon textiles has been a *terra incognita* in the study of Southeast Asian textiles, to the extent that the word Mon cannot be found in the index of the book *Textiles from Burma: Featuring the James Henry Green Collections* (Dell and Dudley 2003). This is not surprising, because ever since the fall of their capital Pegu to the Burmese in 1539, Mon culture has been absorbed by the Burmese and vice versa. Yet throughout their vicissitude, the Mons, like many other ethnic groups without their own country, cling tenuously to their language, history, tradition and cultural norms that give them an identity of their own. Whether they live in Thailand, or in Myanmar, and have become Thais or Myanmar citizens, they always think of themselves as Mons. But for the determination and perseverance of Khun Kasaporn Tramod and Khun Narisa Dejsupa, researchers at the Thai Khadi Research Institute, Thammasat University, and the support of the James H. W. Thompson Foundation, we might have never know the existence of Mon textiles at all.

As is to be expected, textiles of an ethnic minority, living in countries that they cannot call their own, are not materials that will send textiles' lovers into rapture. Woven by rice farmers for their own use, they are generally of cotton and are woven at home. Their looms are described at length by Robert Halliday, a pioneer of Mon study during the first three decades of the last century, in his book, *"The Talaings"* (1997/2000, I). The word *"Talaings"* itself is Burmese, which the Mons considered derogatory (Guillon 1999, 17-18). So, like the Mons themselves, their textiles are humble and prepossessing. They reflect the basic agrarian way of life. Yet one sees their former grandeur in the length and colouring of their clothes. These are the textiles of a proud but subjugated people.

The Mons living in Myanmar believe that their history goes back to the time of the Buddha (Halliday 1923/2000, II: 83-88) and that they gave the Kingdom of Pagan its Theravada Buddhism, culture, art and architecture (Nai Pan Hla 1958, 69-70; Guillon 1999, 114-139). But inscriptional evidences indicate the presence of the Mons in Lower Myanmar by the mid 9th century (Bauer 1991, 34) and art historical evidences suggests, that the Mons may have migrated to Myanmar in the 10th century (Krairiksh 1974, 64). Furthermore, recent researches show that Pagan owed its art and architectural styles not to the Mons, but to north-eastern India (Bautze-Picron 2003, 3-5). Only with the establishment of the Mon Kingdom at Pegu in the mid 14th century that Mon culture reached its zenith in the following century (Aung-Thwin 2002, 48-49).

Although the old Mon speaking people may have been the inhabitants of central and north-eastern Thailand between the 6th and 8th centuries (Bauer 1991, 32-33) and remnants, called Nyak Kur, still survive to this day on the Korat Plateau (Nai Pan Hla 1992, 36-45), most Thai Mons living along the banks of the Chao Phraya (Nichaiyok 2547, 149-235) and the Mae Klong Rivers (Wongthet 1993, 74-112) in central Thailand, trace their ancestry to the series of migrations to escape Burmese repressions between 1595 and 1815 (Guillon 1999, 194-208). According to Robert Halliday, the Mons in Siam called their homeland in Myanmar "Mon Land" *(Dung Mon)*, whereas the Thais called it Burma Land *(Muang Bama)* (Halliday 1992/2000, II: 7). Wherever the Mons settled they maintained the traditions of their forefathers. Halliday states that one or two things that distinguishes the Mons from their neighbours is the tradition of the House Spirit *(kalok hoi)*, as manifested by the little spirit houses and the hanging of the basket containing ancestral clothing and ornaments on the southeast corner post of their houses and the spirit's dance performed in connection with it. *(Ibid.* 9) Halliday, writes:

> *It will be seen that the Talaings as a separate people with laws and government of their own, no longer exist. In Burma it is no longer possible for the casual observer to distinguish from the Burmese. It is only in the matter of language that they greatly differ to any but the closest observer... Close observers in Burma have had to own the almost impossibility of distinguishing the Talaings in mere appearance apart from the Burmese.* (Halliday 1917/2000, I: 25)

Yet this was not the case in the 15th and 16th centuries when Mon dresses and hairstyle were quite distinctive from those of the Burmese. Jacques de Coutre, who visited Ayutthaya in 1595, in the reign of King Naresuan, mentioned in connection with the practice of wearing small bells inserted in the flesh of the penis, which was then prevalent in both Siam and Pegu the following:

That the author of this invention was the Queen of Pegu, because in her day the inhabitants of that Kingdom were much inclined towards the unspeakable sin [of sodomy]. And she made a law, with great penalties, that the women should wear their dresses – which are just like petticoats – open from the navel to the hem, so that when they walked they revealed the whole of the thighs. She did this so that the men would desire them and would refrain from the unspeakable sin.
(Quoted in Smithies 1994, 82)

The same account is also given by Alexander Hamilton, a Scottish sea captain, who visited Pegu in 1710-1711 (Hamilton 1727/1997, 25-26).

This style of wearing the *ganin* must have continued into Thailand into the 19th century, since it is depicted on a door panel of the ordination hall at Wat Bang Namphueng Nok, Phra Pradaeng District, Samut Prakarn Province **(1)** (Muang Boran 1991, 47). The paintings on wood panels at Wat Bangkhae Yai, in Amphawa District, Samut Songkhram Province, from 1814, also show Mon women wearing the *ganin* in the traditional way **(2)** (*Ibid*, 38, 64). The upper part of the *ganin* covers the breasts and opens "from the navel to the hem," which recalls the garments of Māra's daughters depicted on the glazed terracotta plaques from Ajapāla stupa at Pegu, dated 1479, in the reign of King Dhammazeti **(4)**. Some of the women painted at Wat Bangkae Yai also wear the close fitting white jacket. While the men wear plaid loin cloth favoured by Mon men **(3)** (*Ibid*, 42, 46-47).

As for the hair style, Mon men used to shave their hair at the back and sides leaving the central part as if a bowl were upturned on the head. Such was the style that in 1535, after having reigned in Pegu for four years, the Burmese King Tabeng Shwethi cut his hair off after the Mon fashion (Halliday 1917/2000, I: 28).

On the dress worn by the Mons, Halliday reiterated the similarity with the Burmese. "The dress worn by the Talaings in Burma is the ordinary Burmese dress. In that respect they are quite indistinguishable from the Burmese." (*Ibid.*, 27)

1 Mon woman wearing the *ganin* with front opening. Wat Bang Namphueng Nok, Phra Pradaeng District, Samut Prakan Province, 1824-1851.

2 Mural showing Mon woman wearing the *ganin* covering the breasts and opening in the front. Wat Bangkhae Yai, Amphawa District, Samut Songkram Province, 1814.

Opposite: (left to right)

4 Mara's daughters, glazed terracotta plaques from Ajapala stupa, Pegu, 1479.
(Private collection Bangkok)

5 A man wearing a cotton *glik-halone* tied at the waist and gathered up into three folds.

6 A man wearing a cotton *glik-halone* with the end thrown over the shoulder.

3 Two Mon women, one with white jacket and men in plaid loin cloths. Wat Bangkhae Yai, Ampawa District, Samut Songkram Province, 1814.

Indeed, this similarity was recorded by a Thai observer already in 1835. For Khun Mahasidhivohan describing the dress of different nationalities in the inscriptions of Wat Phra Chetuphon, Bangkok, writes that the Mons wore checked garments and jackets similar to the people of Ava. (*Prachum Khlong Kawi* 2462, 40)

Halliday's description of the dress worn by the Mons in Burma is particularly instructive:

The men wear a loin cloth, glik, consisting of a piece of narrow cloth, some eight yards long, sewn in two breadths without cutting. It is put round the body and fastened in with a twist at the waist, and the remaining part of it is gathered up in three folds and hung from the waist in front (5) or simply thrown over the shoulder (6). Old men may be seen on cold mornings with the spare end worn round the shoulders as a shawl. The silk material for this garment is sometimes cut and made into two saluings. To make an ordinary saluing, a piece of cloth, some twenty-two inches wide and four and a half yards long, is woven. It is cut in two and the two breadths joined. The ends are then sewn together and the garment is complete. Cotton is used for workaday wear and silk for special occasions. The upper part of the body is covered with a short white cotton jacket or one of darker material. The head is covered with a bright coloured silk handkerchief put round and the ends tucked in as a turban.

The ganin worn by the women is formed just like the men's saluing, except that it has a broad band of a different pattern on the top and is somewhat smaller than the men's garment. A jacket of white or coloured cotton or silk completes the costume. On festive occasions a bright silk scarf is worn over the shoulders (7). Very old women may sometimes be seen with an open ganin consisting of a piece of silk, almost square, made of two widths joined together. It is sometimes partly laced to keep it from opening too much in walking." (Ibid.)

The *glik-halone* is still worn in the Mon State of Myanmar by bridegrooms, candidates for monkhood in pre-ordination ceremonies, folk dancers (8) and mediums during spirit's dances (9). However, in Thailand today it is only worn during the spirit's dance.

The *glik-halone* have the following characteristics:

1. As its name implies the *glik-halone* is a long loin cloth, measuring between 350 to 700 centimetres. For the same length of cloth must cover the lower part of the body as well as the head (10).

2. The *glik-halone* has a stitch running along its length. On account of the narrow weft dimension of the loom, measuring about 20 centimetres, the Mons stitch two length of clothes together, so that the width of the *glik-halone* comes to about 40 centimetres (11).

3. It clearly differentiates the upper part (*dub*) from the lower hem (*chan*). Since the Mons hold the head to be higher than the feet, the latter, as represented by the lower hem (*chan*), is demarcated by a weft band. As for the head section (*dub*), it is sewn into a "V" shaped pouch which is used for keeping personal belongings and tied up into a knot for safe keeping (12).

125

7 Women wearing a *ganin* with white blouse and red scarf. Kamawet Village, Mudon.

8 Dancers wearing the *glik-halone*. Kamawet Village, Mudon.

9a-b Medium wearing the *glik-halone* during the spirit's dance near Kyaujnataw.

11 (above) *Glik-halone* is made by stitching two lengths of cloth together.

10 (left) A silk *glik-halone* worn covering the head.

12 The head section of the *glik-halone* is sewn into a "V" shaped pouch for the keeping of personal belongings.

4. The colours of the *glik-halone* are limited to the five primary colours, namely black, white, red, yellow and blue.

Fraser Lu also takes the Mon *glik* to be the same as the Burmese *pah-so*. For she writes:

Men in pre-colonial Burma wore a very voluminous pah-so, 400 centimetres long by 150 centimetres wide, made from an 8-metre-long piece of cloth cut in half and sewn along the selvage. It was worn as a sarong with the excess either draped in folds in the front or thrown over the shoulder. One end was sometimes sewn a short way along the selvages to form a 'V'-shaped pouch in which small personal items could be placed. ... Pah-so for everyday wear were made of striped or plaid cotton, but for formal occasions silk was the preferred material, with those patterned in acheik being the most desired by all." (Fraser Lu 2003, 261)

Although the *glik* and the *pah-so* were indistinguishable to Halliday and Fraser Lu, there are reasons to believe that the *glik*, or *glik-halone* (long loin cloth) as the Mons call it today, may have been the original Mon garments. For not only the Mons themselves contended that the *glik-halone* was the national garment of the Mon people (Sub-Department of Mon Culture 1977, 214-215); but the Burmese scholars also agree that Burmese dress evolved from those of the Pyus and the Mons (U Min Naing 2000, 70-72). The researchers believe that the *glik-halone* can be singled out as an example of Mon textiles, because the word is mentioned in the Mon inscription of King Kyanzittha of Pagan (r. 1084-1112), and because it is inseparable from the worship of ancestral spirits and its basic patterns are sanctioned by custom:

1. The word *glik*, or *glait* as it is used in the Mon inscription of Pagan, refers to a loin cloth, such as in Inscription No. 5 of King Kyanzittha which recorded the restoration in 1098 of the *stupa* called Kyik Tala located somewhere in Lower Burma (Duroiselle 1960, 144). Lines 14-16 of this inscription describe women wearing a wrapped-around skirt and a blouse with long sleeves and men wearing white loin cloth *(glait kuchum bomtoin)*. It also mentions 126 Rāmens (Mons) wearing long white loin cloth, carrying metal and earthenware pots (Phe Maung Tin 1972(a)). In the Schwezigon Inscription, the word *glĭk* appears on Face B. line 35, in which King Kyanzittha gave way with his left hand *glit-latak* (cloth that can be worn and wrapped around as well) (Duroiselle 1960, 97, 117 and Phe Maung Tin 1972 (b)). *Glik antak* may have been corrupted to *glit-latak*, which Mons sometimes use today to refer to a piece of long loin cloth instead of the customary *glit-halone*.

2. The *glik-halone* is inextricably linked with the Mons' belief in spirits *(kalok)* in particularly to that of the house spirit *(kalok sñi)* (today *kalok hoi* or *panok hoi* is used instead). Halliday observed, that "It looks as if originally the *kalok* had marked a kind of tribal distinction, though nowadays it is more of a family affair." He elaborated that after the father of a family died:

The eldest brother as being the nearest representative of the deceased father is recognized as the head of the family. In his house are kept the requisites for the kalok. These consist of articles of clothing and adornment and are kept in a basket hung on the dayuin khoroṅ, *or spirit's post* **(13)**. *This, in a house of the Talaing pattern, is the post at the southeast corner. All their brothers with their wives and children are said to be of one* kalok.... *The* kalok *follows only the male line, and when the sisters marry, each becomes attached to the* kalok *of her husband's family.* (Halliday 1917/2000, I: 110-111)

The ancestral spirit is represented by a set of clothing which is called *panok-hoi* in Myanmar and *alok-hoi* in Thailand. It consists of the followings items **(14)**:

13 Ancestral cloths are kept in a case, or a basket, and hung next to the spirit's post. House of Nang Thawil Monda, Bang Kradi, Bang Khunthian District, Bangkok.

14 Set of ancestral clothing.

15 The weaver of a new set of ancestral clothing.

I.   One or two lengths of *glik-halone*. One with a common pattern shared by all ancestral clothes, called *panok*. The other has plaid or checked pat tern particular to the family, called *panok-hoi*.

II. One white long-sleeved jacket with front opening tied by a pair of cords at waist level. The jacket may be black, red or orange in colour and the cords may be as many as five pairs.

III. One white or red head cloth.

IV. One ring with red or white gem stone tied to a cord of the jacket.

V.   One woman's *ganin,* a garment composed of a red waistband, a red skirt body and a lower hem.

VI. Two shawls, one red and one white.

This set of spirit clothes is worshipped by the Mondeh, or the Mons who lived in the region of Pegu (Nichaiyok 2547, 72). Whereas those living in the Dagon (Yangon) area, called Mondung, worship the coconut spirits, while those living in the region of Moattama, called Monya, worship the bamboo spirits (Tun Thein 1995, 15-16). Nevertheless, all three Mon groups in Myanmar keep ancestral clothes which are handed down to the eldest son in the family. If he does not have a son, it would be given to his younger brother to pass on to his son and heir. When no more son is born the family's lineage comes to an end.

If a man wishes to move elsewhere and to start his own family, he must obtain exact copies of his ancestral clothing and ornaments. "The same colours and the same checks and patterns must be used. It is the same *kalok* and must be treated in exactly the same way." (Halliday 1917/2000, I: 113)

Should sickness or calamity befall a family, a village medium *(don)* would be consulted who would then examine the ancestral clothes. If any part of them is found to be damaged, they would have to be changed at once. The change entails a dance to propitiate the spirits and an order for a new set of clothing. The ancestral clothes must be woven by a widow, or her descendants **(15)** with the following specifications:

I.   A quid of betel as a contract for the order.

II. The order must be completed two days before the ceremony.

III. The colour and pattern must be exactly the same as the original.

IV. There would be two lengths of ancestral clothes; one is the ancestral *glik-halone (panok)*, the other is the family *glik-halone* with its own distinctive pattern *(panok-hoi)* **(16)**.
     The ancestral *glik-halone (panok)* generally has horizontal red stripes along the length of the cream-coloured cloth with a vertical with red band indicating the lower hem.
     The family *glik-halone (panok-hoi)* is woven with the family's own plaid or checked pattern.

V.   Only the hands must be used when stiffening the cotton thread with rice water.

VI. While weaving the thread must not be broken.

After the spirit's dance is over, the new ancestral clothes are kept in their usual place by the spirit's post, that is the post at the southeast corner of the house. The damaged set of clothes is then made into cushion covers for monks **(17)** or pillows covers for the use of family

129

16 An order for ancestral clothing consists of two lengths of textiles: one with stripes is the ancient cloth and the one with plaids is the family's garment.

17 Discarded ancestral cloth made into cushions for monks.

members **(18)**. Mon people would not keep other family's ancestral clothes in their home, less they cause them bad luck.

According to a 75-year-old abbot in Paung, ancestral clothes *(panok)* were not woven to be worn. The family's garments *(panok-hoi)*, on the other hand, were worn to show that the wearers belong to the same family. As the Mons were exogamous, they would not marry among themselves. He also said that, after Alaungpaya's attempt to exterminate to the Mons in 1757, the Mons hid their identity by wearing Burmese dress. So the *panok-hoi* with family's plaid or checked patterns is no longer worn; but is used only in spirit's dance.

3. The basic patterns of both the ancestral clothes *(panok)* and the family's garments *(panok-hoi)* are hallowed by tradition. They consist of plaids *(anang khok ngae)*, checks *(anang ni moimai oua moimai)* and stripes *(anang noan)*.

The plaid represents the rice field *(anang khok ngae)* **(19)**. It is said to have been derived from the cut and sewn "rice field" pattern of the monk's robe, as prescribed by the Buddha himself. This belief can be attributed to Theravada Buddhism since it is shared by both Mons and Thais. (Gettinger and Lefferts 1992, 97-100)

The checked pattern is called *(anang ni moi mai oua moi mai)* which means "One square for your and one square for me." **(20)**

The stripes *(anang-noan)* are differentiated into two varieties: horizontal stripes *(anang-noan or anang-halone)* and vertical stripes *(anang kanu)*.

18 Discarded ancestral cloth made into pillow covers for family members.

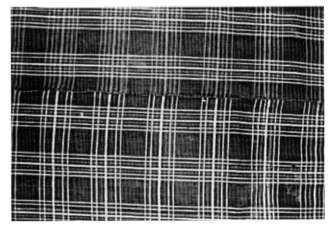

19 Plaid representing the rice fields *(anang khok ngea)*.

20 Checked pattern meaning "one square for you, one square for me."

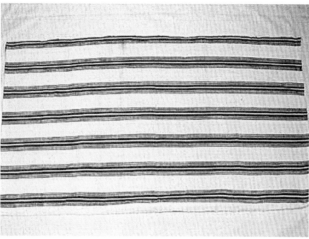

21 Horizontal stripe bamboo pattern.

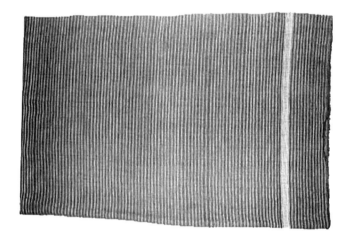

22 Vertical stripes *(anang kanu)*.

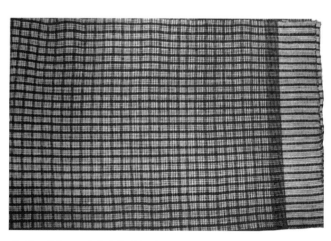

23 Family's *panok-hoi*, Ko Zak, Kyaikmayaw.

The horizontal stripes are sometimes called "bamboo" pattern *(anang-om-toon)* **(21)**. They are on found blankets, sheets and mosquito-nets. Tradition requires that the mother of the bridegroom weaves them as presents for her son's wedding so that his new family with grow and multiply as fast as bamboo.

The vertical stripes *(anang-kanu)* are rarely found on the male loin cloth **(22)**, but are popular with women. The researchers have documented 35 distinctive plaids, and checked patterns belonging to different families in villages in the districts of Kyaikmayaw **(23)**, Mawlamyine **(24),** Paung **(25)**, Mudon **(26)**, Chaung-zon and Thanpyuzayat. Those around Ye have not been studied.

As for the ancestral clothes *(alok-hoi)* in Thailand, they are of plain colour, generally subdue in tone **(27).**

To conclude, the fear of persecution has led the Mons in Myanmar to keep their identity to themselves. But hidden away in baskets, kept beside the spirit's post of their houses, are cloths belonging to their ancestors. These long loin cloths with stripes, plaids and checked patterns are quintessentially Mons. For they embody the belief, hope and fear of an ethnic minority, whose identity is kept alive by history, language and tradition. To these we might add textiles, which represent the indomitable spirit of the Mon people.

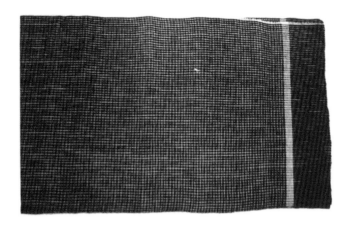

24 Family's *panok-hoi,* Ko Hanat, Mawlamyine.

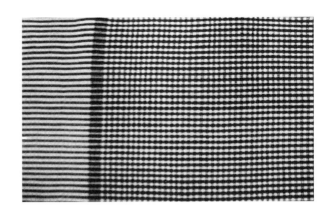

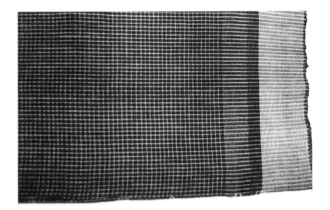

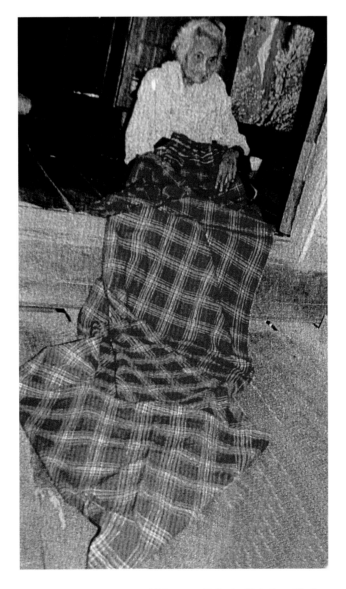

26 An 103 year old women with her grandfather's *glik-halone*, Mudon.

25a-c (above) *Panok-hoi* belonging to three different families in Paung.

Acknowledgements

The "Mon Textiles" project is undertaken by the Thai Khadi Research Institute, Thammasat University, to commemorate the auspicious occasion of Her Majesty the Queen's Sixth Cycle Anniversary. It is funded by the James H. W. Thompson Foundation.

The writer is grateful to the James H. W. Thompson Foundation for funding the research and to Khun Kasaporn Tramod and to Khun Narisa Dejsupa for the informations and photographs of Mon textiles. He is indebted to Dr. Henry Ginsburg, former Curator of Thai manuscripts at The British Library, and to Dr. Richard Blurton, Curator of Southeast Asian art at of the British Museum, for their valuable advice and assistance on the subject.

References

Aung-Thwin, Michael
2002   Lower Burma and Bago in the History of Burma. *The Maritime Frontier of Burm: Exploring Political, Cultural and Commercial Interaction in the Indian Ocean World, 1200-1800.* 25-57. ed. Jos Gommans and Jacques LeiderAmsterdam: Konikklijke Nederlandse Akadmic van Wetenschappen.

Bauer, Christian
1991   Notes on Mon Epigraphy. *The Journal of the Siam Society* 79 (1): 31-83.

Bautze-Picron, Claudine
2003   *The Buddhist Murals of Pagan: Timeless vistas of the cosmos.* Bangkok: Orchid Press.

Dell, Elizabeth and Dudley, Sandra
2003   *Textiles from Burma: Featuring the James Henry Green Collection.* Brighton: The James Green Centre for World Art.

Duroiselle, Chas
1960   *Archaeological Survey of Burma: Epigraphia Birmanica Being Lithic and Other Inscriptions of Burma.* I (2). Rangoon: Archaeological Survey of Burma.

Fraser-Lu, Sylvia
2003   *Burmese Crafts Past and Present.* Kuala Lumpur: Oxford University Press.

Gittinger, Mattiebelle and Lefferts, H. Leedom Jr.
1992   *Textiles and the Tai Experience in Southeast Asia.* ed. Henrietta Cosentino, Washington D.C.: The Textile Museum.

Guillon, Emmanuel
1999   *The Mons: A Civilization of Southeast Asia.* Trans. and ed. James V. Di Croco. Bangkok: The Siam Society.

Halliday, Robert
1917/2000 *The Mons of Burma and Thailand: Volume 1. The Talaings.* ed. Christian Bauer. Bangkok: White Lotus Press.
2000   *The Mons of Burma and Thailand: Volume 2. Selected Articles.* ed. Christian Bauer. Bangkok: White Lotus Press.

Hamilton, Alexander
1727/1997 *Alexander Hamilton: A Scottish Sea Captain in Southeast Asia 1689-1723.* ed. Michael Smithies. Chiang Mai: Silkworm Books.

Krairiksh, Piriya
1974   *Sema* with Scenes from the *Mahånipåta – Jåtakas* in the National Museum at Khon Kaen. *Art and Archaeology in Thailand.* 35-66. Bangkok: Fine Arts Department.

Muang Boran
2534   *Mural Paintings of Thailand Series: Wat Bangkae Yai.* Bangkok: Muang Boran Publishing House.

Nai Pan Hla
1958   Mon Literature & Culture over Thailand and Burma. *Journal of The Burma Research Society.* XLI (1 & 2): 65-75.
1992   *The Significant Role of The Mon Language and Culture in Southeast Asia.* Part I. Tokyo: ILCAA.

Nichaiyok, Sophon
2547   *80 Years of Honorary Professor Suet Gajaseni, M.D.: 48 Years of Thai Råmañña Association.* ed. Sophon Nichaiyok. Bangkok: Thai Råmañña Association.

Phe Mauang Tin.
1972(a)   Trans. and ed. *Kyan Sit Tha Mon Inscription.* Rangoon: University of Rangoon.
1972(b)   *Shwezigon Mon Inscription.* Rangoon: University of Rangoon.

Prachum Khlong Kawi
2462   *Prachum khlong kawi Charuk Wat Phra Chetuphon.* Bangkok: Sophonphiphatthanakorn.

Smithies, Michael
1994   Body Ornamentation and Penile Implants in Siam and Pegu. *The Journal of the Siam Society,* 82 (1): 81-88.

Sub Department of Mon Culture and Literature
1977   *Traditional Culture of Ethnic Minority (Mon).* Burma Socialist Program Party.

Tun Thein
1995   *What should be known about the Mons and other stories.* Rangoon: Aye Printing.

U Min Naing
2000   *National Ethnic Groups of Myanmar.* Trans. Hpone Thant. Rangoon: Thein Myint Win Press.

Wongthet, Pranee
2536   *The Mae Klong Basin: Socio-cultural Development.* ed. Pranee Wongthet. Bangkok: Silpakorn University.

1 Xam Nuea style *sin phii* spirit skirt with white waistband.

Spirit Skirts of the Lao-Tai Peoples of Laos

Patricia Cheesman

Textiles of the Lao-Tai ethnic groups are surprisingly homogenous in their materials, motifs and weaving techniques, despite their far-flung locations with boundaries ranging from northeast Vietnam, to the west in Assam, India, and south in Thailand. It is most likely that these common elements were established prior to the later Lao-Tai migrations away from their early homelands in the Red and Black river regions of southern China and north Vietnam during the 10th century AD. On the other hand, variations in the structure and format of their textiles suggest that they were established later and differ from region to region.

The ancestors of the Lao-Tai peoples living in Laos P. D. R. and neighbouring countries where they have settled, including Vietnam, Thailand, Myanmar, India, and Cambodia, migrated south from the Yangtze River region of China in the 6th century BC. They established the Yüeh kingdoms in southeast China but, as the Han Chinese expanded their empire, were driven further south into the Red and Black river delta regions by the 3rd century BC. The emerging Vietnamese peoples consequently drove them north into present-day Yunnan Province, China. In the 2nd century BC, these migrants founded the Ai-Lao kingdom on the upper reaches of the Red and Black rivers. The Chinese attacked the Ai-Lao kingdom, whose peoples dispersed into north Yunnan in the 1st century AD. However, the Lao-Tai peoples returned to the Red and Black rivers into the hills of northern Vietnam where they began to establish centres of political power known as *muang* by the 6th century AD. Tai records described these later migrations and this unique form of administration based on control over peoples rather than land ownership that gave each *tjau muang* (regional chief) jurisdiction over the population in his region. However, a complex system of tributary relations evolved whereby weaker *muang* paid tribute to stronger *muang,* and thereby increasing the income of the latter and simultaneously creating a system of peaceful co-existence. The original inhabitants of areas occupied by the Lao-Tai in their migrations were brought under the *muang* system, and many of these peoples intermarried and integrated into the Lao-Tai culture and textiles tradition.

The establishment of many *muang* in northwest Vietnam brought together peoples of southern China, northwest Vietnam and northeast Laos in the Red, Black, Ma, and Xam river regions during the 6th century. This powerful Lao-Tai confederation expanded with the influx of more Lao-Tai peoples from southern China in the 8th century and gave rise to the great Sipsong Tjau Tai *muang* in the 14th century. In the 10th century overpopulation led to southern migrations into the Noen, Mekong, Salaween and Chao Phraya river regions, bringing areas of present day Myanmar and Thailand into the Lao-Tai *muang* system of administration by the 14th century.

The 14th-15th century period was a golden age of prominent Lao-Tai *muang* including Sipsong Tjau Tai, Xam Nuea, Phuan, Lan Xang, Sipsong Panna, Lanna, Sukhothai, and Ayuthaya. It was most likely that the variations in the regional styles of clothing and textiles of the Lao-Tai peoples according to the *muang* system were established during this period. Each *muang* had a unique style of dress that was adopted by all the different peoples in the region regardless of ethnic identity to show allegiance to their chief. The regional chiefs established local codes of dress, according to their original *muang* styles from Sipsong Tjau Tai and their relations with the more powerful *muang* of their time. Thus, a material lexicon of migratory patterns and tributary relations was illustrated in the textiles and clothing of the Lao-Tai peoples prior to the French Indochina period (1893-1954 AD), which saw the end of *muang* system.

A group of textiles that stand out as homogenous in all aspects, including their structure, are the spirit skirts of the Lao-Tai peoples of Laos P. D. R., suggesting their origins to the period prior to the 10th century. The spirit skirts, called *sin phii* (spirit tube skirt) or *sin mor phii* (shaman's tube skirt) in the northern regions of Laos and Vietnam, are woven with wide weft ikat bands alter-

2 *Thiang haew* burial house in Tai Daeng burial grounds, Houa Phan province, Laos.

3 *Sin phii* spirit skirt with *thiang haew* burial house motifs on the hem, Nam Noen River, Laos.

nating in red silk and indigo cotton, which are separated by supplementary weft or multi-coloured stripes (1). The waistbands are usually plain red or white fabric or cloth woven in a supplementary warp technique. These latter waistbands are called *hua buan* in Houa Phan province of Laos and are reserved for ritual use only, whereas in Vietnam this type of waistband is commonly used (4). (This kind of elevation in the status of a specific type of textile where their use is restricted is common among the Lao-Tai peoples when the textiles become rare). Often the main body of the spirit skirt is sewn upside down, which is a sign of chaos that befits the life passage ritual at death. The ikat sections of the skirts depict images of burial houses, *thiang haew,* and/or pairs of river dragons, whose bodies form the gables of the burial house (2).

The colours and weaving techniques of the sections separating the ikat bands can be used to identify the origin of a spirit skirt. Sipsong Tjau Tai style spirit skirts have plain stripes of red, green and yellow between the ikat bands that depict clear burial house motifs (5), whereas spirit skirts in the Xam Nuea style have discontinuous supplementary weft between the ikat bands of paired river dragon motifs (6). The Nam Noen style skirts have burial house motifs in the hem piece (3), and Muang Phuan style skirts have continuous supplementary weft bands in yellow, orange or white silk between the ikat bands depicting paired river dragon motifs.

Shamans of the Tai Nuea, Tai Khang, Tai Daeng, Tai Moei, Tai Dam and Tai Waat in Houa Phan province, Lao P. D. R. (the region of the ancient *muang* of Xam Nuea) and the Phuan and Tai Khang in Muang Phuan, or present-day Xiang Khouang province, Lao P. D. R, wore spirit skirts. Although the Tai Nuea, Tai Khang and Phuan have been Buddhists for many centuries, they maintain a fascinating combination of shamanic and Buddhist beliefs and iconography. The greater domination of one of these belief systems seems to vary with the presence of charismatic religious leaders, but the two belief systems exist simultaneously without confusion. This is a unique character of Lao-Tai Buddhism, which evolved by the absorption and overlapping of indigenous beliefs and culture. The shamans themselves became spirits while in trance. When the shamans wore spirit skirts, the spirits of the ancestors accepted the shamans as they travelled to the after world in search of medical cures and advice on all forms of social administration, personal conflicts, and auspicious days for feasts.

Spirits skirts were also involved in funerals. For burial a woman was dressed in layers of clothing, including many skirts. One of the skirts had to be a spirit skirt that would be easily recognised by the ancestors who would consequently invite her spirit into the heavens. Also, the Lao-Tai believed that a deceased female could find her mother-in-law in heaven by wearing this skirt, as the mother-in-law had woven it for her. At the funeral cere-

4 Xam Nuea style *sin phii* spirit skirt with *hua buan* waistband.

5 Sipsong Tjau Tai style *sin phii* spirit skirt from M. Waat, Vietnam.

6 Xam Nuea style *sin phii* spirit skirt with red waistband and ikat design upside down.

7 *Sin mii taa* banded ikat tube skirt with *tiin tii* hem, Nam Noen River, Laos.

monies for both men and women, the deceased's daughters-in-law also wore layers of skirts, whose amount depended on the regional tradition. One of these skirts was also a spirit skirt woven by her mother-in-law, which she would consequently reserve for her own burial. Thus, these skirts are sometimes called *sin luuk phue* – daughters-in-law skirt.

Oral tradition states that the first shamans were women who had spirit helpers in the form of various animal spirits and that men learned the techniques of ecstasy later. Male or female shamans, who have animal helpers and are known as *mor mot* (*mot* shamans), used to dress in spirit skirts when in trance as well as other distinctive items of clothing such as blouses, red belts, and red and white shawls **(14-16)**. Often, men could not fit into the blouses and had to wrap them around their shoulders and sometimes simply tucked the spirit skirt into the front of their pants when dancing in trance.

Two photographs taken by Madame Marthe Bassenne in 1909[1] depict "Kha women" wearing, "the *sine*, small jackets and high bonnets of rolled-up cloths. **(8-9)**" The caption to one of the photographs reads, "A dance of Kha women. **(9)**" Although the people in the photograph are wearing women's clothing, they are recognisably masculine and one of the figures has a woman's blouse wrapped around his shoulders. The men are carrying or wearing white and red belts/shawls that are not seen in the other photograph **(8)**, which also portray "Kha women." Also, their head cloths are not neatly tied and held in place with silver pins through large hair-buns as shown in the other photograph entitled "Kha women," and their tube skirts are tucked in roughly at the waist. It is not too difficult to see that these are men wearing spirit skirts while the women are wearing Xam Nuea style clothing. It is possible that both photographs are of shamans, some men and some women.

It is curious that the dress of the Kha women is Xam Nuea style, rather than that of their own or of the Lan Xang style of Luang Phabang, Lao P. D. R. the area of Mme. Bassenne's visits. In Muang Hun, Udomxay province, northwest of Luang Phabang, the Lao-Tai peoples wove textiles for sale to the Mon-Khmer speaking peoples (known as Kha people to the early French explorers), and their Mon-Khmer shamans wore spirit

8 (opposite) "Kha women. They are wearing the *sine* a Laotian dress, small jackets and high bonnets of rolled-up cloths." Marthe Bassenne's records, 1909.

9 "A dance of Kha women." Actually this photograph shows male shamans dancing wearing women's dress and the *sin phii* spirit skirts.

skirts for their annual spirit appeasing ritual **(11, 17)**. The Mon-Khmer peoples in Laos have not developed their weaving from the back-strap loom and, in order to fit into the dominant Lao-Tai society, they have often relied on Lao-Tai weavers to provide them with clothing and textiles for daily use and their rituals. It is not uncommon to find Mon-Khmer people in all the regions of Laos wearing clothing styles today that have long been abandoned by the Lao-Tai themselves.

There is another skirt found in many regions of the Lao P. D. R. called *sin mii taa,* or banded ikat tube skirt, that can easily be confused with the *sin phii,* or spirit skirt. The *sin mii taa* differs from the *sin phii* in the ikat motifs. The ikat of the *sin mii taa* does not depict burial houses but often includes river dragons in single profiles ascending in a zigzag line **(7)**. Sometimes, the ikat is totally blurred **(24)** or has motifs of flowers, lozenges or other geometric designs **(10, 18-22)**. The *(sin bork)* are banded ikat skirts of the Tai Muang of Vietnam containing crab ikat motifs **(23)**. Theoretically, the shamanic totems have been replaced by Buddhist images, thereby ridding the design of taboos and dress code restrictions.

The river dragon in shamanic beliefs represents female energy and is called *ngueak*. It has always been an important spirit to be appeased and revered in Lao-Tai culture. The ancestors of the Lao-Tai peoples tattooed their bodies with images of this benevolent spirit[2], and they decorated flags of the their *muang* with it. A great variety of textiles incorporate river dragon motifs in numerous positions such as hooded, mating, sleeping, single or paired *ngueak*. Lao-Tai Buddhists absorbed this indigenous mythical creature into their iconography and associating it with the *naak* or *naga* of the Buddhist scriptures. The *naga* not only sheltered the Buddha from the rain during the Enlightenment, but the Buddha himself was incarnated as a *naga* in a previous life. The word *naak* is simply the Lao-Tai pronunciation of *naga*. Thus, it is acceptable that Buddhist textiles have images of the *naak,* including the *sin mii taa*. Buddhist peoples and some shamanic groups, such as the Tai Moei and the Tai Dam, weave the *sin mii taa,* but it is noteworthy that the Tai Daeng do not have a tradition of making them.

The photograph taken in Luang Phabang in the early 20th century of a "Tai Nuea" woman wearing a tube

10 *Sin mii taa* banded ikat tube skirt with *tiin dork,* Bolikhamxay province, Laos.

11 S*in phii* spirit skirt Muang Hun style, Oudomxai province, Laos.

12 Phuan woman, Luang Phabang, early 20th century.

skirt with double river dragon motifs in ikat technique is curious **(12)**.[3] It is likely that this skirt did not have indigo ikat bands, but only red silk ikat bands that were typical of the *sin mii taa* of the Tai Khang and Phuan from Muang Phuan since the woman is wearing a shawl identifiable as Muang Phuan style. Thus, this photograph depicts a Phuan woman wearing a *sin mii taa* and not a spirit skirt. A 1931 photograph that was taken in Muang Et[4] on the Maa river in Houa Phan province shows a young girl wearing a banded ikat skirt **(13)**. It is likely that this is a *sin mii taa,* and the people are Tai Waat and not "Tay Deng" as stated. The hairstyles, hair accessories, and a shoulder cloth seen in the photograph are typical of the Tai from Muang Waat, many of whom have been reported by Chamberlain[5] as intermarrying to the Muang Et area.

The evolution of the spirit skirt structure has led to the *sin mii taa,* which is made in some cases with red silk and indigo cotton ikat bands and in others using all silk or all cotton in their respective colours. The final development of this design is seen in the *sin mii noi* that has narrow bands of silk ikat separated by stripes of plain or twisted yarns. The large serpent-like forms of the *naak,* or river dragon, have been reduced to simple "s" shapes, following Buddhist aesthetics of simplicity **(25-26)**. In the Lao P. D. R. today, there is a fashion for newly made tube skirts in the structure, colour and iconography of the spirit skirts. These can be worn by anyone; the skirts are no longer reserved for use by shamans and as the sacred and awesome clothing of the after world. Antique examples of these unusual textiles have nearly all been traded from their original villages for high prices, and shamanism is becoming a thing of the past.

The few shamans that do continue to call upon the spirits for cures and consultations now wear a tube skirt that is also becoming rare, the *sin muk lai khon* – a textile with human/spirit figures in weft ikat technique framed by supplementary warp and weft **(27)**. One day, the *sin muk lai khon* skirt may become sacred and restricted to use by shamans and spirits only and may even become known as *sin phii*. Future researchers may one day question the shamanic origin of the spirit skirt structure I have recorded as it becomes more commonly used by ordinary people.[7] Change is a natural element of living cultures and the spirit skirts presented here have a significant place in the history of the dress of the Lao-Tai peoples.

13 Tai Waat girls, Muang Et, 1931. *(Musée de l'Homme archives)*

142

14 Male Tai Moei shaman with women's skirt tucked into his pants, a woman's head cloth and a woman's blouse around his shoulders.

15 Female Tai Daeng shaman wearing a spirit skirt for a healing ceremony.

16 Male Tai Daeng shaman dressed in women's clothes at a ceremony to appease his spirit helpers.

17 *Sin phii* spirit skirt Muang Hun style, Oudomxai province, Laos.

18 *Sin mii taa* banded ikat tube skirt Muang Hun style, Oudomxai province, Laos.

19 *Sin mii taa* banded ikat skirt, M. Khang sub-style, Xiang Khoang province, Laos.

20 *Sin mii taa* banded ikat skirt, Ngum river sub-style, Xiang Khoang province, Laos.

21 *Sin mii taa* banded ikat skirt, Xiang Kham sub-style, Xiang Khoang province, Laos.

22 (above) *Sin mii taa* indigo banded ikat skirt, Nam Noen style, Tai Moei, Houa Phan province, Laos.

23 (right) *Sin bork* Nghe An style banded ikat tube skirt, Tai Muang, Nghe An province, Vietnam.

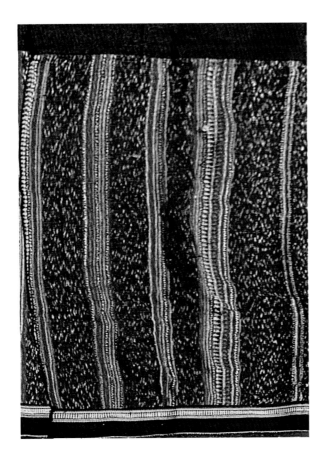

24 *Sin mii* tube skirt with blurred ikat, Sipsong Tjau Tai style, Tai Dam, Houa Phan province, Laos.

25 *Sin mii noi* ikat tube skirt, Muang Phuan style.

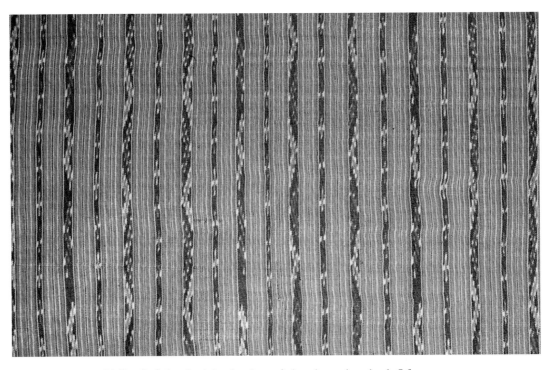

26 Detail of *sin mii noi* showing the *naak* river dragon in a simple S form.

27 *Sin muk lai khon* – a supplementary warp tube skirt with human figures in the weft ikat that is now used by shamans for their rituals.

Footnotes

1 Bassenne, Marthe (Translated by Walter E. J. Tips) (1995). *In Laos and Siam.* White Lotus: Bangkok, pp. 54-55.

2 Cam, Trong (2000). "What can we learn from the Tai ethnic group's names about their origin." *Tai Culture,* Vol. 5, 1: pp. 11-12.

3 Maxwell, Robyn J. (1990). *Textiles of Southeast Asia: Tradition, Trade and Transformation.* Oxford University Press: Oxford, p. 166.

4 Institut de Recherches sur la Culture Lao and Assocoation Culturelle des Routes de la Soie. *Treasure from Laos.* Vientiane, Laos, p. 81.

5 Chamberlain, James R. (1972). "The Origin of Southwestern Thai." *Bulletin des Amis du Royaume Laos:* pp. 233-244.

6 Bunyaratavej, Karen A. (2004). "Baby or Elephant cloth?" In Jane Puranananda (ed.), *Through the Thread of Time: Southeast Asian Textiles.* River Books: Bangkok, pp. 83-90.

7 Cheesman, Patricia C. (2004). *Lao-Tai Textiles: The Textiles of Xam Nuea and Muang Phuan.* Studio Naenna: Chiang Mai, Thailand.

From Girl to Woman
Textiles in Contemporary Phuthai Society

Linda McIntosh

Little is known about the nature and role of the textiles produced by the Phuthai peoples living in central and southern Laos. The study of Phuthai textiles and their production are important as an under-studied aspect of women's roles in Phuthai culture and generally in Tai culture of mainland Southeast Asia. Furthermore, in order to understand changes in textile production and women's associated roles, it is necessary to obtain information about the status of both at the present time.

In Phuthai society, women are the primary producers of cloth. Today, many Phuthai women living in rural areas in Laos continue to weave cloth, but they are also able to buy hand-woven textiles at the local market. Weavers now have the opportunity to buy machine-spun silk thread in the marketplace for silk textile production rather than having to produce their own hand-reeled silk, thus the majority of the households have ceased the practice of sericulture over the past thirty years.

The traditional or stereotypical characteristics defining a good wife and mother have altered as the methods of obtaining cloth change. Traditionally, a girl or young woman possessing advanced weaving skills is considered to be mature, and the quality of her skills and her productivity reflects her ability to be a good wife and mother. Presently, other skills reflect a young woman's maturity and capabilities as a household provider, for example, earning cash income to support her family. The domestic and interregional trade in textiles has grown over the last twenty years after the government relaxed the socialist ideal of self-sufficiency, including textile production, providing avenues to generate income from commercial sales of hand-woven textiles. However, other activities are beginning to provide better incomes than weaving, such as raising and selling agricultural products.

Due to implementation in the 1980s of some Lao government policies, such as universal education and a market economy within the country, girls and women have less time to devote to domestic textile production. This is a result of increased opportunities for a formal education and employment outside the home. Paralleling the behavior of other women in Laos, some Phuthai brides rent their wedding costume in the style of a Lao princess rather than wear an outfit they created themselves since the importance of weaving as a factor determining the character of a woman appears to have decreased.

Despite changes in textile production, the Phuthai continue to use dress and textiles to identify themselves individually and collectively, and incorporate new textiles and styles of dress into their repertoire of cloth. They also classify others according to clothing. One example of this became apparent when I conducted field research on Phuthai textiles in Laos.[1] If I wore trousers in Laos, I was considered to be a foreigner, but if I wore the traditional woman's skirt, *sin,* I am Lao and referred to as a relative (my ethnicity is half Lao, half American).

In the last five years, the popularity of Phuthai hand-woven textiles has grown as items of dress and household textiles among the Phuthai and others. Both private businesses and government entities, such as the Savannakhet provincial tourism authority, promote Phuthai culture including their textiles as a distinct and valuable heritage. The function of cloth is constantly being adapted to the current needs of both the individual and the group, and as the Phuthai experience political, economic, and social changes, their textile production is undergoing transformations. I will first give a background to the Phuthai and textile production before discussing the relationships women have with textiles.

Background

The Phuthai belong to the Southwest branch of the Tai-Kadai ethno-linguistic family, and are related to the Lao and the Thai, the dominant ethnic majorities of Laos and Thailand, respectively. The Phuthai share the belief with other Southwest Tai groups that their ancestors originated from Muang Naa Noi Oi Nuu or Muang Thaeng (present-day Dien Bien Phu, Vietnam).[2] They uphold Theravada Buddhism and shamanic beliefs honouring ancestor and other spirits, which are also similar to the belief systems of other Buddhist Tai peoples.

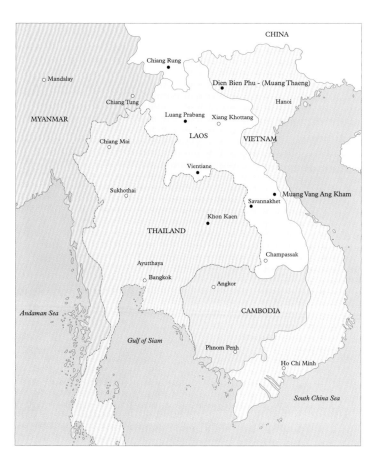

1 Map of Mainland Southeast Asia. Dien Bien Phu, Vietnam, is the origin of the Phuthai. Southerly migrations led the Phuthai peoples to settle in Muang Vang Ang Kham, Laos.

2 Settlements of the Phuthai peoples on the left and right banks of the Mekong River.

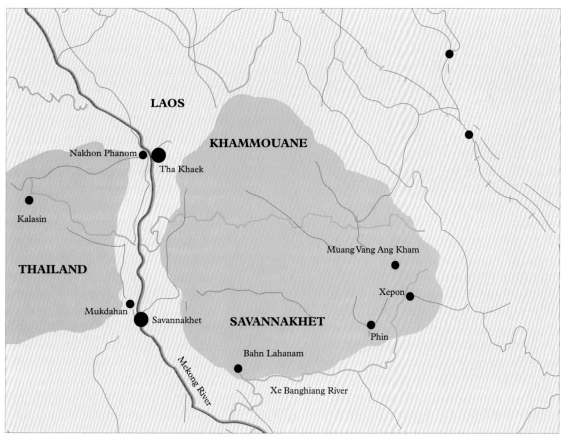

151

3 The *long kong* courting ceremony where the women gather in a communal area and prepare cotton thread after the rice harvest. Songkhone District, Savannakhet Province, Laos.

Southern migrations from Muang Thaeng in early 16th century CE led to the establishment of Muang Vang Ang Kham, located in present day Vilabuli and Xepon districts of Savannakhet province, Laos **(1)**. Historical records describe the leaders of Muang Vang Ang Kham paying tribute to the stronger political entities, such as courts of Annam (Vietnamese) and Lan Xang (Lao), but ruling autonomously with little interference from these stronger kingdoms except during periods of regional political instability. Muang Vang Ang Kham's location on a historical regional trade route, which began on the Vietnamese coast and ended in Burma (Myanmar), gave the Phuthai exposure to other cultures through trade. In the past, the Phuthai traded cattle and gold along this centuries-old trade route.[3]

Sudden migrations of Phuthai to the west began in the 19th century CE. In 1828 Siam attacked Vientiane and other settlements east of the Mekong River after Chao Anou, the king of Vientiane, attempted to retake territory in Siam during the previous year. The Siamese army resettled thousands of prisoners of war, including Phuthai peoples, into Siam on the right bank of the Mekong River **(2)**. In 1833 war erupted between Siam and Annam in Cambodia, leading to more forced migrations by the Siamese of the Phuthai and other peoples living in between the two kingdoms.[4] Many groups resettled in northeast Thailand, and their former rulers retained their power over them in their new home if the resettlement was peaceful. The power of Muang Vang Ang Kham waned because the Phuthai population increased in areas west of this *muang* (city state), including in Bahn Lahanam present-day Songkhone District of Savannakhet province.

Due to excessive bombing and defoliation by chemicals in the area, the Second Indochina War also caused a consequent migration of the Phuthai living in Muang Vang Ang Kham, which is near the Annamite mountain chain and on part of the Ho Chi Minh Trail. However, some Phuthai returned to the area after the end of the war, but settlement is sparse as the city of Xepon was completely destroyed in war and rebuilt several miles away from its original location and the district of Vilabuli restricts access to outsiders. The Phuthai remain the most populous ethnic group of Savannakhet and Kham mouane provinces, but small populations also exist in Bolikhamsay, Salavan and Champasak provinces.

4 Men also join the *long kong* ceremony for merrymaking, such as singing and music. Songkhone District, Savannakhet Province, Laos.

Textile Production of the Phuthai

Phuthai women remain responsible for all aspects of textile production, such as raw materials, dyeing, and weaving the fabric for clothing, bedding and gifts. They plant indigo and cotton, important secondary crops, grown at the same time as rice, the primary crop. Sericulture is still practiced by a few families, but the raising of silk has declined in the last thirty years. Some informants blame the cessation of sericulture on the use of pesticides for farming and exposure to herbicides in Muang Vang Ang Kham area during the Second Indochina War. However, other factors may have discouraged villagers from raising silkworms, such as changes in the marketplace.

The process of producing cotton thread has held cultural significance to Tai groups, including the Phuthai. The courting ritual *(long kong)* occurring during the dry season after the rice harvest revolves around the production of cotton thread. Women gather on a veranda or underneath a house in the evening to socialize while they go through the steps of making cotton thread, such as ginning, carding, and spinning **(3)**. Men entertain them, singing and playing music **(4)**. Young men and women are able to socialize in an acceptable manner in this setting since it is not appropriate for members of the opposite sex to socialize alone if they are not married.

Indigo is the primary natural dye the Phuthai consistently use and is planted alongside cotton at the beginning of the rainy season. The weavers prepare fresh indigo dye towards the end of the rainy season. Individual women have their own recipes for making indigo dye either kept fresh in ceramic jars or made into a paste **(5)**. The dyers nourish the indigo dye as if nuturing a child and knowing when she is sick or hungry. Other plants materials have been used to create other natural dyes, but in many villages inexpensive, synthetic dyes have replaced natural dyes.

The Phuthai came into contact with foreign raw materials due to their proximity to the regional trade route described earlier. Fine Indian cotton and metallic threads from both India and China are found in early 20th century textiles. After the 1975 Communist Revolution, there has been a return to using local materials since Laos' neighbouring countries of Thailand and China embargoed Laos for political reasons, cutting off the supply of imported goods. During the early years of

153

5 An indigo dye master dyeing cotton threads in a fresh indigo basin. Songkhone District, Savannakhet Province, Laos.

the communist regime, the government also encouraged its citizens to be self-sustaining and promoted cotton textile production instead of sericulture since silk is considered to be a high status marker, especially of the royalty and aristocracy. However, the government began to relax its policies in the 1980s, and development projects and private businesses have rekindled silk textile production. With the introduction of a market economy in 1986, different types of threads have been available in the markets of Laos, including polyester and rayon from China and Thailand, increasing the range of raw materials available in the country for textile production.

Women's Dress

Women in Laos continue to define their individual and group identity by dress. One example as mentioned earlier is the way that the Lao designated my ethnicity based on the style of dress that I wore. The women, including in Phuthai villages, consider me to be Lao (or Tai) when I wore the traditional Lao skirt, or *sin,* although I am Lao-American. If I wore trousers they considered me to be a foreigner. However, their ethnic identity remained unchanged whether they wear pants or traditional dress.

When questioned, Phuthai informants identify Phuthai woman's dress as *sin mii sue lap lai,* or the traditional skirt decorated with weft ikat and a blouse of indigo cotton decorated with supplementary weft red silk material. The *sin mii* is decorated with weft ikat in the mid-section and is made from silk or cotton **(6)**. If made from cotton, the dye used on the threads is usually indigo and the skirt would be worn daily. Women reserve a silk *sin* for special occasions. Most Phuthai women ceased to weave silk *sin* approximately thirty years ago and rely on the intra-regional trade to provide such clothing. The Phuthai also wear traditional skirts made from other techniques, such as supplementary warp, discontinuous and continuous supplementary weft, plain-weave stripes, and warp ikat. The *sue lap lai,* or indigo-dyed cotton blouse decorated with silver coins and supplementary weft patterned red silk, is rarely made or worn today. A tailored, indigo-dyed cotton blouse without any embellishment has become a substitute.

The traditional skirt or *sin* contains group-identifying characteristics. (The structure of the skirt is in three parts: the head or waistband; the body or midsection; and the foot or border.) The Phuthai waistband generally contains stripes and a red background, but the waistband may be made from two separate pieces of material in which one is white cotton and the other is striped **(7)**. The body or midsection is patterned with weft ikat or other types of techniques. Phuthai women also use a variety of skirt borders. The Phuthai commonly use the *tiin*

6 Phuthai women wearing traditional skirts decorated with weft ikat in the midsection for the Buun Bang Fai or Rocket Festival. Songkhone District, Savannakhet Province, Laos.

7 (left) This striped, red waist-band, *hua sin*, is in the Phuthai traditional style. Vilabuli District, Savanna khet Province, Laos.

8 (below) This warp-faced skirt border, *tiin* (*hao*), comes in several styles (see skirt borders in 6). Vilabuli District, Savannakhet Province, Laos.

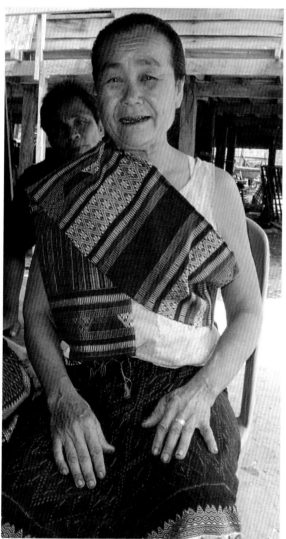

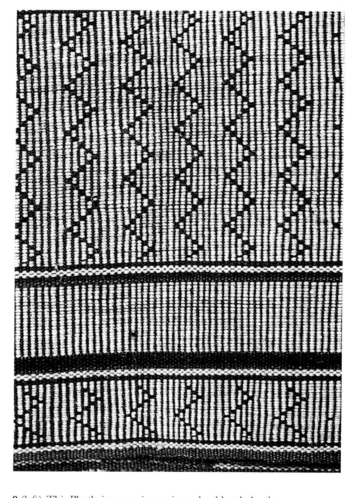

9 (left) This Phuthai woman is wearing a shoulder cloth, *phae daam*, that she wove herself. This *phae daam* upholds the original colours and style of the Phuthai shoulder cloth. Vilabuli District, Savannakhet Province, Laos.

155

hao border, which is a narrow, warp-faced textile that is primarily white on an indigo or black background **(8)**. Phuthai women wear other types of borders woven with different techniques, such as discontinuous supplementary weft. The width, colours, and design of the border are dependent on current fashions within the local community and national trends.

The shoulder cloth of the Phuthai also holds ethnic identifiers in its patterns and colors. This shoulder cloth, or *phae daam,* normally has a red ground, and the tone of the red varies according to the raw materials and dyestuff **(9)**. Supplementary patterns are in yellow, purple, white, and green. Patterned rows alternate in different colours and end with the pattern of an integral fringe called *soi saa.* The shoulder cloth is woven in either silk or cotton, or a combination of these materials. Occasionally, metallic threads are also woven into this textile, and contemporary pieces are sometimes made with synthetic dyes and threads.

Stylistic variations in shoulder cloths are apparent between different areas of Savannakhet Province, Laos.

In the Phuthai villages around Muang Vang Ang Kham, the Phuthai homeland, the shoulder cloth contains multiple rows of patterning. However, the shoulder cloth found in areas closer to the Mekong River (west of Muang Vang Ang Kham) has minimal rows of motifs, and the patterned rows are separated by equal widths of plain weave. This type of shoulder cloth found in the western part of the province resembles the Lao shoulder cloth or *phaa biang* **(10)**.

Ceremonial Textiles

Phuthai women also produce textiles for ceremonial use or for special occasions. Some women wear these textiles reserved for special occasions as a shawl wrapped around the body while listening to Buddhist sermons at the temple **(11)**. The *phaa daam* is similar in structure to the Phuthai shoulder cloth *phae daam,* and the difference between these textiles is their size. *Phaa* refers to a wide cloth and is made from a length of cloth which is folded, cut in half, and then sewn together along one side to create the desired width. *Phae* is narrower than *phaa* and the

10 This shoulder cloth, *phae bing,* is worn by a woman living in Songkhone District, Savannakhet Province, near the Mekong River displays influence from the textiles of the Tai-Lao.

11 This elderly Phuthai woman is wearing a shawl or *phaa daam,* which she made as a young woman. Phuthai women wore a shawl during the winter while listening to Buddhist sermons at the temple. This display was an opportunity to show off a woman's weaving skills. Vilabuli District, Savannakhet Province, Laos.

156

12 Detail of a supplementary warp patterned shawl or *phaa jong.*

13 Details of a continuous supplementary weft patterned shawl or *phaa lai.*

width of one hand-woven textile. The *phaa daam* is no longer produced in Savannakhet Province, Laos. Other ceremonial textiles, such as the supplementary warp-patterned *phaa jong* (12) and the continuous supplementary weft-patterned *phaa lai* (13), continue to be woven by the Phuthai in this province. The Phuthai use the *phaa jong* and *phaa lai* to designate auspicious or sacred space in the home and at the temple.

In order to accumulate merit women weave or purchase textiles to donate to the Buddhist temple. Women present textiles to male relatives when the men are ordained as monks or to monks already living at the local temple. These textiles include bedding and textiles for the monks' and novices' personal use. Generally, certain rituals designate when donations are acceptable, such as annual festivals or funerals. Buddhist laywomen also offer textiles woven for specific uses in the temple, such as for manuscript wrappers and banners. During the period of my field research in 2004, I did not observe production of manuscript wrappers or temple banners. The informants state that material is purchased at the local market

for presentation to the temple. This applies also to monks' robes; Phuthai women have ceased to weave cloth for the robes and buy ready-made robes instead. Traditional Phuthai manuscript wrappers and the banners have white cotton background and are woven with supplementary weft patterning in red and black separated by bamboo slats.

Household Textiles

The Phuthai also produce cloth for domestic use. Many household items are available at the market so if families can afford to buy them they will take the opportunity to do so. For example, women no longer make mosquito nets, and their pillows are usually purchased too. However, Phuthai girls and women of all ages continue to weave material from handspun cotton for the home. This checked or striped material is used as bedding, such as mattress covers, blankets, and all-purpose cloth. The all-purpose textile, *phae taa loo,* functions as a belt, head cloth, baby carrier, and towel, for example. I also have observed this material being made into banners that are donated to the Buddhist temple. In such cases the textile takes on an auspicious meaning as a medium to honour the dead and to allow the distribution of merit, crucial in Buddhist beliefs.

Textile Production and Gender Roles

The social roles created through the making of hand-woven textiles continue today but has been adjusted to fit the ever-changing needs of society. The physical characteristics of textiles have also been altered over time due technological advances and availability of materials for example. Hand-woven textiles continue to play a part in

14 Weaving handspun cotton fabric, Xepon District, Savannakhet Province, Laos.

15 Material for pillows made for a bride's trousseau. Vilabuli District, Savannakhet Province, Laos.

society from birth until death. A Phuthai mother swaddles her newborn child with a hand-woven cloth, *phae taa loo,* and this cloth also serves as a baby carrier, cradle sheet, and towel, plus other uses, as the child grows **(14)**. Hand-woven textiles serve as household items, such as bedding, offering physical protection to the body, but their presence in the gift exchange during weddings and Buddhist ordinations symbolizes their importance of the rites of passage. The effort devoted to make finely woven materials for these ceremonial occasions helps to signify the importance of the events.

In the past, a Phuthai man presented woman with a sleeping mat, two pillows, and other household items when asking for her hand in marriage. A bride-to-be would then weave paired sets of household textiles for her future family as well as gifts for the groom and his relatives. The number of paired items depended on the status and wealth of the families. Presently, many of these goods are purchased from the market, but both wedding parties agree on the number of items to purchase for the exchange of gifts. As stated above, Phuthai women have ceased to make mosquito nets and pillows, purchasing them at the market, but some single girls continue to make pillow covers for their trousseau **(15)**.

In the past, a bride also wove her wedding outfit, usually the *sin mii mai suea lap lai,* which was what she would have worn for any special occasion. Today, many brides rent or buy their dress since their wedding day is the only day they can dress as a princess in present-day communist Laos. Thus, many Phuthai brides wear a Luang Phabang royal court-style outfit, similar to brides of other ethnic groups in Laos. Grooms either wear a princely outfit, although today no longer woven by the bride or his mother, or they dress in an international style of shirt and trousers.

The Phuthai continue to use hand-woven textiles for special events. Although the men wear an international style of dress, they often wear a hand-woven shoulder cloth to symbolize the importance of an occasion. Some women continue to weave cloth to wear for special events, but they also have the opportunity to buy hand-woven material at the market. The use of hand-woven textiles is also evident during holidays, such as temple festivals and other religious ceremonies. In such cases the textiles are used to demarcate auspicious space and are presented to the temples and to respected relatives as gifts **(16)**

In traditional Phuthai society, girls did not have the opportunity to receive a formal education. Boys earned an education at the Buddhist temple where girls were not permitted to study. In the early twentieth century the French colonial administration in Laos introduced a universal education system, but secondary schools were often located in major urban centres and not in rural areas. Parents were often reluctant to allow girls to live away from the family in order to attend school. The majority of girls thus received a non-formal education in the home based on gender roles, especially on how to be a good daughter, wife, and mother. Textile production was one component of this non-formal education. The present government in Laos has expanded the education system, but the absence of secondary schools in the rural areas still exists. Many girls living in the countryside do not attend secondary school if there is not one in the vicinity of their village (85% of Laos' population lives in a rural environment). Girls living in rural areas begin to learn the steps of textile production as an adolescent after finishing primary school, thus, continuing non-formal education concerning gender roles in a home setting.

This non-formal education teaches that a woman who provides for the basic needs of her family is a good member of society. In the past women sold produce and even textiles on a small-scale basis at the local market to earn a small income for her family. However, now that a market economy is strong in Laos and cash income is important for the well being of her family, a wife and mother needs cash to maintain this well-being. Many women work outside the home in order to earn a living and often move to other cities or even other countries to fill low-level positions. This income allows women to buy inexpensive, hand-woven and factory-made textiles from the market since women spend their time earning money and cannot devote their time to weaving.

The local market has been a source for materials and hand-woven textiles from other areas in Laos and in the region. Phuthai weavers are beginning to produce textiles for the market, finding that their textiles have value if sold locally, nationally and internationally. Private businesses and government entities in Savannakhet Province promote Phuthai textiles as high quality and distinctive products. Women are able to fulfill their roles as a provider for their family by returning to hand-woven textile production as a commercial enterprise. This allows them to continue to be preservers of their heritage. Adolescents who learn how to weave have the opportunity to stay home or in the village and weave to earn an income. They will also be able to pass on the traditions to subsequent generations.

16 A *baisrii* or *suu khwan* ceremony held during the Lunar New Year. A *phaa lai* demarcates sacred space under the offering and a new *phaa lai* textile is presented as an offering. The women participating in the event are wearing clothing reserved for special occasions.

Textile production has experienced changes due to transformations in the education system, technology, and the market economy. Hand-woven textile production has become a mode for women to earn an income and provide for the family. The position as income earners has given women the opportunity to alter their position in their families. In traditional Phuthai society, women usually were responsible for family finances, but as a major provider of income their roles as decision makers for the family will certainly increase. Women are also learning new skills from the management responsibilities of commercial textile production and sales that can be applied in other situations. A girl's skills as a weaver can continue to reflect the quality of her future role as a wife and mother but is expanding to involve the potential to earn an income depending on her skills, productivity and business sense.

Footnotes

[1] The author, Linda S. McIntosh, conducted field research in Thailand and Laos in 2004 on the Phuthai with the generous suport provided as a grant from the James H. W. Thompson Foundation.

[2] A. Thomas Kirsch. "Phu Thai: A Case Study of Religious Syncretism in Northeast Thailand." PhD Dissertation, Harvard University (1963).

[3] The National Highway 9 of Laos follows this historical trade route. For more information on trade in this region during the 19th century see Etienne Aymonier. trans. Walter E. J. Tipps. *Isan Travels and Northeast Thailand's Economy in 1893-1894.* Bangkok: White Lotus (2000).

[4] Kennon Breazeale and Snit Smuckarn. *A Culture in Search of Survival: The Phuan of Thailand and Laos.* New Haven, CT: Yale University Southeast Asian Studies (1988).

Bibliography

Aymonier, Etienne. trans. Walter E. J. Tipps. *Isan Travels and Northeast Thailand's Economy in 1893-1894.* Bangkok: White Lotus (2000).

Breazeale, Kennon and Snit Smuckarn. *A Culture in Search of Survival: The Phuan of Thailand and Laos.* New Haven, CT: Yale University Southeast Asian Studies (1988).

Harmand, Franois-Jules. trans. Walter E. J. Tipps. *Laos and the hilltribes of Indochine: Journeys to the Boloven Plateau from Bassac to Hu through Laos, and to the origins of the Thai.* Bangkok: White Lotus (1997).

Kirsch, A. Thomas. "Phu Thai: A Case of Religious Syncretism in Northeast Thailand." PhD Dissertation, Harvard University (1963).

McIntosh, Linda S. "Ho Chi Minh Trail." In David Levinson and Karen Christensen, et. al (eds.), *Encyclopedia of Modern Asia.* New York: Scribner's (2002).

Monks' Robes in Rural Northeast Thailand
Relic and Memory

Leedom Lefferts

One of the most distinctive set of clothes in Theravada Buddhist Southeast Asia is monks' robes **(1)**. The saffron, earthen, colour of these robes, the ways they are made, their style of wearing, and the quantity of cloth all serve to separate their wearers from the surrounding lay population. While this is a remarkable costume in today's world, little has been written about it or about the ways by which this attire comes to the people who wear it.

Theravada Buddhist monks' robes, *traichiiwaun* (often shortened to *chiiwaun*), reveal two paradoxes, one in their inherent nature and the other in how they are viewed today. The first is that these pieces of cloth – designed to be worn by the adepts of a faith dedicated to renunciation – embody power, prestige, and status. It is quite clear that men wearing the three robes designated by the Buddha as the uniform of those who would go forth to carry his findings into the world are accorded respect, authority, and power far beyond that of any person in lay attire, no matter how ornate. However, paradoxically, the Buddha specified that these robes should be made of patches precisely so that they would be without worth, so that they would have no commercial value and no one would covet them or envy those who wore them. During the Buddha's lifetime and certainly since, these robes have become distinguishing symbols of the power of his thoughts and of the organization of monks and novices, the Sangha, *phrasong,* who personify and carry on these thoughts.[1]

The second paradox contained in monks' robes is how cloth of such importance can be so neglected in textile studies. Paralleling Robyn Maxwell's discussion of *Talismanic Textiles in Islamic Southeast Asia* (this volume), monks' robes are "virtually invisible" in the corpus of analysis and critique undertaken about the textiles of the Theravada Buddhist peoples of mainland Southeast Asia. Articles on monks' robes that outline their modes of construction and the ways by which they are presented to those who wear them are infrequent, even though the robes' wearers play prominent roles in the societies of Thailand, Cambodia, Laos, Burma, and southern China

1 Monks on morning rounds wearing complete sets of three robes, *traichiiwaun,* and carrying bowls, *baat,* with layman wearing man's skirt, *phaa sarong,* and shoulder shawl, *phaa komaa,* for politeness. June 1980, Baan Dong Phong.

where Theravada Buddhism dominates. Without question, textiles of laypeople who have achieved status and prestige through more mundane channels, including wearing textiles for attendance at Theravada Buddhist ceremonies where monks in these robes officiate, receive greater attention than the textiles of the men for whom becoming a monk is an extraordinary lifetime event.

The purpose of this paper is not so much to explore the second paradox, of the relative neglect of these textiles in the study of Southeast Asian cloth, as to assist in its rectification by shedding light on the first issue, how these robes could become such important markers of status and power for the men who wear them. Perhaps by so doing, this paper will bring about a productive discussion of the roles and meanings of monks' robes and an appreciation by scholars of religion and material culture of the power of these objects in the world of Southeast Asian textiles.

The paper searches for understandings concerning the ways by which these robes confer status, meaning, and engagement with the supernatural. It focuses on how these robes are given and used today in Northeast Thailand – the occasions when these robes are presented, statements used on these occasions, and the expectations of the donors of these robes regarding the purposes of these gifts. Perhaps through a discussion of the modes by which monks' robes come to their wearers we may come to understand how they carry status and power – in other words, how these extra-mundane pieces of cloth become endowed with charisma.

At the outset, it must be made clear that all robes are gifts. While Theravada Buddhist monks can sew and dye cloth, they are enjoined from weaving. All the cloth that comes into their hands must be secured from one of two sources: either it is obviously discarded cloth that no lay person is using or it is purposely given to them. Prior to the industrial revolution cloth for monks' robes, as for most Southeast Asian cloth, came from women's work: from the growing of cotton or a bast fibre such as hemp, or the raising of silk worms, through the production of yarn to the weaving of white cloth, one purpose of which was for use as donations to be made into monks' robes.[2]

Today, while the vast majority of monks' robes are made in factories and purchased ready-made and dyed, many are presented by women. Women remain the basic channel through which textiles (as well as food; monks may not cook)[3] are obtained by monks.

However, monks' robes are not donated at will or randomly to their wearers. The Buddha stated that monks may have only one set of three robes, *traichiiwaun,* T, L (*tichiiwaun,* P[4]), within their maximum of eight possessions. The three robes are the single-layered upper robe, *chiiwaun,* T (*siiwaun,* L, *uttarasanga,* P); lower garment, *sabong,* T, L (*antaravasaka,* P); and double-layered upper robe, *sangkhatti,* T, L (*sanghati,* P).[5] These robes can be presented only on certain defined occasions. Each ordinand must come prepared with a set of robes in order to be ordained; this takes place in the *Bun Buat,* or ordination. Monks' robes cannot be given during the three-month long Rains Retreat *(Pansaa),* from mid-July through mid-October. One set may be presented during the month following the Rains Retreat, at the *Bun Kathin* ceremony. If robes are presented at other times, these presentations must be surrounded by a number of ritual signifiers, chief among which is that the cloth is defined as "found", either as "unowned" in a forest *(Bun Phaa Paa),* or as part of the rags of a corpse *(bangsukun).* All of these restrictions came about as injunctions by the Buddha as he founded his organization of followers, ensuring that they would be renunciants who followed the Middle Path and wore cloth modestly.

Today in rural Northeast Thai Theravada Buddhism the occasions for donations and the words and behaviors that are used at those times signify two basic themes: the first theme is a remembrance of these robes as relics of the Buddha and his injunctions to those who would carry on his discoveries concerning the nature of existence. I term this a theme about *relics,* remembrances of the life and death of the person who founded this Way, *"expressions and extensions of the Buddha's biographical process".*[6] The second theme arises from a desire on the part of the donors to make these donations in the memory of their ancestors so that the merit made through giving these robes may bring about a better existence for those who have gone before. I term this a theme about *memory.* As we explore the occasions during which robes are given, we are concerned with the interaction of relic and memory. In this way, we may come to understand some of the depth of meaning contained in these cut-and-sewn pieces of cloth and the power they have when worn by certain men.

This paper is written using information obtained during ethnographic fieldwork in the region known as Northeast Thailand (or Isan). This region, bordered by Laos across the Mekong River to the north and east and to the south by Cambodia, is known for its religiosity; most of the monks in the Thai Sangha come from Northeast Thailand, even if they inhabit temples, *wat,* in Bangkok or outside of Thailand in England, Australia, or the United States. The members of this village where I worked, Baan Dong Phong, located towards the centre of Isan, are ethnically Lao who have been part of the Siamese/Thai Kingdom for well over 100 years; thus they are called Thai-Lao. Today their ethnicity has diverged from that of their Lao relatives on the left bank of the Mekong; much has changed under the onslaught of educational, economic, linguistic, media, and religious systems controlled from the Kingdom's capital, Krungthep Mahanakorn (Bangkok).[7]

Although this paper dwells on the array of ceremonies through which robes find their way to the members of the Sangha, it must be made clear that there are many ceremonies for other purposes in the Thai-Lao Theravada Buddhist calendar.[8] The ceremonies detailed here are of particular interest because they – more than others – involve exchanges focused on monks' robes. The interplay of relics and memory involved in the gifting of these robes and cloth that could be made into them provide much of the dynamism found in contemporary Thai-Lao Theravada Buddhism.

Monks' Robes as Relics

Monks' robes can be understood as relics of the Buddha because he is the one who appointed their use and constructed their design. Just as monks are transmitters of the sayings of the Buddha and perpetuate the texts by which he announced and codified his discovery, monks' robes signify the stability of these findings by reaffirming the designs and meanings he established 2500 years ago. Strong[9] notes two different origin stories for the Buddha's robes, paralleling the two different ways, noted in the previous section, that monks' robes may be obtained. The one is through discarded cloth. At first, the *bodhisattva* who would be come the Buddha wore a robe:

> made of the discarded garments of ten *pratyekabuddhas* who passed into *parinirvana*.... (S)ix years later ...that robe became worn out ... (H)e looked around and found, in a cremation ground, the discarded cloth *(pmukla)* that had enveloped the body of a servant girl who had died ... The *bodhisattva* took the cloth, washed it, and sewed it together under a tree at a spot that became known as *Pmuklasvana* ("[The Place of] Sewing-the-Dustheap-Robe").

The other method by which the Buddha obtained robes (after he had achieved Enlightenment) was through gifts, from wealthy donors or from other monks who had received these robes and who exchanged those with him.

It becomes clear through these stories that the Buddha's robe is not a permanent object, passed down from monk to monk,[10] but, rather, especially in the Theravada tradition, something consumed through use that must be re-constructed according to a pattern. Thus, even as the monks who wear robes embody the continuity of the Buddha's discoveries, the robes themselves are subject to constant re-creation.

Bun Buat

The ordination ceremony is one site for beginning to understand how monks' robes entre into use by a member of the Sangha. Replicating the life-course of the *bodhisattva* who would become the Buddha, the ordinand must appear with a set of robes and a bowl. He initially approaches the Preceptor for the ordination carrying the robes in his bent forearms. After an initial greeting, bowing, he presents his robes to the Preceptor and takes refuge in the Triple Gems (the Buddha, Dhamma, and Sangha) and requests the "Going-Forth" (*Pabbajj*, P.). Three times he states, "I request the Going-Forth. Having taken these ochre robes, please give me the

Going-Forth, out of compassion for me" **(2)**. Following instruction in the Triple Gems and "the five basic objects of meditation," the Preceptor takes the smallest piece of cloth, the shoulder cloth worn across the left shoulder, *amsa*, T, L, and puts it over the ordinand's head. The Preceptor then returns the remaining robes to the novice (*neen*, T. L.; *sumanera*, P.) and tells him to go to a suitable place and don them **(3)**.[11]

Even though this regimen ensures that each ordinand has the requisite number and kinds of articles for ordination, the procedure by which an ordinand receives the robes to entre the ordination ceremony is not prescribed. Among Tai cultures generally as well as specifically within the Northeast Thai-Lao context, a mother (or her sur-

2 Ordinand presenting his set of robes, *traichiiwaun*, to Preceptor at beginning of ordination. July 2005, Khon Kaen Province.

3 Preceptor placing shoulder cloth, *amsa*, over ordinand, returning other robes to him and requesting that he don them. July 2005, Khon Kaen Province.

162

rogate) presents these robes to her son as he enters the ordination hall.

Tambiah[12] and others have noted that having a son become a monk is one of the most meritorious acts in which a mother can engage. The link between mother (and father) and son is made explicit in the preparations and rituals leading to the ordination. For the mother, this focuses on the robes; for the father, the focus is on the monks' bowl.[13]

For young men, entrance into the Sangha involves a drastic separation from their previous role in a family and projects them – ensures that they "Go-Forth" – into the world as different beings.[14] Moreover, these young men, as members of the Sangha, become responsible for a vital aspect of their parents' lives: by becoming a monk a young man becomes able to communicate with and transmit his parents' appreciation for the lives they have received to their parents and more distant ancestors, *"bidaa maandaa (P.), puu yaa taa yay (T. L.)."*

This intermediary role is impressed on these young men in the soul integration ceremony, *sukhwan,* that occurs the day or evening before ordination. The *sukhwan* separates the young man from his family and community as it confirms his movement into the monkhood. Yet this ceremony also involves the reintegration of the ordinand with his *khwan,* spirit; this reintegration is symbolized by tying white strings around the ordinand's wrists. The ordinand pays respects to his parents by asking for their blessing, *karawa,* and presenting a dish on which five pairs of candles and flowers are placed, *kan haa.*

The ceremony's officiant, the *mau phraam,* while calling the ordinand's *khwan,* enjoins the ordinand to remember his future role as an intermediary between the laity and their ancestors. He reminds the ordinand of how his parents raised him and gave him things and how they now give him the things by which he becomes a monk. He especially enumerates the monks' robes, *traichiiwaun,* and bowl, *baat,* which are required for a young man to entre the monkhood (4).[15]

Often an ordination takes place in remembrance of a parent or other relative, "ordination of (name of ordinand) to make merit on behalf of (name of relative)" *". . . ngaan ubosombat . . . phua uthit suan kuson dae . . ."* In this case, the ancestors are specified and named. The robes used on such occasions, while coming from the mother, are specifically meant to clothe a man who, in remembering his deceased relative, makes merit on that person's behalf.[16]

4 *Mau Phraam* (back to camera) conducting *sukhwan* ceremony. Ordinand's mother is on left and father on right; some village women also make merit by participating in ceremony. July 2005, Baan Dong Phong.

The presentation of the robes to the ordinand occurs the next day, usually in the morning, when the ordinand and his familial celebrants and sponsors arrive at the ordination hall. Led by a monk, the ordinand and his relatives circumambulate the ordination hall three times in a clockwise direction prior to entering. The mother (or her surrogate) holds the robes that the ordinand will don while his father (or a surrogate) carries the bowl wrapped in cloth (5). When I ask women why they carry the robes in this three-fold circumambulation, they say they are responsible for the robes, the cloth that they once produced and now purchase as complete sets. They say that men carry the bowl while women carry the robes; each parent does this so that, when they die and are in hell, they can think of the thing they carried and be raised to heaven.[17] Each gender has its parallel role in the presentation of requisites to the new member of the Sangha: the robes signify that a young man has become a member of the Sangha; the possession of a bowl designates him as a monk.

The gifts of robes and bowl that take place during a *Bun Buat* replicate the complicated series of exchanges between laypeople, their soteriological goals, and monks that is at the heart of Theravada Buddhism. The gift of robes helps create a being able to provide a focus for merit-making and the betterment of a lay person's life through the constant reminder that this special being is a representative of the Buddha. The gift of the robes also assists in recapitulating the drama of the *bodisattva*'s renunciation of his home life which permitted his journey to Enlightenment and discovery of The Way.

5 Mother of the ordinand carries the robes under a special ornate cover, while his father carries monks' bowl, wrapped as a *naak*, serpent (See Lefferts 1994). July 2005, Khon Kaen Province.

6 Monk marking robe, *chiiwaun,* to determine it for his use. July 2005, Baan Dong Phong.

The ritual of robe-giving preceding the ordination recapitulates this crucial biographical moment.

Following ordination, a monk must determine, *phinthu,* P, his robes, declaring them his own and the sole set that he possesses. This ritual must be accomplished before going to bed on the day the robes are received; otherwise, he is in violation of one of the 227 rules of the *Pattimokka* that govern his behavior as a monk. Determination takes place through the monk's recitation of a vow for each of the robes and his bowl. Usually prompted by another monk who knows the procedure, he recites the vow, makes a mark in either blue or black pencil in a corner of the cloths to distinguish them from those of other monks, and then rubs the cloth or the bowl (6).[18] This must be done each time a monk takes possession of a new robe and is part of the formula by which the Buddha enjoined his followers to a life of moderation.

Bun Kathin

Most ordinations take place in the months and weeks preceding the beginning of the Rains Retreat which spans mid to late July to mid to late October. During the Retreat monks may not entre or leave the monkhood nor may they receive substantial gifts, such as robes. The Buddha saw that many of his followers were bedraggled and in need of new robes by the end of this period. He declared that the month following the end of the Rains Retreat could be used to dispense equally, among all the monks who had endured the Retreat within the confines of a single *wat,* the cloth which was available there, once it had been made into robes.[19]

Today in rural Northeast Thailand the *Bun Kathin* is a ceremony in which a major sponsor usually provides the wherewithal, including the robes, for the monks who have spent the Rains Retreat in a particular *wat* (7). If no sponsor comes forth, the villagers band together to produce the donations.[20] Aggacittta Bhikkhu, a Malaysian Theravada Buddhist monk, notes[21] that the Buddha specified that the cloth for a single robe is to be given to a designated monk in a wat (8). Tambiah found, for his Northeast Thai village, as do I in my fieldwork, that a single set of robes is donated to the appointed recipient. However, additional robes and other cloth can be presented following the donation of the main set of robes.[22] The focus of the ceremony, following the Buddha's prescription, is on the presentation of new robes to the monks (and novices) who stayed together through the Rains Retreat. In this way, the Kathin as celebrated in Northeast Thailand is equivalent to the ceremony established by the Buddha and is thus a "relic" of his doctrine.

Many times, however, a sponsor or sponsoring family comes forward to undertake the ceremony in memory of important family members who have died. The ceremony thus evolves into a memorial for the deceased, *uthit suan kuson.* In such cases a ceremony to the memory of the deceased, *Bun Chaek Khaaw,* with his or her ashes, is held at the sponsor's house on the days leading up to the *Bun Kathin.* More usually, as we shall see shortly, *Bun Chaek Khaaw* are held from February through April; holding a *Bun Chaek Khaaw* immediately prior to a *Bun Kathin* means that a family takes upon itself considerable responsibility as well as the opportunity to make a great deal of merit for deceased family

7 Sponsor carrying *kathin* robes during parade through village. November 1981, Baan Dong Phong.

8 Monks accepting *kathin* robes which will be turned over to the designated recipient. November 1971, Baan Dong Phong.

members. This responsibility together with this merit can be seen as equivalent to a major wealthy Bangkok sponsor's coming to hold a Kathin in the village.

Bun Phaa Paa

The Festival for Forest Cloth, *Bun Phaa Paa,* builds on the specific incident in the *bodhisattva*'s life when he discovers and utilizes cloth that has no owner in order to make his robes. Northeast Thai-Lao and other Tai groups use this ceremony as a means to hold an important ceremony equivalent to a *Bun Kathin* for a particular *wat*. Since only one *Kathin* per *wat* can be held during the month after the Rains Retreat, the *Bun Phaa Paa* provides a way to do much the same during the remainder of the festival calendar. The donation of robes provides the ritual focus for the event. To ensure that the scene is appropriately set, usually a small replica of a tree is provided on which a model of a gibbon made of a towel is hung. The travelers/pilgrims who have organized this event bring this tree and the gibbon to the *wat*. Thus, a *Bun Phaa Paa* is a relic ceremony is turned by the agency of particular sponsoring individual or organizations into a way to make merit. As monks receive these robes, they recite a specific *pamsukula* chant for unowned cloth.

Monks' Robes as Memory

The ordination, *Bun Buat,* and ceremonies designed for donating robes, *Bun Kathin* and *Bun Phaa Paa,* are the major occasions in which monks' robes are given as reminders of specific injunctions and events stemming from the Buddha's life. These ceremonies and the robes that are dispensed are relics of injunctions of the Buddha as he established his findings in the world.

However, Thai-Lao participate today in a variety of additional rituals for robe presentation not encompassed by these three ceremonies. Those other rituals follow the Buddha's injunction that robes may be fashioned from a corpse's burial garments. That possibility came about because of specific events in the life of the *bodhisattva* who became the Buddha and refers to the permissible ways to make monks' robes that he detailed after Enlightenment. The *bodhisattva* first obtained his robes from "the discarded garments of ten *pratyekabuddhas*." After that cloth wore out and while he was still a *bodhisattva*, he looked around and recovered cloth "from the body of a deceased servant girl (in) a cremation ground" **(9)**.

After Enlightenment, even as he affirmed that monks could wear new robes presented by wealthy donors, as in the *Bun Kathin* ceremony, the Buddha re-affirmed that monks could utilize cloth obtained from charnel grounds. The opportunity presented by utilizing cloth discarded in cemeteries provides a major pivot for the prominence of monks' robes as gifts in contemporary rural Thai-Lao Northeast Thai culture. These opportunities permit the employment of the robes as vehicles for memorializing the deceased and making and transferring merit to them. This paper holds that, while a significant amount of the importance of monks' robes as objects of status and myth comes about because of the position of robes as relics of The Buddha, much additional power comes from this association with the super-

165

9 The Buddha removing clothing from the corpse of a deceased servant woman. Panel 6, Upper register, Lacquer Pavilion, Suan Pakkad Palace, Bangkok; taken January 1991.

natural, through the transference of merit associated with presenting monks' robes and other cloth while making merit in the name of the deceased. These presentations are known in Thai and Lao as *bangsukun*.

One important ceremony that includes *bangsukun* occurs as part of cremation,[23] *ngaan sop*. During a *ngaan sop*, three occasions occur in which *bangsukun* can be given. Two of these involve presenting objects wrapped in white cloth; the third includes the presentation of the single-layered upper robe, the *chiiwaun*. White cloth presented in these ceremonies is designated to be made into monk's robes.

The first presentation of *bangsukun* occurs in the final blessings prior to cremation, when gifts – necessities wrapped in a white cotton cloth to be used by the deceased's spirit as it moves from this world to the next – are made in the name of the deceased by relatives. The *bangsukun* is placed on the coffin, *sop*, and connected to the sitting place for the monks by a white cotton string, *saay sin* (*saay sinchana*, P.) **(10)**. The dedication of the *bangsukun* – the white cloth and the things it contains, entrusting these to the monks to assist the spirit in its travels – occurs in a recitation led by the temple's lay leader, *tayok wat*. The white cotton string connected to the *bangsukun* is held by the monks as they perform the *Pamsuklagth*, P, chant **(11)**.[24, 25]

The second *bangsukun* is possibly more familiar since it is often shown on TV when members of the Thai Royal Family present *chiiwaun* as *bangsukun*. On this occasion, robe, *chiiwaun*, are laid on the coffin by members of the deceased's family, other relatives, and the sponsor of the event, and retrieved by members of the Sangha. During this occasion each monk recites the *Pamsuklagth* for the dead as he retrieves the robe, holding a monks' fan, *taalapat*, P, in front of him as he engages in the recitation **(12)**.

The third occasion for *bangsukun* at a funeral occurs during the retrieval of the deceased's ashes, usually three days after cremation. Again, as on the first occasion, a collection of useful items is given for the deceased person's travels in the world of the spirit, *look winyaan*. The presentation occurs when the ashes of the deceased have been laid out and configured as a body. The items are wrapped in white cloth, placed on the ashes, and connected by the white cotton string, *saay sin,* to the monks so that the things may be accepted by them in the name of the deceased person **(13)**. The *bangsukun* leaves with the monks when they depart the scene.

10 *Bangsukun* atop coffin connected to seating place of Sangha by white cotton string, *say sin.* January 2005, Baan Dong Phong.

11 Abbot of *wat* receiving *bangsukun* previously accepted by Sangha. January 2005, Baan Dong Phong.

12 Presentation of monks' robe, *chiiwaun,* as *bangsukun* during funeral; donor kneels to the monk's left as the monk, holding a fan, recites *Pamsuklagth.* June 1982, Baan Dong Phong.

167

13 *Bangsukun* presented during retrieval of deceased's ashes. *Bangsukun* is connected to Sangha members by white cotton string, which they hold during chants. March 2005, Baan Dong Phong.

Over the years since I have been observing Thai-Lao funerals, I have seen a change in the pattern of *bangsukun* presented at *ngan sop*. Not until the past decade or so has the presentation of the single-layered upper robe, *chiiwaun*, become the norm. Earlier, only the presentation of things wrapped in white cloth took place. Now, *bangsukun* has evolved to such an extent – probably due to increased wealth – that "great" *bangsukun*, *mahaa-bangsukun*, are often held. Twenty *chiiwaun*, in groups of four, are placed on the deceased's casket and presented by the sponsors to similar numbers of members of the Sangha. To complete the *mahaabangsukun*, a twenty-first, complete, set of three robes, *traichiiwaun*, is presented by the major sponsor to the senior monk.

Bun Chaek Khaaw

In the Northeast Thai village context, the deceased's descendant households hold a festival known as *Bun Chaek Khaaw* or, more formally in Pali, *uthit suan kuson*. This follows the retrieval of the ashes that takes place following cremation, after a length of time determined by the pressures of time and the availability of appropriate funds. The Thai-Lao name for this festival gives its local meaning, gifts of cooked rice, *khaaw*, accompanied by other food, in the name of the deceased to members of other households who come to the festivities. The Pali name refers to it as a memorial for the deceased.

The purpose of the *Bun Chaek Khaaw* is to transmit the deceased's ashes from the place where they have been kept temporarily following cremation and recovery to the *wat*, where they will be permanently stored in an appropriate location.[26] This festival is accomplished in the name of the deceased; it brings merit to the deceased as well as the sponsors, usually current household members. *Bangsukun* is given on this occasion. This includes many of the items presented during *ngaan sop* for the use of the deceased, such as soap, soap powder for washing clothes, toothpaste, tooth brush, etc. However, the items also include a charcoal stove, rice steamer, sticky rice basket, *nam plaa* (fish sauce), a complete set of clothes appropriate to the deceased's gender, and other necessities for life, including a *prasaat phung*, a small, doll house-like structure in and around which are placed these things that will be useful for the person in the next world, *look winyaan* **(14)**.[27] White cloth is not presented in this *bangsukun*. All of these items, as well as the ashes of the deceased, are accepted by the members of the Sangha and end up at the *wat*, from which some may redistributed and others used as appropriate.

Finally, *bangsukun* takes place on any occasion when a dedication is made in remembrance of the deceased with members of the Sangha as celebrants. *Bangsukun* can be given after food is presented to the Sangha during a normal morning service, or when a festival for a specific household, *Bun Hien*, is held **(15)**. These items are given to the Sangha, even though many are inappropriate for the personal use of monks or novices.

When *bangsukun* items are accepted by the Sangha, they become purified, *borisut*, of their associations with lay people. Members of the Sangha reconstruct the meanings of these things through the chants they perform. Monks said that materials presented during a *ngan sop* or *Bun Chaek Khaaw* can be redistributed or used for whatever task deemed appropriate in the *wat*.

When I asked laity about the purpose of *bangsukun*, the immediate response was that these items are for use of ancestors, often specifically named, in *look winyaan*. When asked what the monks do with this material, laity said that the monks either use it themselves or give it away. Many items are saved and used as prizes in lottery drawings, *soi daaw*, during festivals, where people pay money to draw chances for goods. When I asked specifically about the donated cloth items, I was told that they are used in *soi daaw* or given away, or the cloth can be used in the *wat*.[28]

The white cloth that has been used to wrap objects presented as *bangsukun* and other items for personal use,

14 *Bangsukun* for delivery to *wat* at end of *Bun Chaek Khaaw*, including *prasaat phung* and necessities for life in the next world. July 2005, Baan Dong Phong.

15 *Bangsukun* presented during household ceremony, *Bun Hien*, consisting of items intended for ancestor's use in the next world. June 2005, Baan Dong Phong.

including *chiiwaun,* are kept by the abbot in a cabinet. He gives these away as appropriate. The white cloth can be used to make monks' robes if necessary. Because it was presented as *bangsukun* and donated in a person's name, it is meant to be used by a monk or novice and is not for general *wat* use. Such white cloth is kept separate from other white cloth which comes into the *wat*'s possession.[29]

I am familiar with an additional instance of the term *chiiwaun* for which I have not been able to ascertain the context. I have not been present in a Tai-Lue community (in North Thailand, Laos, or Sip Song Panna, Yunnan Province, China) to witness the presentation of small, sometimes elaborately decorated pieces of cloth that surround Buddha statues, termed *siiwaun.* These textiles bear a slip of paper inscribed with the name of the deceased and a dedicatory statement **(16a, b)**. One end of the cloth is attached to a short pole placed upright in the back of a wooden block, sometimes carved into the shape of a turtle. This construction is placed near the main Buddha statue in a *wat*. On the basis of information already available about the presentation of cloth in Theravada Buddhism, it seems reasonable to hypothesize that that these *siiwaun* are presented as *bangsukun* for the commemoration of specific ancestors. They are one of the ways by which women make merit by weaving. Different Tai cultures dedicate *bangsukun* in different ways. However, these exchanges of the living with the deceased through cloth and the mediation of the members of the Sangha form a basic, underlying framework within Tai Theravada Buddhist cultures.[30]

16a Miniature monks' robes *chiwaun*, displayed before a small Buddha statue. May 1990. Sip Song Panna, Yunnan Province, China.

16b Writing on paper attached to back of *chiwaun* dedicating cloth to the memory of the marker's ancestor. May 1990. Sip Song Panna, Yunnan Province, China.

169

Conclusion

Monks' robes connote status, power, and engagement with the supernatural through their construction – the "design" and earthen colour coded into them – and by the meanings associated by laity to their donation to the Sangha. These donations are governed by a series of rules that limit gratuitous gifts to Sangha members, who have renounced most of the objects of this world. At the same time these rules evoke events in the experience of the Buddha and thus provide references to analogous events in the lives of the donors. The resulting restrictions on donations, together with the opportunities provided for doing so, help to imbue these otherwise modest scraps of cloth with meanings far above their monetary worth.

As the Buddha attained Enlightenment and then remained to establish the mechanisms by which his findings would be perpetuated and disseminated, he drew upon his experiences to codify his findings and actions for others. Monks' robes and the rituals by which they are obtained are the relics of these codifications and give meaning to these cloths. As contemporary men and women donate these garments and then deal with those who wear them, the conditions under which the Buddha codified these relics reverberates through the words and actions of monks and laity.

However, these robes carry additional weight, as memorials of the donors' mothers, fathers, and more distant ancestors and deceased relatives, on whose behalf the cloth and other items presented at the same time are donated to assist them in their lives in the next world.

The study of Southeast Asian textiles provides opportunities to examine in detail the exchanges between the complex constructed worlds of the cultures of this region.[31] Monks' robes within Thai-Lao Theravada Buddhism provide "a materiality that enables ideas and realities."[32] Monks' robes facilitate the creation and perpetuation of relationships between Northeast Thai-Lao and members of the Sangha, providing ways for these people to continue to obtain their soteriological goals. Additionally, these same robes are major vehicles for maintaining the reality of these people's relationships with their ancestors. Monks' robes convey and energize Thai-Lao people's relationships with their ancestors in material form. This imaginative expression becomes available to us through the examination of cut and sewn rags secured from dust-bins and charnel grounds.

Leedom Leeferts is a Professor of Anthropology *Emeritus,* Drew University; Research Associate, Department of Anthropology, Smithsonian Institution. Contact address: 132 12th Street, SE, Washington, DC 20003, USA.

References Cited

Aggacitta Bhikkhu
2001   *Kathina Then and Now.* Taiping, Perak, Malaysia: Buddha Dharma Education Association, Sasanarakkha Buddhist Sanctuary (web site: http://sasanarakkha.cjb.net) Gittinger, Mattiebelle and Leedom Lefferts.
1992   *Textiles and the Tai Experience in Southeast Asia.* Washington, D.C.: The Textile Museum.

Hayashi Yukio
2003   *Practical Buddhism among the Thai Lao: Religion in the Making of a Region.* Kyoto Area Studies on Asia, Center for Southeast Asian Studies, Vol. 5. Kyoto: Kyoto University Press.

Lefferts, Leedom
1993   "The Power of Women's Decisions: Textiles in Tai Dam and Thai-Lao Theravada Buddhist Funerals." *Southeast Asian Journal of Social Science* 21(2): 111-129.
1994   "Clothing the Serpent: Transformations of the Naak in Thai-Lao Theravada Buddhism" IN, Milgram, L., and P. Van Esterik, *The Transformative Power of Cloth in Southeast Asia.* Montreal: Canadian Council for Southeast Asian Studies, Toronto: The Museum for Textiles, pp. 19-38.
1996   "The Ritual Importance of the Mundane: White Cloth among the Tai of Southeast Asia." *Expedition* 38(1): 37-50.
2004   "Village as Stage: Imaginative Space and Time in Rural Northeast Thai Lives." *Journal of the Siam Society* 92:129-144

Mahmakuta Rajavidylaya
2544/2001 *Pli Chanting – with translations.* Bangkok: Mahmakuta Rajavidylaya Press.

Davids, T. W. Rhys and H. Oldenberg
1881   "Seventh Khandhaka (The Kathina Ceremonies), Mahâvagga, VII." *Sacred Books of the East,* Vol. 17. Oxford: Clarendon Press, pp. 147-163.

Songsrii Praphatthaung
2537/1994 *Moradok Sing Thau Nay Phraphutthasaatsanaa (Heritage of Woven Things in Buddhism).* Bangkok: Fine Arts Department.

Strong, John S.
2004   *Relics of The Buddha.* Princeton Princeton University Press.

Tambiah, S. J.
1970   *Buddhism and the Spirit Cults in Northeast Thailand.* Cambridge Studies in Social Anthropology 2. Cambridge: Cambridge University Press.

Thaamarangsii, S. W.
n.d. *Monphithii.* Bangkok.

Van Esterik, Penny
1986   "Feeding Their Faith: Recipe Knowledge among Thai Buddhist Women." *Food and Foodways* 1(1): 198-215.

Vajiraññavarorasa, Somdet Phra Maha Chao Krom Phraya
2532/1989 *Ordination Procedure and the Preliminary Duties of a New Bhikkhu.* Bangkok: Mahamakuta Rajavidyalaya Press.

Vatcharin Bhumichtr
2001   *Healthy Salads from Southeast Asia.* Trumbull, Connecticut: Weatherhill.

Footnotes

1 This paper does not discuss the details of the construction of monks' robes nor of other cloth used as part of Theravada Buddhism. See Gittinger and Lefferts 1992, pp. 94-141, and Songsrii 2537/1994.

2 See Lefferts 1996 for a discussion of the varied ritual uses of white cloth.

3 See Van Esterik 1986 for a discussion of the presentation of food to members of the Sangha.

4 Terms are given in vernacular Thai (T) and Lao (L), followed by the original term in Pali (P). Unless otherwise noted (and except for obvious English expressions), italicized terms are Thai-Lao.

5 Gittinger and Lefferts 1992, pg. 97.

6 Strong, 2004, pg. 5, italics in original.

7 I focus on this village, where I have lived intermittently since 1970, because the people there, including the successive abbots and members of the Sangha who reside in the *wat* and the ritual specialists who operate there, the *mau phraam,* ritual Brahman, and *tayok wat,* Buddhist lay leader, have allowed me to partici pate, observe, and ask questions about how they do things. My original research was not on religious issues; I came to this through the study of textiles, which I see as one way to under standstatuses, roles, and abilities to exercise agency. This paper is part of that exploration. Thanks go to my village friends, to the many others who have helped me, and to the National Research Council of Thailand which has sponsored my research.

8 See Tambiah 1970 and Hayashi 2003 for listings of the annual cycle of Northeast Thai Theravada Buddhist ceremonies.

9 Strong, 2004, pg. 216.

10 Strong 2004, pg. 218, notes "in East Asia, especially in the Chan/Zen tradition, the 'transmission of the robe' (and to a lesser extent of the bowl) . . . became one of the primary means of asserting the passing on of one's lineage . . .".

11 See Vajirañanavararosa 2532/1989 for a complete account of the ordination procedure, in Pali and English. The wearing of robes designates a man as a member of the Sangha, either as a novice or a monk. The possession of a bowl, delivered during the second part of the ceremony, the *Upasampada,* designates a monk.

12 1970, pg. 147.

13 Often a sponsor, who may not be a family member, may finance much of the ordination expense. However, even in the ceremonies I have witnessed, the mother and father still held the robes and bowl and gave them to their son.

14 For a description of how a young man becomes an ordinand and an analysis of the roles of textiles in that transition, see Lefferts 1994.

15 I wish to extend my gratitude to Chan Sangop Somumchaan, *tayok wat* of Baan Dong Phong, for his gift of the handwritten texts of his many recitations and chants from which this summary is taken.

16 This ordination is not to be confused with the ordination of, usually, young relatives of the deceased as novices for the short duration of a funeral. That is called ordination in order to pull the casket of the deceased, *buat chung sop.*

17 "The mother will see the robes of her child (and) she will rise from hell to heaven;" "*Mae cha hen phaa chiiwaun kaun luuk, cha khun na lok pay suwan.*"

18 S. Thaamarangsii, Monphithii, n.d., pg. 171.

19 Davids and Oldenberg, 1881, Mahavagga, VII, 1, 2.

20 Additionally, a village may organize a *Chula* or Great Kathin, during which, in twenty-four hours, women harvest cotton, produce yarn, and weave white cloth to be donated to a *wat.* Gittinger and Lefferts 1992, pp. 102-103, Vatcharin, 2001, pp. 7-10.

21 2001.

22 When a monk receives a new robe or set of robes, he must discard his previous set and determine the new one.

23 Or, in case of a sudden death, burial.

24 Songsrii 2537/1991, pg. 11, shows a photograph of monks receiv ing white cloth unwrapped directly from a corpse, noting that this occurred originally, *tae doem,* T. This cloth is called *bangsukun chiiwaun.*

25 This chant differs in words but not in substance between the *Mahanikaya* and *Thammayut* orders in Thailand. There is also a *Pamsuklagth* for the living, recited by monks prior to a person's death as a kind of "Last Rite"; Mahmakuta Rajavidylaya, *Pali Chanting – with translations,* 2544/2001, pg. 53.

26 Not every household can afford a *Bun Chaek Khaaw.* Sometimes to save on expense and time the Bun is held in the days immedi ately following the recovery of the ashes. At other times, the festival may not be held at all and. Instead, at an appropriate time, the ashes are deposited in a reliquary *stupa* or hollow fence post at the *wat* boundary with the requisite number of four monks and immediate family members participating in a small service.

27 The *prasaat phung,* literally "honey shrine," fulfills the same function as a *hau yen,* "cool house," in Thai Dam funerals (Lefferts 1993, pg. 119).

28 I specifically asked about the use of cloth to wrap palm-leaf manu scripts, *hau khamphii.* White cloth and women's skirts, *phaa thung* or *phaa sin,* are preferred because they are sufficiently wide to securely wrap the stack of palm leaves in a manuscript. Utilitarian/shoulder cloth, *phaa komaa,* is usually not wide enough. Men's skirts, *phaa sarong,* can be used because they are sufficiently wide, but few are donated. I was told there were no special meanings involved in using women's skirts; they are the more numerous donation and they more adequately fulfill the requirements of securely wrapping a manuscript than most other donated cloth. See also Gittinger and Lefferts, 1992, pp. 121-123.

29 White cloth not destined for monks' robes, but kept for utilitarian purposes, such as providing the necessary covering for table tops and altar shelves on which rest important things, *khong dii,* is held in its own repository so it will not be confused with the white cloth that can potentially be used for monks' robes. Much of this cloth comes to the *wat* through ceremonies auxiliary to funerals, such as the white flag used when a deceased's ashes are brought to the *wat.*

30 See Lefferts 1993.

31 Lefferts 2004.

32 Kastalena Michelaki, discussant comments, Panel 3-095, "Ceramic Ecology XIX", Annual Meeting, American Anthropological Association, Washington, D.C., 3 Decembe 2005.

Female Lower Garment or Holy Manuscript Wrapper?
The Role of Women in a Buddhist Society

Suriya Smutkupt

For people living in many parts of Laos and Thailand, and especially for Thais from the northeastern area, the *pha sin*[1], a woman's tubular skirt **(1)**, and the *bai lan*[2], religious manuscripts **(6)**, find their origin in two extremely different cultural contexts. The *pha sin*, woven by women and used to wrap their lower body is of a worldly nature, while religious manuscripts belong to the sacred world of Buddhism. Therefore, the idea that traditional Isaan people would wrap sacred *bai lan* in *pha sin* would seem unthinkable. Such a combination seems entirely inconsistent with beliefs, because theoretically, the two should not even be mentioned in the same context. And yet, the practice of wrapping religious texts in women's lower body garments is commonly found **(2)**. How could two such opposite objects be linked together in such a way? What is the rationale behind this idea?

2 Examples of Buddhist palm leaf manuscripts (*bai lan*) wrapped in *pha sin*. Rama IX Chalerm Prakiet Library, Nakorn Rachasima. (Photo: PP)

By focusing on the relationship between *pha sin* and *bai lan,* this paper will examine contemporary anthropological theories about gender in terms of the ideas, practices and beliefs of Isaan people. However, it must be noted that in recent times there has been a decline in the importance placed on *bai lan* manuscripts and the teaching undertaken through the use of these scriptures. Although the tradition of wrapping manuscripts in *pha sin* is disappearing, in many parts of Isaan it is still possible to find these sacred scriptures stored in the manuscript cabinets of old temples. Sadly neglected, most of the wrapped manuscripts are in a state of deterioration, torn and covered with dust **(9)**.

With education, modern technology and greater influence from central Thai culture, the role in Isaan of the temples, Buddhist monks, religious knowledge and ancient wisdom has been greatly reduced. In particular, as the *bai lan* were written in ancient scripts such as the Buddhist *dhamma* script, Kom (Khmer) script and Thai Noi script, few people today can read them. The knowledge and use of these archaic scripts is disappearing, as are the meanings and importance of manuscripts wrapped in *pha sin* from the memory of modern-day Isaan people.

1 Temple mural scene showing Isaan women wearing tubular skirts (*pha sin*) and making offerings to the monks on a holy day (*wan pra*). Mural from Wat Taku, Nakorn Rachasima, early 19th century. (Photo: Paisarn Piammattawat)

Traditionally, academic research about these manuscripts has focused on their significance in terms of religious meaning and beliefs. From their study, scholars have attempted to glean information about the way of life and attitudes of the people who created them. They categorized, compiled and preserved the manuscripts as historical evidence. This paper, however, considers these manuscripts in a very different context, placing emphasis on the significance of wrapping the manuscripts in *pha sin* in terms of local beliefs and customs.

In this paper two important issues will be considered:

1) The issue of symbolism The *pha sin* represents the female gender, while religious manuscripts are representative of the male gender, authority and expertise. Thus, logically it should be taboo to associate the two items together. A woman's lower body garment would seem not to have any place in a manuscript cabinet in Buddhist temple. However, for Isaan culture, this is an exceptional situation and cannot be resolved theoretically.

2) The issue of gender The manuscripts wrapped in a *pha sin* help us to understand the role of gender in Isaan culture in former times. The use of a woman's *pha sin* in a religious context serves as a forceful "cultural signifier" in explaining male-female relationships. These wrapped manuscripts indicate to us that the relationship between men and women in the past was not an authoritarian or totalitarian with fixed division of genders roles as might be believed.

In order to clarify this discussion, it is important to note that the *pha sin* used to wrap manuscripts were never worn prior to being employed for this purpose. However, even though these textiles were new and unused, in general textiles woven for a woman's use were not normally associated with the sacred. In terms of the symbolism inferred by this, it is important to note that the Isaan people have created an exception or special criteria to allow the sacred and the profane to be used together. While women are prohibited from being ordained as Buddhist monks, their skill at weaving wonderful and beautiful textiles provides an option for women to employ their craft to gain merit according to local Buddhist beliefs **(3)**.

The traditional view about Thai society is that the two genders are very separate and that the social roles of men and women are very different in terms of historical, cultural and social contexts. The general view is that Thai males played a significant role in politics and government, while women remained at home, where their dominate role was related to family and society. In real-

3 Scene from the City Pillar Shrine in Nakorn Rachasima showing Isaan woman weaving. *(Photo: PP)*

ity, the situation might actually be the opposite, with a much more complex social relationship between the two sexes taking place. In the past, the role of gender in Thai societies, including in Isaan society, has been that men and women helped and supported each other, even if their roles are clearly divided. Certain mechanism found in religious beliefs, traditions and various social institutions help both genders come to terms with each other's role and create a balance between the sexes.

Taking the view that the two genders work and support each other in social relationships is a much more realistic approach, especially in terms of the question of manuscripts being wrapped in *pha sin*. In this case, women play the important social role of supporting religion especially through their support of the men who enter into the monkhood.

In order to better understand the use of *pha sin* manuscript wrappers, it is necessary to consider the significance of *bai lan* manuscripts in Isaan, especially in the period before the social and educational reforms introduced during the reign of King Rama V (1868-1910). The *bai lan* manuscripts are the "books of the Isaan people of the past". They require special care and treatment because the palm leaf used in their making is a natural, fragile material and not durable. The knowledge stored in these manuscripts contains its own uniqueness. Only the few literate persons who could read and write could use these manuscripts. They were the monks, persons who had studied in the monastery, those educated in religious scripts and members of the court.

4 Rare mural scene showing two men playing an Isaan musical instrument (*can*). The men wear hipwrappers (*chong kraben*), called a *pha yao* in Isaan. Mural from Wat Taku, Nakorn Rachasima, early 19th century. *(Photo: PP)*

Bai lan manuscripts contain important information about literature and traditions of the past **(4)**. They include religious chants, legends, the *jataka* (stories about the former lives of the Buddha), and medical texts. These manuscripts were stored in Buddhist temples and kept for various religious rites and rituals. In addition, there were certain persons who could read these manuscripts, namely the *mor dhamma*,[3] *mor suad*[4] and *mor ya*.[5] These were persons who had been previously ordained but were no longer in the monastery. They thus kept these manuscripts in their possession in their homes.

While there were large numbers of *bai lan* manuscripts to be found both in the temples and in the homes of learned people, generally women never had anything to do with their production or use. Women could not be ordained; therefore literacy among women was limited. Generally women never inscribed, read or studied these sacred texts.

However, women did have an important role to play in the use of *bai lan*. These manuscripts were the original books of the Isaan people and were created before the age of modern printing technology. The woven tex-

tiles, especially the *pha sin* which the women made to be given to the temples to wrap the manuscripts have the same function as modern book covers. Their use was to protect the book so that it could be kept for a long time. However, unlike today's modern book covers, the textiles created by the women to protect the manuscripts are a visual reminder of their beliefs systems, traditions and religious rites. Thus the *bai lan* manuscripts and *pha sin* cannot be separated from each other.

The role of Isaan women was to be the listeners of the recital or chant of religious manuscripts. They participated in the creation of manuscripts by donating woven *mud mee* (ikat) textiles to wrap manuscripts. In research made in seven provinces between 1987-1991, 2,500 *bai lan* manuscripts were counted. Of these, 500 were wrapped with *pha sin.* The remaining was wrapped in other kinds of textile such as *pha kao ma* (rectangular textile used as a sash or in other utilitarian ways) **(5, 11)**, *sarong* (man's tubular loin cloth) or kept in cabinets or wooden boxes. In particular, the manuscripts in Srisaket and Roi Et provinces were found to be wrapped in *pha sin* and were very well preserved. Additionally, two other

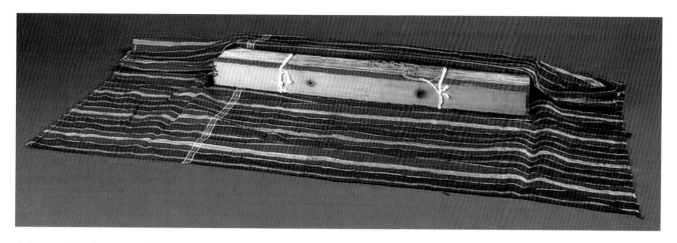

5 Rectangular all-purpose cloth used by men and women *(pha kao ma)* were also donated to temples for wrapping *bai lan*. Rama IX Chalerm Prakiet Library, Nakorn Rachasima. *(Photo: PP)*

provinces which are important economic centres, Nakorn Panom and Ubon Ratchathani have a strong tradition of wrapping manuscripts in *pha sin*.

The Rama IX Chalerm Prakiet Library in Nakorn Rachasima province is one of the largest sources of old Isaan manuscripts. The collection is reported to include 6,549 bundles of manuscripts and 18 Thai *samut* (books). They cover various subjects on Isaan life including past local history, texts on ancient styles of massage, astrology, medicine, local legends and stories, Buddhist *jataka* stories and other literatures. As a large number of these manuscripts are found wrapped in *pha sin,* this clearly points to the fact that this was a popular tradition in Isaan.

Even a number of old sayings which emerge from the daily life and cultural context of Isaan people indicate the importance of this tradition. One saying states, "become rich from offering alm of bananas, become a *phrajao* (lord) from offering alm of *pha mad mee* (ikat textiles)." Another saying which has an ironic double meaning is "whoever wants to be a scholar must unwrap the *pha sin* off" or "whoever wants to be a scholar must go to unwrap the *pha sin* off at temples." This saying has a sense of risqué humor, because the term "taking a *pha sin* off" can mean removing the skirt from a woman. However, is strictly forbidden for a woman to take her skirt off in the temple area. And, of course, when a man becomes a monk, he must renounce relationships with women.

The fact that these sayings are part of the local culture points to the popularity and common practice of using women's *pha sin* to wrap manuscripts. These sayings also show the relationship between the two genders in the sense that "men can entre the monkhood while women who are deprived of such an opportunity can use

their skills to weave *pha sin*. From the proceeds of their weaving, women can donate money to the temple for the creation of sacred manuscripts, and they can also donate the textiles for wrapping them. It is also believed that only the *pha sin* of devout believers should be used to wrap manuscripts. The *pha sin* being donated for wrapping manuscripts can be made of cotton, silk or silk with golden treads. The material used and the weaving techniques tell much about the social status of the person making the offering (7).

As the manuscripts are considered sacred, there are specific regulations with regard to their care. The cloth used to wrap manuscripts can be made from all types of thread; however the textiles must be new and if not new, must be unused. Women believed that even though they have killed many silk larvae to make the thread to weave textiles; they can compensate for this and make merit by donating their weavings to the temple. One monk explained that *pha sin* are used because they are considered to be the most beautiful and the best material for wrapping manuscripts. In addition, a woman's long hair was also donated to temples to be used to tie up the manuscripts. Once again this is considered as a way for women to make merit.

There are also many rules about the use of manuscripts. On special occasions and on every *wan pra*[6] (holy day) respect will be paid to the manuscripts. There are also beliefs about what is not permitted when using or handling manuscripts such as while moving manuscripts, the whole bundle should be removed and carried in a position which is not below chest level. Women and children are not allowed to touch them, and no one is permitted to sit or lie down on manuscripts.

In Isaan, the use of *pha sin* to wrap manuscripts points to the role of women in supporting Buddhism and

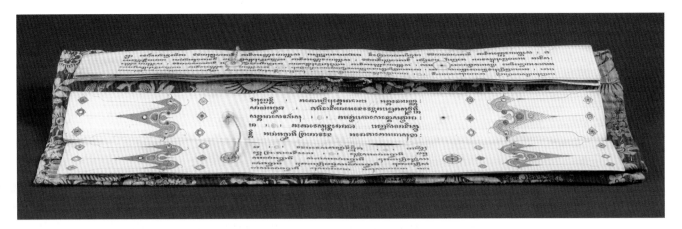

6 A fine example of a palm leaf manuscript *(bai lan)* opened to one of the pages. Rama IX Chalerm Prakiet Library, Nakorn Rachasima. *(Photo: PP)*

7 A beautiful old ikat textile *(pha mad mee)* used to wrap a manuscript. Rama IX Chalerm Prakiet Library, Nakorn Rachasima. *(Photo: PP)*

local communities. This gives women a place in Buddhism, an otherwise male dominated belief system. Buddhists believe that being born a man is one of the qualifications to become a *Boddhisattawa* (Buddha to be), thus it is considered that to be born a man is superior. Traditional Theravada Buddhism as practiced in Isaan has no ideological structure for women. They do not fit into the qualifications for being a *Boddhisattawa*, and are thus overlooked by this concept.

However, as a supporter of Buddhism, women play a vital role. We see older women making merit by giving alms to the monks. They gather at the temples to do chores, cooking, chanting prayers, weaving prayer flags or monk robes and supporting temples with monetary donations.

The use of a woman's textile to wrap religious manuscripts points to a positive relationship between men and women. In the nurturing of Buddhism, it shows the support the sexes give to each other in Issan villages. Wrapping manuscripts in *pha sin* is an example of how women support men and vice versa, and how they work together to support Buddhism. This social relationship has great significance both in the past and present.

It can be further noted that although men and women in traditional Isaan culture have different statuses, this does not mean there was sexual oppression or one sex taking advantage of the other **(8)**. Traditional mechanism ensured that sexual oppression did not develop. However, more recently when these Issan people have migrated into cities and traditional cultural values are

176

affected by modern culture, sexual oppression appears to develop.

In conclusion, a number of important cultural values can be understood from studying the practice of wrapping manuscripts in *pha sin*. First of all, this custom demonstrates a supportive relationship between genders with Buddhism serving at the centre of this cooperation. The tradition also points to the value and significance placed on books, literacy, transfer of knowledge and ancient wisdom. Showing respect to *bai lan* demonstrates that the highest value is given to knowledge and literacy. Isaan people held great respect for those who could read, write and had special knowledge. Especially respected were those with knowledge of both worldly and religious matters.

The knowledge found in the manuscripts wrapped in *pha sin* consists of the cultural and religious knowledge of the community **(10)**. This is different from the knowl-

8 Scene from the City Pillar Shrine in Nakorn Rachasima showing an Isaan couple working together pounding rice. *(Photo: PP)*

9 Partially folded textile showing how the *pha sin* is wrapped around a manuscript. Note how the silk textile has deteriorated with age. Rama IX Chalerm Prakiet Library, Nakorn Rachasima. *(Photo: PP)*

10 A *bai lan* with Buddhist *dhamma* script opened here in fan shape. This was originally tied together by strings at either end so that the pages could be opened like an accordion. Rama IX Chalerm Prakiet Library, Nakorn Rachasima. *(Photo: PP)*

11 Tiny bamboo sticks have been inserted into a *pha kao ma* to strengthen the textile for use to wrap and protect a *bai lan*. The Rama IX Chalerm Prakiet Library, Nakorn Rachasima. *(Photo: PP)*

12 A manuscript completely wrapped in a *pha mad mee* and tied closed with sacred string. Rama IX Chalerm Prakiet Library, Nakorn Rachasima. *(Photo: PP)*

edge and skills acquired in modern-day education. Knowledge wrapped in *pha sin* responds to the needs of the whole communities and helps to develop the potential of men and women in the provinces.

The wrapping of manuscripts in *pha sin* gave Isaan women a way to support Buddhism **(12)**. This opened a cultural channel which allowed them to participate in Buddhism by being able to donate the best thing they could create to help to support society and Buddhism. Women wanted to learn about and participate in the teachings of the *dhamma*. They wanted to participate in making merit in Buddhism. Unlike modern feminists who use protest to gain what they want, they were comfortable with the role they played in their society. Based on the socio-agricultural conditions, they played an important role, equal to that of men in supporting *dhamma*. In their goal to achieve enlightenment, society allowed women to make merit in various forms and on different occasions according to their status and role as daughters, mothers and women elders.

The role of Isaan's women in Buddhism has lessened gradually as the use of *bai lan* manuscripts disappears and the centre of the community is no longer in the temple compound. The entire social structure has changed as Isaan women migrate from their communities to become workers, unskilled labors or even to work in the sex trade. Men have also left their communities to seek work in the cities or overseas. As a result the relationship between men and woman has changed drastically.

Manuscripts wrapped in *pha sin* played an important role in traditional Isaan society, demonstrating the significance of women in a Buddhist community. Under-

standing this allows us to see the transition of economic and social relationship in terms of symbols. With globalization, Isaan men have forgotten the value of these manuscripts, and Isaan women no longer weave the *pha sin* to contain them. Becoming citizens of globalized communities, these men and women of Isaan face fierce competition and will need to learn to new ways to survive in a society vastly different from the one that wrapped religious manuscripts in women's *pha sin*.

Footnotes

[1] A *pha sin* is a woman's tubular skirt which is made from woven cloth joined by one or two seams.

[2] Palm leaf manuscripts traditionally used for recording Buddhist texts or cultural records and information.

[3] Persons well versed in *dhamma* (Buddhist teachings).

[4] Persons well versed in praying or chanting.

[5] Persons well versed in traditional medicine treatments.

[6] Celebrated on the full moon and waning moon days.

Royal Brocades in the Siamese Court

Thirabhand Chandracharoen

The subjects of the Kingdom of Siam traditionally believed that the monarch wielded supreme power and was the embodiment of divine rule. Such beliefs resulted in a strict and complicated set of decrees relating to royal status and dress code, or sumptuary law. This paper will consider the way royal brocade textiles were used to reinforce such views.

For the Siamese court, it was necessary to represent the monarch to the public as if he were a divine being who presided over and maintained order in the realm of gods and goddesses. In order to do this, various conventions were employed such as addressing the king through the use of a special royal language; royal music was played with sacred musical instruments when the king appeared in audiences; the throne hall was constructed to symbolize Mount Meru, the heavenly mountain; and royal vehicles or thrones were decorated with various auspicious mythical animal forms and shapes **(1)**. Finally, and most importantly for this paper, textiles, their use and the rules concerning the way they were worn were significant instruments in creating the image of the monarch as representing a part of the divine cosmos on earth.

The Siamese court since the Ayutthaya period (1351-1767) and until the Rattanakosin period (1782-present) has reserved the use of certain types of magnificent textiles uniquely for the king, members of the royal household and the nobility for specific occasions and events. The use of these textiles varied according to hierarchical order and social status.

Royal and court textiles were either produced locally within the kingdom or imported. Locally produced textiles, especially the exquisite brocades produced in southern Thailand, were woven for use in such royal ceremonies as the tonsurate or *so-gun* ceremony. This hair-cutting ceremony was held as a rite of passage for a young prince or princess to symbolically mark the end of childhood **(2)**. Some royal textiles were made by regional vassals under Siamese sovereignty. For instance, the *pha poom* or ikat textile produced by the Cambodian or

1 HM King Prajadhipok (Rama VII) at his coronation, seated on the Budtankanchanasinghat Throne which symbolizes Mount Meru. *(National Archives)*

Khmer vassals of Siam was worn for normal audience with the king **(3)**. Other royal textiles were imported from various foreign countries which can be categorized into two distinct types:

1) Textiles made in a foreign country for its own local market, such as the gold brocades from India known as *tard, atlad, khemkhab* or *khimkhab* and *yiarabab* or *zarbaft*. These brocaded fabrics were fashioned into court uniforms **(4)**.

180

2 HRH Prince Prajadhipok at his tonsurate ceremony, wearing gold brocade *pha nung* and *tard* jacket. *(National Archives)*

4 A brocade jacket made from imported Indian *yiarabab* cloth and worn during Siamese court ceremonies. *(National Museum, Bangkok)*

3 Siamese court nobility wearing *pha poom* ikat hip wrappers for audience with the king. *(National Archives)*

5 Ceremonial brocade cloth (*pha lai yang*) used on special royal occasions. *(Private Collection)*

6 Brocade made using golden thread. *(Private Collection)*

2) Certain imported textiles specially ordered and made to Siamese patterns such as *pha lai yang*. These textiles, including those painted and printed in India, were used for full ceremonial royal events such as when the king traveled around the city or when he granted audiences to foreign ambassadors **(5)**.

Due to the rich variety of textiles available, the Siamese court was able to implement a strict, precise and complicated set of protocols for court dress. These rules reflect identity and concepts developed over centuries and unique to the Siamese. From the Ayutthaya period through the brief Thonburi period, and then on to the present-day Rattanakosin or Bangkok period, most of the court etiquette relating to the monarch and royal household has been maintained in all respects as in former times. This includes the sumptuary law or dress code. As the range of textiles used in the Siamese court for royal attire and uniforms of high-ranking nobility and officials is too great to discuss in this given space, this paper will only consider *pha yok* or brocades.

For the Siamese who live in the central plains and the upper part of the southern peninsula, the term *pha yok*, or brocade, is used to describe textiles on which the design has been made with supplementary threads, raised over a plain silk ground. When the brocade design is woven with ordinary silk, it is called *pha yok mai* or silk brocade **(7)**, and when it is woven with gold threads, it is known as *pha yok tong* or gold brocade **(6)**.

Throughout the 417 years of the Ayutthaya period, people involved with the Siamese court were well acquainted with *pha yok*. When the capital city fell to the Burmese in 1767, documents in the royal libraries and objects kept in the Siamese court's inventories, including textiles, were destroyed. Today only scant evidence concerning textile use of that period can be found in old records. Fortunately some documentation remains in the present-day Siamese court which proves that the court of Ayutthaya was familiar with brocaded fabrics and that that their use was prescribed as royal attire for the king, the royal household and as uniforms for court officials.

Important documents from the Rattanakosin period such as chronicles, royal commands to arrange ceremonies, correspondence between departments, copies of royal letters, list of items considered as tribute, memoranda of foreign ambassadors, legends and literature are well maintained in the National Library and the National Archives. They are extremely useful for textile

7 Brocade made of ordinary silk. *(Private Collection)*

8 Central panel shows flower motif worn by commoners.
(Private Collection)

research. Our information about royal brocades has become much clearer after studying these records and examining those brocades which remain in the collections of the National Museum and the royal treasures which are kept in the Grand Palace. In addition, more information has been obtained from private collections and manuscript wrappings in temples throughout the kingdom.

From such research, we can assume that the reason the Siamese Court chose to use brocades for various royal occasions was due to its particular qualities. Such rich and elegant textiles reinforced the the elevation of kings to divine status. In addition, the use of such sumptuous fabrics for interior decoration in the palace helped create the image of otherworldliness on earth.

Special supplementary weft techniques are used to raise the designs above the plain silk ground. Theses supplementary wefts can be woven with either natural dyed silk or gold or silver threads, thus creating an exquisitely beautiful fabric that emphasizes a wearer's high social status.

An almost unlimited ranges of designs were created. Geometric patterns, flowers and plants, and the *kranok,* a stylized design derived from a flame or lotus are just

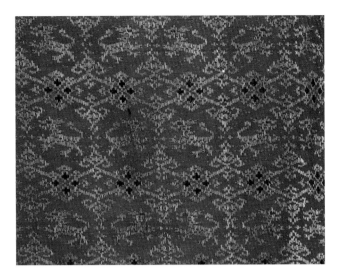

9 Mythical *singha*. *(National Museum Chaiya, Surat Thani)*

10 Mythical *garuda*. *(Private Collection)*

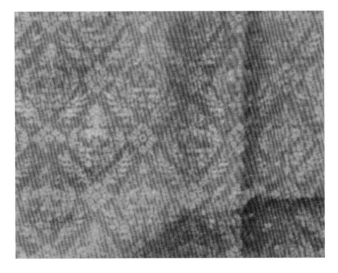

11 Mythical *thep-panom*. *(Private Collection)*

some of the many examples. Certain floral motifs were used by commoners **(8)**. Others were reserved for the king, the royal household and nobility. These featured mythological animals from the *himavatta* (holy forest), such as *naga* (serpent or big snake), *hera* (half-serpent, half-dragon), *hamsa* (swan), *garuda* (half-man, half-bird) mount of Vishnu, *kinnaree* (half-woman, half-bird), *kinnara* (half-man, half-bird), *singha* (lion), and *thep* (celestial deities or beings) in various postures such as *thep-panom* (paying respect), *thep-parum* (dancing), and *thep-tue-chor* (holding flowers) **(9, 10, 11)**.

The use of gold thread also contributed to the concept of divine status of a king. As it was often imported from abroad, it was considered particularly valuable and as such beyond the reach of commoners.

In addition, certain types of brocade could not be produced within the kingdom and had to be imported, thereby making them also out of the reach of commoners due to their cost. Thus the use of imported brocades served as one of the indicators of the user's social status.

There is evidence that during the Ayutthaya period, imported brocades were ordered from China, India and Persia. Later in the Bangkok period, the major sources of imported brocades were China and India. In contrast, no clear evidence exists to show where the centres of domestic brocade production were during the Ayutthaya period. By the early Rattanakosin period (1782-1851), however, it is certain that the major centre for brocade production was in the upper part of Siam's southern provincial region, with Nakhon Si Thammarat as the heart. The Bangkok court favored the skills of southern weavers who were highly respected for their ability to weave fine brocades.

Several government documents dating to the early Bangkok Period confirm the importance of southern Siam as a major source of brocades. These include orders for brocades for court use and delivery notes for brocades sent to the court from Chumporn, Chaiya (now in Surat Thani), Nakhon Si Thammarat and even from as far south as Songkhla province. In one letter dated Tuesday, May 22, 1860, Phraya Sri Saowaraj Pakdi informed the Governors of Songkhla, Chaiya and Chumporn that His Majesty the King had graciously expressed his wish to obtain brocade fabrics with the *rajawat* design **(12)**.

The court was responsible for the cost of procuring the raw materials for weaving. In some cases the government provided the raw materials. Other times, the provinces procured their own materials and the costs were reimbursed by the court. There were various documents which discuss this issue.

Brocades woven by skilled weavers from the upper southern provinces can be distinguished and differentiated from other imported sources by the following characteristics:

Plain weave

The local loom with only two heddles created a plain ground textile. By increasing the number of heddles, the range of designs became more complicated **(13)**.

China and India produced a greater variety of brocades than Siam through the use of loom with three or more heddles. Weaving with more than two heddles created a twill or warp-faced cloth, where the warp threads are more visible on the front side of the textile. This kind of fabric was called '*tuan*' or 'satin' and could be used to create many designs. Supplementary weft patterning appeared only on the right side of the fabric.

Local Silk

Since the weather in Southern Thailand was not suitable for growing mulberry trees and for raising silkworms, most raw silk thread was produced in the Isaan (northeastern) region of the Kingdom.

Imported silk from China or India was finer but was used in smaller quantities because of its high cost. It is evident that textiles woven with imported silk threads were thinner and lighter due to the fineness of the silk.

Thai Design

Local weavers produced textiles with designs similar to the traditional or royal designs because they were a part of and understood the local culture. However, textiles woven by foreign weavers deviated from Thai designs. Different types of loom were used resulting in different kinds of fabrics.

Colour

Locally-produced brocades were in more somber colours when compared with the colourful Chinese and Indian brocades. Chinese brocades used colours not popular in the south such as bright yellow, pink, orange, purple and bright green **(14)**. Indian brocades also featured colours seldom used in the south, such as purple and bright green **(15)**.

After conducting a study of old textiles, I found that court brocades from the southern provinces could be categorized into the following groups:

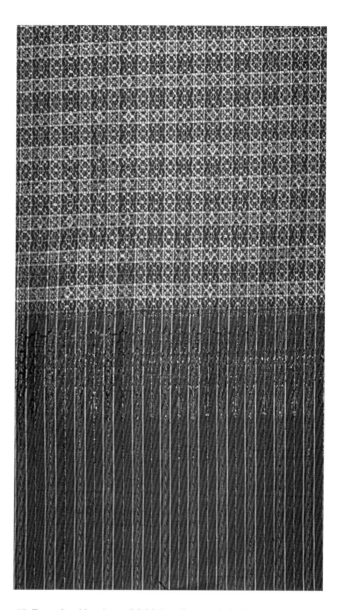

12 Brocade with *rajawat dok lek* (small pattern) design made in southern Thailand over 100 years ago. *(Private Collection)*

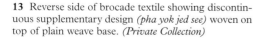

13 Reverse side of brocade textile showing discontinuous supplementary design *(pha yok jed see)* woven on top of plain weave base. *(Private Collection)*

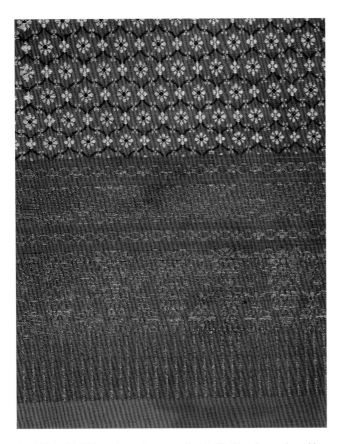

14 Colourful Chinese brocade woven for the Thai market and used by a member of the royal family during the reign of King Chulalongkorn (Rama V). (*Private Collection*)

15 Golden brocade woven on navy blue silk base, made in India for Thai royalty and used during the reign of King Chulalongkorn (Rama V). (*Private Collection*)

18 Old textile from southern Thailand showing the *rajawat dok yai* (large pattern) or *rajawat kom* design. (*Vimanmek Collection*)

Brocades with free designs

In this case, weavers freely created the designs with supplementary wefts, without any restriction. For this kind of fabric, supplementary weft technique was generally used in certain areas or the whole length of cloth. Brocades with both supplementary weft and warp are rarely found **(16)**.

Brocades with small square designs

These are called *pha yok jed see* or seven-coloured brocade. They are made using a discontinuous supplementary weft technique. Weavers could choose to add supplementary weft threads in many colours **(17)**.

Brocades with designs over the plait ground

This kind of fabric is made using the supplementary weft technique over the plait ground. With this technique, the overall pattern of the design would look like slanting plait. This type of fabric is given a special name of '*rajawat* brocade' **(18)**.

The large quantities of brocades ordered from the southern provinces for court use during the early Rattanakosin period were used in the following ways:

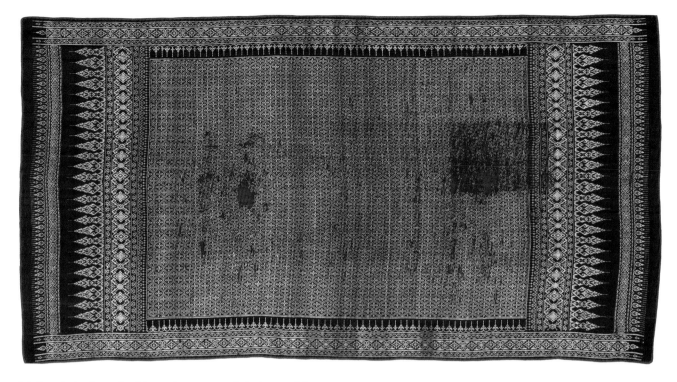

16 Free design brocade with supplementary weft design on plain weave background. *(National Museum, Bangkok)*

***Pha nung* (hip wrapper)** To use as *pha nung,* the fabric should roughly be 300 x 90 cm. For normal occasions, there are two ways for men and women to wear *pha nung.* The first is *nung jeeb* **(19)** and the second *nung chong kraben* **(20)**, while a third style, *nung loy chai* was used for casual attire and private occasions. For important ceremonies, the manner of wearing a *pha nung* is more complicated such as *nung jeeb chong wai hang hong* for young princes or princesses during tonsure ceremony **(21)**, *nung bao khun* for *Phraya Raekna* (the senior official undertaking the role of ploughing the rice field on behalf of the king in the Royal Ploughing Ceremony) and the *Phraya Yuen Chingcha* (senior official in the role of welcoming Shiva on behalf of the king in the Royal Swing Ceremony) **(22)**. There were also rules for the way elephant handlers, who ride on the neck of the elephant wear *pha nung.* In this case, there were even manuals which explained various elaborate styles of wrapping a *pha nung,* depending on the type of elephants as well. The *pha nung* used for this purpose was of a special dimension, 170 x 350 cm; two pieces were woven and sewn together to form a large *pha nung* **(23)**.

17 Plain weave brocade with supplementary discontinuous design created with patterns of small squares. *(Vimanmek Collection)*

187

19

20

19 HSH Poonpismai Diskul wearing a hip wrapper in the *nung jeeb* style on the occasion of her tonsurate. *(National Archives)*

20 Chao Chom Manda Chum with her daughters HRH Adhron Thipayanipha (right) and HRH Sujidra Paranee (left). Chao Chom Manda Chum and Princess' Sujidra wear *chongkraben*, while Princess Adhorn wears a European style dress. *(National Archives)*

21 HSH Bim Rambai Rabibadhana in the *nung jeeb chong wai hang hong* style on the occasion of her tonsure ceremony. *(National Archives)*

21

22 Phraya Pradipat Bhubal in ceremonial attire. Underneath his coat he wears a *yierabab* jacket and gold brocade *pha nung*. *(National Archives)*

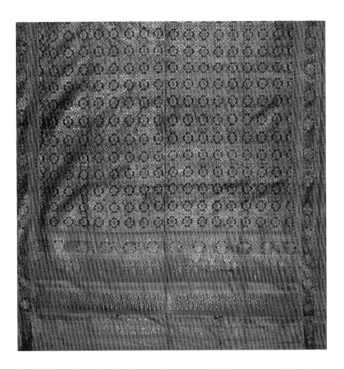

23 Golden brocade double-panel ceremonial *pha nung* used for handling elephants. The two identical lengths of silk have been sewn together along a middle seam. *(Vimanmek Collection)*

24 Waist sash *(pha kaad eaw)* decorated with small square pattern designs. *(Private Collection)*

25 Shawl or sash *(pha hom)* decorated with *rajawat dok lek* design. *(Private Collection)*

The Siamese court categorized brocades that were mainly used as *pha nung* into two categories: the first category was for distribution to nobility, officials and occasionally used as tribute. The second type, called *sompak yod* was used as official uniforms to show ranks.

Pha hom (sash* or *shawl) is of the same size as the present day men's all-purpose cloth or *pha kao ma*, measuring 70 x 185 cm. It is used as a shawl for both men and women or as women's sash or breast cloth **(24)**.

Pha kad eaw (waist sash) is a long narrow piece of cloth, measuring 40 x 185 cm, for men to tie around their waist **(25)**.

***Pha ched pak* (handkerchief)** is a square piece of cloth, measuring from 40 x 40 cm to 65 x 65 cm. It is used for wiping betel nut juice or stains from the mouths or for tucking at the waist to look fashionable. It can also be used for wrapping things like a betel box **(26)**.

Cherng pha nung* or *sang wien yok measuring 300 x 20 cm, is an end border piece. It is a long piece of fabric woven especially to attached as a border of *pha nung chong kraben* **(27)**.

No clear evidence documents how the Siamese court ordered brocades from China and India. However, circumstantial evidence from textiles and documents help provide an idea of how such orders were made. The Siamese court employed merchants to act as middlemen

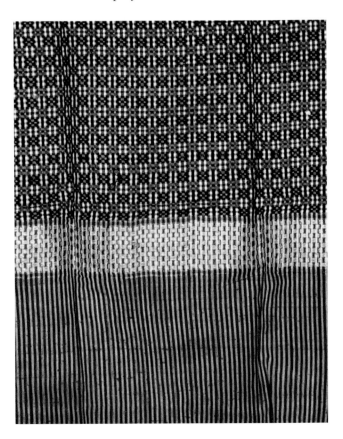

who ordered textiles and delivered the finished products to the court. The orders were sent with instructions, desired designs and fabric samples. In some cases, foreign weavers created designs especially for the Siamese.

From the preserved pieces and old photographs, Siamese brocades of the early Bangkok period court ordered from China were mainly textiles with free designs to be used as *pha nung*. *Pha yok jed see* or seven-coloured brocades and *pha yok ta rajawat* or brocades with *rajawat* design were not found.

Other interesting evidence about the order of Indian brocades comes from descriptions of costumes used for a version of the *Ramayana* written by His Majesty King Rama I. For this classical performance called the *E-Nao*, it is mentioned in various records that the characters in the play wore costumes made from various Indian brocades. The different types of imported Indian brocades are as follows:

Atlad is woven with the popular mango motif throughout the fabric. Some are found with designs in gold thread while others are woven with gold and silver threads. This type of brocade does not have borders or end panels and is used for making trousers, shirts, or other items **(28)**.

26 Silk handkerchief or cloth used to wrap objects *(pha ched pak)*. *(Private Collection)*

27 Long strip of brocade cloth *(cherng pha nung or sang wien yok)* which would be sewn on to the edge of a *pha nung. (Private Collection)*

29 Striped golden brocade *(khimkhab* or *khemkhab). (Private Collection)*

28 *Atlad* brocade showing popular mango motif. *(National Museum, Bangkok)*

30 Golden brocade *(yierabab* or *zarbaft)* with silk satin weave background, imported from India and used during the reign of King Chulalongkorn (Rama V). *(Private Collection)*

Khimkhab* or *khemkhab is a striped textile woven using only gold threads, or gold and silver threads. The use of *khimkhab* is similar to that of *atlad*; it is for making trousers, shirts, or other items **(29)**.

Yierabab* or *zarbaft is a type of brocade with borders and end panels, which was used as *pha nung*. However, it could also be ordered in bolts without borders and end panels for making trousers, shirts or other items. *Yierabab* was also ordered only as a hem piece or *sang wien* to be attached to the *pha nung* **(30)**.

Tard is another type of brocade. The textile used in making supplementary patterning is made from flat metal strips of gold-plaited silver or gold-plaited copper or silver and silver-plaited copper **(31)**.

Other types of materials the Siamese court ordered from India which could be categorized as brocades are *mashru, pattala* and *jamdani*.

Conclusion

The Siamese court appreciated the value, beauty and uniqueness of brocades. These woven textiles responded to the court's need to uphold the status of the monarch as he avatar of a god who descended to the earth to rule and protect his subjects **(32)**. The Siamese court thus chose brocades as an important instrument, together with other types of fabrics, to create this image.

To obtain these important textiles, the Siamese court ordered brocades from the southern provinces of Thailand and also imported them from foreign countries such as China and India. As they were made-to-order for royal use, court brocades had unique characteristics which differentiated them from textiles worn by commoners.

The resources of the Siamese court allowed the extensive use of brocades woven with gold thread. In contrast, commoners, unable to afford gold thread, used plain silk brocade, with occasionally some gold designs woven into the end panels.

The Siamese court reserved certain motifs for the use of the king, the royal household and the nobility. These designs included mythical creatures from *Himmavatta* or holy forest such as *naga, hera, hamsa, garuda, kinnaree, singha* and deities in various postures. Brocades for commoners were generally decorated with geometric designs, flowers, plants and *kranok*.

The study of the brocades used in the Siamese court provides important insight into the Thai monarchy and Siam's rich cultural heritage. These unique textiles played a vital role in establishing the status of their royal wearers and creating the image of a majestic god-like king and court.

31 *Tard* brocade made by using supplementary patterning woven with flat metal stripes. *(National Museum, Bangkok)*

32 HRH Prince Kitiyakara Voralaksana in formal royal attire, wearing a tailored jacket made of golden *yierabab* brocade from India. His wife (left) HSH Apsara Samarn (Devakul) Kitiyakara and their daughter, HSH Kamala Pramodya Kitiyakara are attired in a fashion popular with ladies of the court during the reign of King Chulalongkorn (Rama V). They wear western-style lace blouses with traditional *chong kraben* (trousers created by wrapping a piece of silk around the waist, passing it through the legs and securing it with a belt) of imported Chinese brocade silk. *(National Archives)*

References

Chandracharoen, Thirabhand (1996). *Brocade Textile from Southern Region of Thailand during the Early Rattanakosin Period*. Individual Study of Faculty of Archaeology, Silpakorn University.

Chandracharoen, Thirabhand (2004). *Tied Together: Khmer Lao and Thai Mudmee Textiles*. Bangkok, Thailand: The James H. W. Thompson Foundation.

Gittinger, Mattiebelle (1992). *Textiles and the Tai Experience in Southeast Asia*. U. S. A.: Schneidereith & Son.

Religious and Status-Marking Functions of Textiles among the Tai Peoples of Vietnam

Michael C. Howard

The textile tradition of the Tai peoples of Vietnam has its origins among the ancient Daic speaking peoples (Kam-Sui, Kadai, and Tai languages) in China. These peoples are associated with various early kingdoms located along the Yangtze River, such as those of the Shu, Ch'u, Wu, and Yueh, stretching along the coast of China south into northern Vietnam. The Tai of the Lo clan settled in the Red River delta region of northern Vietnam in the 6th century BC (Madrolle 1937: 313-14, 319), whose emblem was the gray heron commonly found on Dong Son era bronzes. This bronze tradition in Vietnam is associated with these Yueh Tai and is part of a much larger bronze tradition among the Yueh of southern China. In the 3rd century BC, Nam Cuong, a Tai kingdom established in southern Guangxi, China, and northern Vietnam, has its capital Nam Binh located in present-day Cao Binh commune, Hoa An District, Cao Bang Province, Vietnam. (1, 2) Thuc Phan, a ruler of Nam Cuong conquered the neighbouring Tai kingdom of Van Lang around 258 BC, and then extended his territory into the lowlands of the Red River delta. His enlarged kingdom is commonly known as Ou Lo or Au Lac. The Qin general Zhao Tuo (or Chao To; Trieu Da in Vietnamese), who conquered the Tai territories to the north and established his own kingdom of Nam Viêt, defeated Thuc Phan in 208 BC in what is now Nghe An Province, Vietnam (3, 4) The descendants of the Tai peoples of Yueh and Ou Lo today include the Tai-speaking peoples called Zhuang (Chuang) in China and Tay, Nung, and Thai in Vietnam.

1 Portion of the original wall of the Nam Binh citadel, Cao Binh Commune, Hoa An District, Cao Bang Province.

2 Shrine kept by Thuc Phan's descendants within the Nam Binh citadel grounds.

3 Cuong temple near Cua Lo, Thanh Hoa Province.

4 Thuc Phan's shrine within the Cuong temple.

5 Supplementary weft hook and rhomb pattern on a Tai Muang *sin bok* from Quy Chau District, Nghe An Province (woven in the 1940s). This pattern is referred to as the *bok khau lang* (bell flower).

6 Supplementary weft hook and rhomb pattern on a Tai Dam *sin tah lan* from Quan Son District, Thanh Hoa Province (woven in the late 1970s).

Traditional Patterns

There are no examples at present of early Tai textiles with discernible patterns, and Chinese sources are vague. What we know about ancient Tai dress comes mainly from human figures on bronze items. These figures tell us that women wore head cloths, blouses, and decorated tube skirts, and men wore decorated loincloths (see Le 1990: 169-74). Only basic outlines of the patterns are discernible. More recent textiles from Vietnam and China, along with oral traditions, allow us some insights into the nature of the patterns found on textiles in the past. Also important is the conservative nature of Tai aesthetic tastes. In a discussion of Tai Dam patterns, Hoang (1988: 61-62), comments that the Tai Dam consider deviation from established patterns as damaging a beautiful thing and indicates that a woman has lost her Tai character.

There are two types of Tai textile patterns that are of particular relevance for the present discussion. The first category includes relatively realistic depictions of animals and, sometimes, of plants. The other category encompasses geometric or abstract patterns that are viewed as representations of plants and animals (often only a part of an animal, such as the forehead of a tiger or the foot print of a dog). The hook and rhomb, the eight-pointed star, and a number of other patterns are associated with the early Daic Bronze Age kingdoms mentioned above **(5-8)**. Tai informants in Vietnam generally relate particular plants with these geometric patterns. While the eight-pointed star elsewhere in Asia symbolizes the sun, the Tai commonly identify it as the fruit *mak phay* (a smooth-skinned fruit found in the forest that is eaten mainly by birds) or with various types of flowers. These patterns are generally viewed as special and even auspicious but do not have a particular sacred or religious status association. However, there are exceptions. One Tai informant from Thanh Hoa Province said that a pattern that she had woven of an eight-pointed star within a series of diamonds and diagonal rows of hooks represents *bok ben khoa hom,* which she noted is the flower of the tree from which coffins are made **(9)**. *Bok ben* refers to the flowering tree *Duabanga sonneralioides,* while *khoa hom* refers to a chest and lock. This large pattern is surrounded by fairly abstract representations of what she identified as *to bi* (dragonflies).

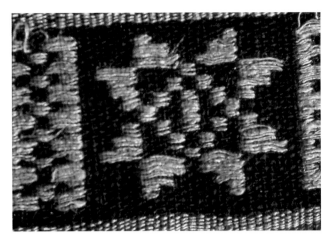

7 Supplementary weft eight-pointed star pattern on a Tai Mai Chau *sin mi* from Mai Chau District, Hoa Binh Province (woven in the 1930s).

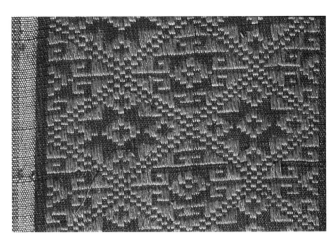

8 Supplementary weft eight-pointed star pattern on the hem-piece of a Tai Mai Chau *sua tin sao* from Mai Chau District, Hoa Binh Province (woven in the 1930s or earlier).

9 Supplementary weft *bok ben khoa hom* pattern on a Tai Dam *phai pha* from Quan Son District, Thanh Hoa Province (woven in the mid1980s).

10 Weft ikat funeral hut and artificial tree pattern on a Tai Mai Chau *sin mi* from Mai Chau District, Hoa Binh Province (woven in the 1930s).

One pattern that falls somewhat between the geometric representations of plants and realistic depiction of animals is a pattern said to represent an artificial tree and the roof of the structure built over a grave. **(10, 11)** The funeral hut is referred to as *thieng heo* in Tai Dam. Such artificial trees are made of bamboo and then are decorated in various ways. The Thái erect them for various ceremonies and festivals, including funerals. When erected for funerals the tree is called *ko heo* by the Tai Dam (*heo* = funeral). At funerals, after praying in the house, the tree is erected at the gravesite. Sometimes the weaver produces a fairly accurate image of this artificial tree, but usually the depiction is fairly abstract. This pattern usually is found on a woman's *sin mi* style of tube skirt, woven using a weft ikat technique arranged in a band that is bordered with plain stripes and narrower bands of geometric, floral supplementary weft patterns. If the tree pattern is in indigo dyed ikat, the alternating ikat bands are in a rust red colour and vice versa. These alternating bands that do not contain the tree motif may have patterns realistically depicting important status-marking animals (i.e., gray herons or dragons) or more abstract figures. In any event, the tree pattern is found only on skirts with special significance, indicating the high status of the wearer or to be worn at special events such as funerals.

Realistic animal patterns appear on a variety of types of cloth, using a range of weaving techniques. These include: supplementary warp patterning on skirt waistbands; supplementary weft and weft ikat patterning on skirt bodies, supplementary weft patterning on blankets, head cloths, and skirt borders. As I have noted elsewhere this portrayal of animals is "often fairly realistic" and, although younger informants sometimes have difficulty with identification, "many older informants are able to

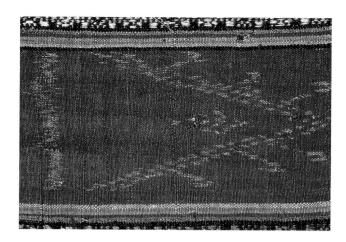

11 Weft ikat funeral hut and artificial tree pattern on a Tai Thanh *sin mi* from Con Cuong District, Nghe An Province (woven in the 1930s). After the weaver died her daughter kept it to display when praying to her ancestors at New Year.

12 Supplementary weft pattern of civets on a Tai Muang *sin man* from Que Phong District, Nghe An Province.

give very specific identities for the type of animal being portrayed and to do so in a manner that clearly indicates that they are not simply guessing" (Howard 2004a: 137).

Animals depicted realistically in Tai weaving include dragons (22-25), civets (12), monkeys (13), deer (14), elephants, turtle, phoenix, fish, frogs (16), spiders, butterflies, grasshoppers, horses (39), and a variety of birds (17-19). Such animals may have a special place in the Tai belief system with important sacred or spiritual qualities, but this is not always the case. Also, such a link to the sacred may no longer be known. The monkey motif is a popular on blankets that is woven by a woman and friends and relatives prior to her marriage and by newly married women. This motif is associated with the desire of a newly married couple to have children that are as jovial as a monkey. The civet motif is commonly found on skirts and blankets of the Tai Muang of Nghe An Province that is associated with hunting since the civet is popular to hunt. These are contemporary beliefs concerning these animals, and any older notions seem to have been forgotten.

The spotted deer, called *to quang bok* (flower deer) in Tai Dam and also known as the dapple deer or Japanese deer, symbolizes the fire god in Tai legends, and it is considered auspicious to encounter such a deer. Its image is found on Dong Son era bronzes and on Tai textiles (20, 21). It is a popular pattern on skirt hem-pieces and blankets of the Tai Muang of Nghe An Province (see Howard and Howard 2002: 259, fig. 181; 264, fig. 200). At least in the recent past, this textile motif does not represent status but simply portrays a sacred image.

The water dragon and gray heron images have had clear links in the past with the Tai feudal elite and reli-

13 Supplementary weft pattern of monkeys *(to linh)* on a Tai Dam *pha lai* from northwestern Thanh Hoa Province.

14 Supplementary warp pattern of a small deer (described generically as *to quang*) on a Tai Mai Chau waistband (*hua lanh tu* or *hua to*) from Mai Chau District, Hoa Binh Province. The small triangle patterns are called *mak ven* and depict fruit from a vine.

197

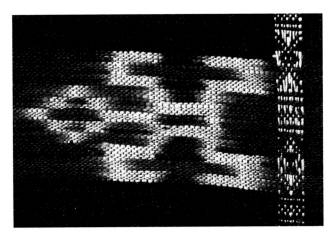

15 Warp ikat figure of a human on Tai Dam skirt material for a *sin muk mi ko* from Thanh Hoa Province.

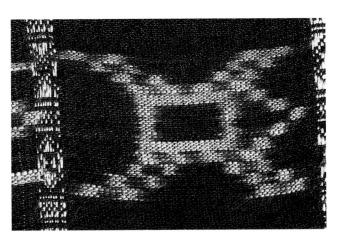

16 Warp ikat figure of a frog on the same piece of cloth illustrated in Fig. 15.

17 Supplementary warp pattern of a pair of birds facing one another on a Tai Dam waistband *(hua lanh tu* or *hua to)* from northwestern Thanh Hoa Province.

18 Supplementary weft pattern of a bird (referred to by one informant as a chicken, *to kay* or *to cay*, and falling generally within the category of birds with an upright tail) on a Tai Muang head cloth *(khan Tai)* worn on special occasions from Con Cuong District, Nghe An Province.

19 Supplementary weft pattern of a small bird on a Tai Dam shoulder bag from Quan Son District, Thanh Hoa Province (woven in 1996).

20 A spotted deer on a Dong Son era ceremonial bronze ax head.

21 An embroidered spotted deer on a Tai Muang hem-piece *(tin sin)* from Con Cuong District, Nghe An Province (made in 1996).

gious beliefs. Water dragons are associated with females and are responsible for transporting the spirits of women to the spirit world at death. Formerly, the dragon *(to hong luong, to ngueak, or to ngawk)* pattern was reserved for members of the feudal nobility, and the rationale for this sumptuary rule is readily apparent since dragons embody great power. The dragon pattern never appears on a piece of cloth in close proximity to other animal motifs. Tran (1978: 37, 110-11) has identified numerous dragon patterns found on Thai (members of the Southwestern branch of Tai) and Muong (a non-Tai ethnic group) waistbands but noted that they are all generally similar – i.e., a wavy mane, a narrow body with bent back, a long wavy tail, and four legs. **(22, 23)** This has led Tran (1978: 73) to remark that they all come from the same original source and variation reflects regional differences to some extent. Tran also comments that these dragon patterns are distinctly Thai, differing from dragon motifs from the Kinh and Han cultures. In the pattern, the dragons always appear in pairs, sometimes, with

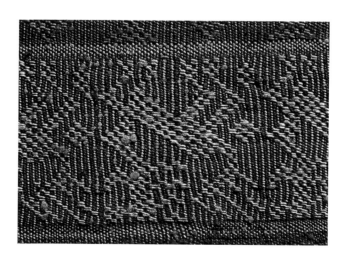

22 Supplementary warp pattern of a water dragon on a Tai Mai Chau waistband *(hua lanh tu* or *hua to)* from Mai Chau District, Hoa Binh Province (a relatively old piece and a fine example of the dragon pattern). It also features the *mak ven* patterns.

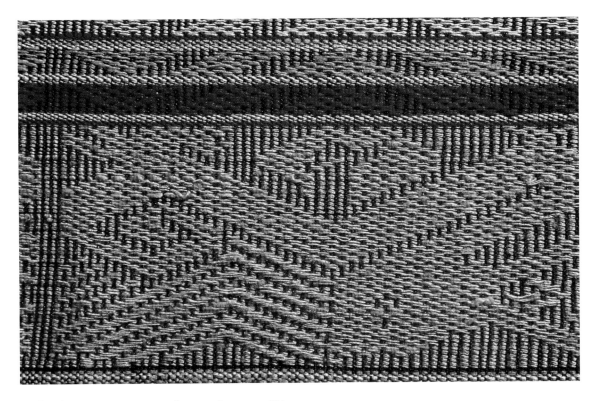

23 Supplementary warp pattern of a water dragon on a Tai Dam waistband *(hua lanh tu* or *hua to)* from Quan Son District, Thanh Hoa Province (woven in 1997).

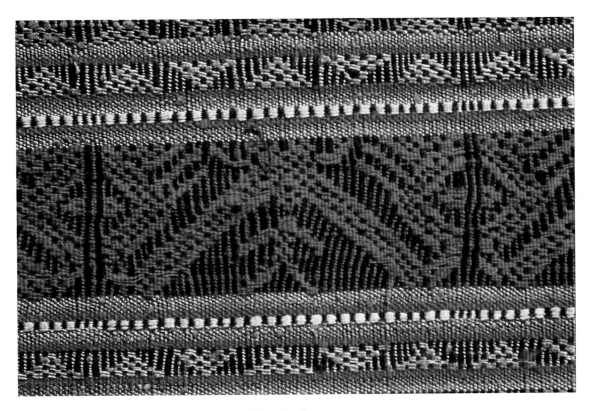

24 Supplementary warp pattern of water dragons with entwined tails over human figure on a Tai Mai Chau waistband *(hua lanh tu* or *hua to)* from Mai Chau District, Hoa Binh Province.

25 Old waistband cloths (early 1950s or older), each with versions of water dragons with entwined tails pattern. They are stitched onto the waistband of a Tai Dam *sin tah lan* from Quan Son District, Thanh Hoa Province (woven in the late 1970s).

26 A gray heron pattern on a bronze bell from the early Dong Son period.

entwined tails (**24**, **25**). Dragon motif woven in supplementary warp appears on the middle waistbands, *hua lanh tu* or *hua to* (*hua* = head, *tu* = gate or door, and *lanh phai* = strip of cloth), of Thai skirts. This pattern is also incorporated into the design of weft ikat bands of *sin mi* tube skirts and is woven in supplementary weft on skirt hem-pieces of skirts and on blankets.

The gray heron *(Ardea cinera)* is prominently featured on many Dong Son era bronzes, and it symbolized the Lo clan, one of the dominant ruling Tai clans mentioned above (**26**, **27**). This bird is also associated with males, transporting male spirits upon death. In the past use of its image on women's skirts was restricted to the noble class. Presumably, only women of the Lo clan wore skirts decorated with this bird motif at one time, but noble women from other clans later wore similar skirts. Examples of these skirts with this pattern come from western Thanh Hoa Province, and production has ceased some time ago. In the eastern part of this province, the Cuong temple marks the site where the Tai ruler Thuc Phan, containing shrines dedicated to Thuc Phan and his general Cao Lo (**3**, **4**). The mountain adjacent to the shrine is called Hac Mountain (its original Tai name has been lost). *Hac* (Vietnamese) refers to the bird appearing on the Dong Son bronzes and is often translated as crane, but a more accurate meaning would be a noble bird. This bird of the imagination may be compared with birds called *co* (Vietnamese), which are common field birds. A gray heron that appeared at the Cuong shrine during a festival in honor of Thuc Phan in 1995, has encased in Thuc Phan's shrine, after being shot and stuffed, and is referred to as *hac* (**28**). The same type of bird appears on

27 A gray heron pattern on a bronze bell from the later Dong Son period.

28 The gray heron that appeared at the Cuong temple in a glass case next to Thuc Phan's shrine.

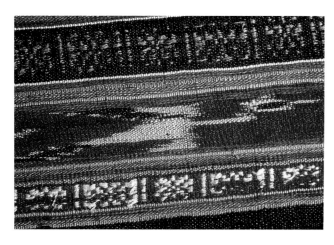

29 Weft ikat pattern of a gray heron on a Tai Dam *sin mi* from north-western Thanh Hoa Province (early 20th century/late 19th century).

30 The weft ikat gray heron and tree of life patterns on the same *sin mi* as (29).

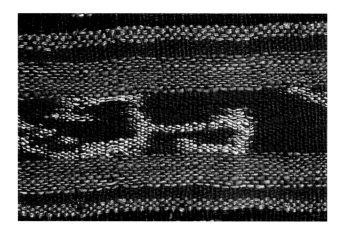

31 A relatively crude weft ikat gray heron pattern on a Tai Dam *sin mi* from northwestern Thanh Hoa Province (probably from the mid-20th century).

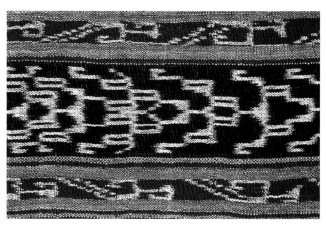

32 The same weft ikat gay heron and weft ikat patterns in adjacent bands.

early Thai textiles in ikat technique. The bird is not presently common to this area of Vietnam, but in the past it would migrate to this area. Legends associated with the Lo clan state that members of the clan migrated along the coast much like the bird.

An accurate portrayal of such a bird is illustrated on a *sin mi* that dates from the late 19th century **(29, 30)**. Another skirt from the same area that is as old as the mid-20th century features a more abstract version of the bird in only two colours (white and rust red) **(31, 32)**. The weavers of Ban Lac village have recently sought to reproduce this pattern. However, they have only been able to produce fairly crude representations of the bird in two colours with an alternating weft ikat band of the hook and rhomb pattern and not the funeral house and tree **(33)**. Relatively abstract versions of the same gray heron motif also is also found on tube skirts from Laos and Lao

Khrang tube skirts *(sin mi ta)* woven in Thailand also sometimes feature this motif. In the case of older Lao Khrang skirts the motif can be fairly realistic, woven in green or black thread for the bird's body with white accents surrounded by red, but newer examples are more abstract and are usually woven with only two colours.

The frog is another animal that figures prominently on bronze drums but not on other bronze items (see Schafer 1967: 254). Regarding recent textiles, the frog pattern is depicted mainly on tube skirts of the Thai living in Thanh Hoa and Nghe An provinces. Only married women wear this pattern since it symbolizes fertility. **(15, 16)** Dore (1993: 243-44) discusses frog-man images on textiles in Southeast Asia, including reference to the festival of the frog goddess *(sit ya kue)* of the Zhuang and its link to fertility.

33 A pair of weft ikat gray herons alongside a weft ikat hook and rhomb pattern on skirt material woven in 2000 by a Tai Mai Chau woman from Mai Chau District, Hoa Binh Province.

The Ceremonial and Status-marking Use of Textiles

Very little remains of the religious beliefs surrounding textiles or of the religious practices for which special textiles were used among Tai peoples in Vietnam. The use of textiles as markers of secular or religious status has also disappeared. Traditional beliefs and practices that survived the wartime period and then the consolidation of communist control in northern Vietnam are rapidly being undermined today by economic changes.

Tay and Nung The Tay and Nung have been more Sinicized than the Thai in the past. Sinicization resulted in significant changes in their weaving traditions and the inclusion of many Han cultural elements into their religious beliefs and practices, which is a mixture of Confucianism, Buddhism, and Taoism, as well as belief in spirits. Of the two groups, the Nung have retained more of their traditional culture than the Tay, but many traditional Nung cultural elements have come to survive only in remote communities. Tay and Nung elites in the past tended to adopt Sinicized dress. One sign of such change among the population in general was the widespread adoption of trousers by women, replacing the traditional tube skirt. In the past women in virtually all Tay and Nung households wove cloth for domestic consumption, but this situation began to change in the mid-20th century. Weaving is now relatively rare among the Tay and survives only in a few communities, although efforts have been made to revive weaving. Weaving is more common among the Nung but has ceased in less remote villages.

The Tay weave on a frame loom, whereas the Nùng usually weave on a combination back-strap/frame loom (*ahn thuhc*) **(34, 35)**. Neither group has woven with supplementary warp or ikat techniques for an extremely long

203

34 A Tay woman from Hoa An District, Cao Bang Province, weaving supplementary weft patterned cloth on a frame loom.

35 A Nung An woman from Quang Hoa District, Cao Bang Province, weaving on a combination back-strap and frame loom.

36 An elderly Tay woman selling baby-carriers *(an um luk)* at the Quang Hoa District market.

time – to the extent that there is no memory of ever having used these techniques. They do, however, still employ supplementary weft techniques to decorate cloth intended for use in making blankets, baby-carriers, head cloths, and shoulder bags for the tourist industry. Other decorative techniques are embroidery and tritik, a resist-dye technique. Both the Tay and Nung use embroidery to decorate priest's robes and the Nung Zin of Lao Cai Province embroider some of their special occasion clothing.

The Tay and Nung have ceased to uphold many religious beliefs associated with weaving. An example of such beliefs is in the traditional restrictions regarding sericulture, such as a person who raised silk worms should not look at or visit people or animals that have recently given birth. Also, when returning from a funeral a person must avoid silk worms for several days. Dietary restrictions included prohibitions from eating snakes by all members of the family and bamboo shoots, taro, scallions, and a number of other food items when the silk worms were ready to spin cocoons.

Textiles previously played an important role in the life cycle of Tay and Nung. Textiles were among the gifts exchanged during marriage. In Tay marriages, the groom's family presented un-dyed was cloth to the bride's mother to compensate her for raising the girl. The mother would later dye the cloth and when her daughter had her first child the mother would make a baby-carrier and swaddling clothes from this cloth. Commercial cloth has now replaced hand-woven for baby's accessories, although older women occasionally still weave the decorative cloth attached to baby-carriers **(36)**. Sometimes, the groom's family gave red fabric, *kua hung* or to remove all bad things, to the bride's unmarried brothers and sisters.

Tay children were sometimes given special shirts, which priests covered with auspicious and protective symbols. In response to questions about such shirts, Nung Phan Sinh informants in Lang Son Province told David Wangsgard (a Simon Fraser University PhD. student) that Nung priests pray into the shirts but write on them. Wangsgard comments that "perhaps they were telling me this to distinguish themselves from the Tay (differences are pointed out to me more often than are similarities)."

Some variation exists in traditional Tay funeral practices (Abadie 2001: 81; Howard and Howard 2002: 54-55). Generally, the corpse is placed on a mat and then covered with the mosquito net commonly used by the deceased. The oldest man in the community is delegated to tie the corners of the mosquito net in order to cover the body. Next, a priest covers the body with pieces of plain white cloth (usually with the head and feet left exposed). In keeping with the beliefs of Sinicized cultures, the Tay believe that a male has seven life principles, and a female has nine. Thus, a respective number of pieces of cloth are

37 A Tay altar screen *(phun man* or *phuhn man)* from Na Giang District, Cao Bang Province (woven between 1900 and 1910). The supplementary patterns were woven with imported French silk thread.

38 Detail from the altar screen in **(37)** showing the central supplementary weft floral pattern.

placed over the body, depending on the sex of the deceased. On the second day of the funeral, a small hut is constructed in an open area near the deceased's house, and a model prison is made from white cloth in the shape of a triangle near this hut. Within the prison is a banner on which is written the name and age of the deceased is placed. A priest then prays for the deceased's spirit to be released by the god of hell. The priest stabs the prison with a sword and grabs the flag, thereby releasing the spirit of the deceased. Those in the funeral procession (the ceremony including the procession is called the *slong pi)* dress in white.

In traditional Nung funerals the deceased is buried in new clothing and wrapped in white cloth *(phai fon*: Nung Phàn Sình) and the children of the deceased wear white clothing inside out. In Nung Loi funerals, the deceased's children bring the pieces of white cloth to cover the body. The eldest male child places his cloth over the deceased first followed by the remaining children in descending order by age and sons before daughters. The Nung Chao do not adhere to the seven-nine formula and the Nung An place the deceased's blankets and mosquito nets in the coffin.

The Tay and Nung use two types of special cloth and clothing for religious practices: large pieces of cloth that are hung as part of the family altar and special clothing worn by priests. Most Tay refer to the family altar screens as *phun man* or *phuhn man (màn* = a curtain; *pha pay*: Tai Dam). In the past, both Tay and Nung households have had such screens when a woman (or her mother) wove them prior to marriage. When the bride goes to her new husband's house she must present this cloth to be hung at the ancestral altar in the husband's house to express respect for the husband's ancestors. The Tay have ceased to weave such textiles. I have illustrated an example of a

39 Detail from the altar screen in **(37)** showing the supplementary weft pattern of a horse.

screen from Na Giang District, Cao Bang Province, which was woven during the first decade of the 20th century **(37)**. The screen is decorated mainly with supplementary weft floral patterns. These include four eight-pointed blossoms *(pet kip)* at each point of the diamond **(38)**. There is a small square kernel in the centre of the diamond that is surrounded by straight flower stems *(bok dau)* and near the stems are six-petal wild flower motifs *(bok cham)*. At the bottom of the cloth is a row of large horses *(tu ma)* **(39)**. Few of these woven screens exist. The Tay Thu Lao of Lao Cai province now use patterned commercial cloth from China which they call "peacock cloth" since it is decorated with peacocks and flowers on a red ground. Efforts have been made recently to revive the weaving of supplementary weft patterned cloth using old patterns in Hoa An commune, Ha Quang district, Cao Bang province. Members of the weaving co-operative have also returned to using such cloth as altar screens **(40, 41)**.

41 Detail of the supplementary weft patterning on the altar screen in **(40)**.

40 A household shrine at the Tay weaving co-operative in Hoa An District, Cao Bang Province with an altar screen woven in 2004.

The Tay and Nung have a variety of male and female religious specialists (Be, Nguyen and Chu 1992: 227-54). The broad term for a priest in Tay is *tao,* but the names differ for specific types of priests. In Nung Phan Sinh a priest is generally called *kuhn slay* and a female spirit medium is *da then*. Writing in the early 1920s, Abadie (2001: 87) mentioned that the highest-ranking priest *(p'u giang)* wears "an embroidered turban on which he places a miter-shaped hat." In addition to such hats, Tay-Nung priests wear special robes (*slua tao:* Tay; *slu tao*: Nung) decorated with Buddhist and Taoist motifs. Priests embroidered, painted or drew the patterns on the coats. The main patterns on Tay priest's robes (see Diep 1997: 29-50) include the four most important supernatural animals: dragon (*tu luhng*), phoenix (*tu phung* or *tu fuhng*), unicorn and turtle (*tu tao* or *tu pha*). Other supernatural animals consist a horse with a dragon head and a unicorn with a dragon head. Realistic animal motifs include the tiger (*tu slua* or *tu slu*), horse (*tu ma*), fish (*tu pa*), and butterfly (*tu buhng-ba*). Buddhist symbolism is depicted as a turtle carrying Buddhist *sutras*, a horse with a dragon head underneath the Bodhi leaf and human figures sitting on the Bodhi leaf. Nung robe are illustrated with dragon, long-tailed phoenix, horse with a dragon head and cock's tail, man on a horse and horse with a dragon head being ridden by a man patterns. Hats are often decorated with the phoenix (sometimes resembling

42 Nung Phan Sinh priest wearing a funeral robe.

43 Nung Phan Sinh priest wearing the same robe backwards to show the back of the robe.

44 White Tai woman and her daughter near Lai Chau town wearing traditional white blouses *(sua kom)* with silver buttons *(mak pem)* that were made in the 1940s.

a cock), dragon or unicorn with a dragon head and the tail of a cock.

David Wangsgard interviewed Nung Phan Sinh priests about their robes, which are now quite rare. The funeral robe that is illustrated is the only one of its kind in the village and apparently in the entire district and it belongs to the oldest of the village's priests, who shares it with other priests, and was made by his grandfather **(42, 43)**. The same priest owns a yellow robe with painted patterns that is worn at ceremonies held for the ill. Another style of robe that is also worn at funerals is a lighter shade of blue than the one shown in **(42)** and **(43)**. Wangsgard noted that it "followed the same pattern as the men's indigo shirts, minus pockets and collar, i.e. four-panel shirts with narrow, wrist length sleeves. The robe is split of either side to about the hip. In the centre of the back of the robe is a single motif of the loin-horse looking creature encompassed by a square frame. This same motif is also in the centre of the back of the robe in the photographs." When he asked the village priests about the identity of the animal he was told simply that it was an imaginary, mythical animal. Continuing the description of the robe: "On each of the front panels there is a single phoenix motif. All the motifs are embroidered. The robe is fastened by two ties in the front, like the robe in the photographs."

207

45 Three married Black Tai women from Tuan Giao District, Dien Bien Province.

Thai I find it useful to divide the Thai (members of the Southwestern branch of the Tai) in Vietnam into two groups, northern and southern (see Howard and Howard 2002). The northern Thai have lost most of their older textile traditions, although they have retained far more than the Tay and Nung. They have ceased to weave decorative techniques, such as warp or weft ikat or supplementary warp or weft, although they appear to have used them in the past. Pieces of cloth with patterns made with such techniques are occasionally encountered as heirlooms.

It is relatively common for White Tai women to wear white blouses that open down the front (*sua kom*) while Black Tai women now wear the same style of blouse that are a variety of colours **(44, 45)**. Northern Thai women fasten their blouses in a variety of ways but the most common means is with an odd number of silver or aluminum buttons, *mak pem* (*mak* = fruit, flower, branch; *pem* = to attach). The two parts of a pair of buttons is sometimes viewed to symbolize reproduction. The left side is male (*mak pem po; to po* = male), and the right side is female (*mak pem me; to me* = female). The northern Thai formerly wore robes (called *sua/xua luong* in most areas, *slua thong* in Yen Chau) for celebrations, to greet visiting notables, or simply in the house when it was cold **(46)**. These are rarely worn today, but older women keep them to wear at funerals. A man's robe usually fastens on the right side whereas a woman's robe is a pullover tunic. They are normally made of cotton, but in the past wealthy people would make them of silk.

Both males and females serve as priests in Black Tai society. Black Tai priests in Son La Province at present often wear normal clothing while praying, but sometimes they add a few special items. These include a long head cloth, which covers the face and a red waist sash. Both of these items are decorated with birds, snakes, dragons and flower patterns. Priests also carry an amulet in the belt. Female priests in Muang Thanh adorn their heads with a special cloth made of four pieces of coloured fabric when talking to the souls of dead. Its ends are decorated with a saw-tooth shape and the centre is made from a piece of supplementary weft-patterned cloth. The fringe consists of coloured cloth and shiny objects. Hoang (1988: 24-25) refers to a special head cloth, called a *pieu khoan*, which is worn by female priests in other areas during the *kin pang* ceremony. This head cloth has patterns in alternating colours drawn on its ends with a rice stem. If the patient is male there are seven patterns on each end, and if the patient is female then there are nine patterns. The patient of the ceremony presents the textile to the priest. If the patient is female she wears it and dances during part of the ceremony. If the patient is male, his mother or wife wears the head cloth during the dance. Patterns painted with rice stems are also sometimes found on *khan mon*, a white coloured cloth that is made by a bride and given to her husband's brothers at their wedding to be used as handkerchiefs at ceremonies.

A variety of other objects are also used during prayers in curing ceremonies. If a woman is ill, these include underwear, jewelry, long pieces of plain white cotton cloth, replicas of the silver waist chains made out of bamboo and nine cloth soul rings. The priest presents white cloth and ornaments to a spirit to buy back the soul of the sick person. After the priest finishes praying, each female relative gets one soul ring and places it on the wrists of the sick person so that her soul does not depart the body. In the past the use of shoulder bags *(thong)* was limited to priests but this restriction disappeared with the advent of communist rule in 1954.

Textiles play an important role at weddings. A woman may spend two to three years preparing clothing and other cloth prior to her wedding to serve as gifts and as part of her dowry. It is customary to select the nicest blanket, mosquito net, mat and pillow to use in the *su pha* ceremony, which takes place before the wedding. In this ceremony a new shirt of the groom and a blouse of the bride are placed on a mat with their sleeves crossed. The groom then gives the bride a pair of silver bracelets. All of these gifts are shown to the guardian spirit of the house. On her wedding day a woman wears new clothing made by her mother or her. Under the panel of the right side of her robe is a small bag containing special gifts, such as a hairpin from her mother and an amulet from her uncle. Typical amulets include the dried innards of a forest worm that is referred to as *bong kin phi, phi kin bong* (worm eats ghost, ghost eats worm) or the dried hand of a baby gibbon called *mu nang mi* (hand of the noble gibbon). After marriage these amulets are attached to her children's baby-carriers.

Black Tai funerals require special clothing. For a funeral, the deceased is dressed in new clothing and then placed on the mat on which they slept when alive and covered with a white cloth. In some areas, the deceased's face is covered with a new head cloth, which is referred to as a *pieu pok na*, when the body is placed in the coffin.

46 White Tai woman near Lai Chau town wearing a typical White Tai robe (woven in the 1940s).

If the deceased is a man, his face is covered with one head cloth. A woman's face is covered with two head cloths, including a head cloth that she often wore when alive.

It is considered inauspicious to make funerary clothing to be worn by members of a family of the deceased before the person dies. Thus, only after a death do the deceased's female relatives make the appropriate clothing for family members. Family members wear different-coloured clothing during the funeral, depending on the relationship between the wearer and the deceased. When

209

47 Tai Mai Chau *sua tin sao* from Mai Chau District, Hoa Binh Province.

48 Detail of the supplementary weft patterning on the hem-piece of the *sua tin sao* in **(47)**.

a woman's parents die, she wears the same colour as her brothers' clothing. In the case of the death of her parents-in-law, a woman dresses in a collarless and hemless white blouse with string ties, an everyday style of skirt and a plain white head cloth. If she is the eldest daughter-in-law, however, she puts on a *sua hieu luong* or filial piety robe and a black or dark indigo blue head cloth to firmly establish that she will serve her in-laws in the sky world. A woman who becomes the eldest daughter-in-law makes these robes for her future in-laws and presents the robes to them on her wedding day. There are two types of robes, but both feature loose long sleeves with wide cuffs differing from the straight long sleeves of other robes. The *sua hieu luong* is loose with open sides and multi-coloured appliquéd stripes. The dark indigo blue or black *sua hieu luong dam* is a pullover tunic opening down the chest.

A special type of short pullover tunic, called *sua nhinh,* is often hung in the house where the funeral is held to ensure that the deceased's soul remains inside during the funeral (Le 1990: 92-93). The soul is believed to reside in the *sua nhinh* before ascending to the sky

world. The bodice consists of dark indigo-dyed cloth, but the sleeves may be a different colour. A younger daughter-in-law often sews these shirts and gives them to her parents-in-law. It is also customary to hang a piece of the living spouse's clothing (often something that was worn every day) on the deceased's grave to assist in the recognition and reunification of the couple when the surviving spouse dies and travels to the sky or after world. If a woman remarries, her former husband's clothing is burnt. The Black Tai sometimes suspend other items of the deceased's clothing from a tree located near the house where the funeral is held.

Southern Thai women of Moc Chau, Mai Chau and communities immediately to the west along the Ma River in northern Vietnam, wore a distinctive type of short-sleeved, pullover robe, *sua tin seo,* for their parents'-in-law funerals **(47)**. In the past, the upper portion of these robes was made of loosely woven and thin, red or gold colored silk cloth. Women have discontinued using such robes, but the upper portion robes worn now is usually made of commercial cotton cloth (see Howard and Howard 2002: 246, fig. 135). The hem of the robe

49 Detail of other supplementary weft patterning on the hem-piece in **(47)**.

includes a wide strip of hand-woven cloth that is elaborately decorated with supplementary weft patterning **(48, 49)**. The wearer of the robe or her mother-in-law may have woven this piece of cloth or sometimes it was a gift from the wearer's husband, who obtained it through trade. In addition to the robe, the daughter-in-law will wear a plain dark coloured tube skirt and blouse. She should not wear any jewelry. Female priests also wore these robes when praying at funerals to call upon the deceased's soul and invite it to have a meal and when the deceased is taken to the grave site. Along with these robes, the priest would also wear a cloth necklace with a small pouch *(thawng sanh)* carrying a magical charm or amulet (see Howard and Howard 2002: 238, fig. 106). The pouch is usually sewn closed and contains several potent items such as a tiger's tooth, a piece of the "Sky God's hammer" (found when lightening strikes a tree), pangolin scales and seashells. Boar tusks may also be attached to the necklace.

A man also wears special clothing of a plain white robe when his parents or parents-in-law die, but this tradition is disappearing (see Howard and Howard 2002:

237, fig. 101). The robe is loose fitting and may open down the front or at the side with knotted strings or ties. The hem of the robe is not stitched, but left rough. The son or son-in-law adorns his head with a plain white cloth.

The southern Thai from other parts of Thanh Hoa and Nghe An provinces have somewhat different traditions of dress for funerals. Among the Tai Muang, there are differences in the customary dress for funerals between those living in northern and southern parts of Nghe An Province. In Chau Tieng Commune, Quy Chau District of northern Nghe An Province, deceased men and women are specially dressed for their funeral. A dead man's funeral clothing includes two robes of an black cotton, inner robe with a stand-up collar, ties on the side and an inner lining of plain white cotton cloth. The thin, white cotton outer robe opens down the front with long sleeves and cuffs made of pieces of plain black and red cloth. A plain red cotton belt is worn around the waist. Usually, in the case when two such garments are worn, one (in this case the outer robe) probably represents an older tradition, while the other (in this case the inner robe) seems to be a more recent adaptation.

51 Detail of the embroidered patterning on the hem-piece of the *sin lai mai* in **(50)**.

50 Tai Muang *sin lai mai* from Quy Chau District, Nghe An Province (woven in the mid-1970s).

In Quy Chau, deceased women are dressed in a plain black cotton robe, *sua nhao*, which opens down the front and has plain white cotton lining, over a plain black blouse and two skirts. The outer skirt is a known as a *sin lai mai* that has a check-patterned, cotton body and an embroidered hem with a black background **(50, 51)**. This special skirt is usually made by a woman's mother-in-law to be worn by her at her parents'-in-law and her own funerals. A plain black *sin lai* is worn underneath the *sin lai mai*. The deceased is also adorned with two head cloths *(khan)*. One of these head cloths is plain and the other is decorated. Quy Chau women wear special clothing when attending their parents'-in-law funerals. All daughters-in-law are expected to wear identical skirts, *sin bok* or a *sin lai mai,* which are usually made for them by their mother-in-law. They also wear a sleeveless, plain red cotton blouse with a plain white band at the bottom, called *sua deng*. In the village of Ban Hoa Tien, all daughters-in-law wear *sua deng* of the same length, but in some other communities the eldest daughter-in-law wears a long blouse while others wear shorter ones.

Tai Muang women in Con Cuong and Tuong Duong Districts of southern Nghe An Province have a tradition of weaving cloth with weft directional bands of supplementary weft and weft ikat patterning mentioned earlier. The Tai Muang reserve use of this cloth is used exclu-

212

sively for making the centerpieces of skirts to be worn at funerals, *sin phi*. A *sin phi* has the usual, plain white Tai Muang waistband, a midsection with supplementary weft and weft ikat patterning of the *sin mi* type and a hempiece that is either plain or embroidered black fabric (**52, 53**). There are two varieties of the supplementary weft patterning on these skirts. One type consists of triangular and diamond-shaped patterns in several different colours of silk thread. The other is woven with black and white thread and is referred to as *muk* patterning although it is supplementary weft and not supplementary warp weave. The Tai Muang believe such patterns are suitable only for clothing worn at funerals. All daughters-in-law at the funeral are expected to wear identical skirts, which are usually made by their mother-in-law. The women wear a long-sleeved, dark coloured blouse with this skirt, and their hair is put up with pins without a head cloth.

The southern Thai in Thanh Hoa province attach no such special significance to the *sin mi* style of skirt or to *muk*-like patterning found on the skirt. A *sin mi* may be worn at funerals, but women also wear them on many other special occasions. It would seem that in the past Thai women throughout this area to wear particular styles of *sin mi* at funerals, but this tradition is now breaking down.

Almost none of the younger women in Con Cuong and Tuong Duong Districts today have the skills to weave the patterned cloth for the *sin phi*. In Yen Thanh village, Con Cuong District, the last traditional *sin phi* was woven in the 1970s, for example (**53**). Older pieces that have not been sold to traders are now kept as heirlooms, but a few new examples have been produced. Efforts have been made recently by a non-governmental organization to revive weft ikat weaving in this village, but such cloth is intended primarily for the commercial handicraft market and not for use in making *sin phi*.

The southern Thai weave two basic types of long supplementary weft cloth, called *pha khit* or *pha deng* when made at least partially of silk with a red ground and *pha lai* when made of cotton with a white ground. Among the uses for such cloth is to serve as screens or covers for coffins. It is considered appropriate to use *pha khit* for men and *pha lai* for women. When used for a funeral, the cloth is interred with the coffin. The Tai Muang in northern Nghe An Province use a type of textile, called a *man bang,* as coffin covers or screens when it is on display in the house of the deceased prior to burial (**54**). Patterns on these textiles usually include a large cross-like pattern representing a tree with flowers, smaller cross-like pat-

52 Tai Muang *sin phi* from Thuong Duong District, Nghe An Province.

terns representing flowers, and, sometimes, small animals. In the past, not all families owned *man bang* and would have to borrow one from a neighbour. The cloth then would be returned to its owner with a gift of buffalo meat. The amount of meat would depend on the wealth of the family. Even fewer families have their own *man bang* today since many of them have been sold to textile traders. Entire villages now do not have a single *man bang*. In recent years plain commercial cloth has replaced the hand-woven material as funeral screens.

53 Tai Muang *sin phi* from Con Cuong District, Nghe An Province (woven in the early 1970s using newly introduced aniline dyes).

Conclusion

The Tai of Vietnam have an extraordinary textile heritage that is rooted in the religious beliefs and feudal structure of their ancient Bronze Age civilization. An amazing amount of this heritage survived well into the 20th century, especially in the more isolated communities of southern Son La, western Hoa Bình, western Thanh Hoa and Nghe An provinces. Unfortunately, the social and political upheaval that the Tai experienced in the mid-20th century and subsequent social and economic changes have meant that much of this heritage has disappeared. Moreover, the rate at which this heritage is disappearing seems to have accelerated in recent years to the point that relatively little now remains except in the memories of a dwindling number of elderly people.

Reforms in Vietnam in the 1990s created opportunities for cultural revival among the Tai, but at the same time they also led to economic changes that have served to further undermine cultural traditions. There have been efforts to revive traditional weaving in a number of Tai communities, such as those of the Tay of Hoa An District in Cao Bang Province and of the Thai of Mai Chau District in Hoa Binh Province. This has meant that versions of some ancient patterns have been revived, albeit not always woven with the same skill as in the past. Some ancient patterns, such as the dragon on waistbands of the Southern Thai, did not require to be revived since they are even more popular now. Yet what has survived or been revived is such a small part of the Tai textile repertoire. Thus, while the dragon pattern is popular on Southern Thai waistbands, it has become rather standardized and many of the other patterns that formerly appeared on these waistbands have ceased to be woven, to the point that it is becoming increasingly difficult to find even very old women who can identify examples of them. In fact, even though patterns may survive, the knowledge of their meaning or significance has largely vanished.

It is still possible to carry out research about these patterns and their ancient meanings and the traditional ceremonial uses of types of cloth and clothing in order to fill in the many gaps that exist in present knowledge about them. However, as time passes this is rapidly becoming more difficult as those who possess the knowledge grow older and die. It would be a pity now to lose such knowledge after its being passed on from generation to generation for over 2,000 years.

Note

I have used Hoang Tran Nghich and Tong Kim An, *Tu Dien Thai-Viet* (Hanoi: Nha Xuat Ban Khoa Hoc Xa Hoi, 1990) for spelling Thai words and Vy Thi Be, Janice E. Saul, and Nancy Frieberger Wilson, *Nung Fan Slihng-English Dictionary* (Manila: Summer institute of Linguistics, Asia Area office, 1982) for spelling Nung words.

References

Abadie, Maurice, *The Races of Upper-Tonkin from Phong-Tho to Lang Son* (Bangkok: White Lotus Press, 2000). [Originally published in French in 1924.]

Be Viet Dang, Nguyen Van Huy and Chu Thai Son (eds.), *Cac Dan Toc Tay, Nung o Viet Nam* (Hanoi: Viên Khoa Hoc Xa Hôi Viêt Nam, Viên Dân Tôc Hoc, 1992).

Diep Trung Binh, *Patterns on Textiles of the Ethnic Groups in Northeast of Vietnam* (Hanoi: Cultures of Nationalities Publishing House, 1997).

Dore, Amphay, "The frog-man and the diamond: A comparative analysis of two weaving patterns of Southeast Asia," in S. Prangwattha nakun (ed.) *Textiles of Asia: A Common Heritage.* Bangkok: Office of the National Culture Commission, Ministry of Education; Chiang Mai: Centre for the Promotion of Arts and Culture, Chiang Mai University, 1993: 224-248.

Gittinger, Matttiebelle and H. Leedom Lefferts, Jr., *Textiles and the Tai Experience in Southeast Asia* (Washington, DC: The Textile Museum, 1992).

Hoang Luong, *Hoa Van Thai* (Hanoi: Nha Xuat Ban Van Hoa Dan Toc, 1988).

Howard, Michael C., *Textiles of Southeast Asia: An Annotated & Illustrated Bibliography* (Bangkok: White Lotus Press, 1994).

_____, "Searching for the identity of the bird on Dongson drums," *Arts of Asia,* vol. 34, no. 2, 2004a, pp. 136-142.

_____, "A comparative study of the warp ikat patterned textiles of mainland Southeast Asia," *Textile,* vol. 2, no. 2, 2004b, pp. 176-207.

Howard, Michael C. and Kim Be Howard, *Textiles of the Daic Peoples of Vietnam* (Bangkok: White Lotus Press, 2002).

Huang Shoubao, *Ethnic Costume from Guizhou: Clothing Designs and Decorations from Minority Ethnic Groups in Southwest China* (Beijing: Foreign Languages Press, 1987).

Le Ngoc Thang, *Nghe Thuat Trang Phuc Thái* (Hanoi: Nha Xuat Ban Van Hoa Dan Toc, 1990).

Madrolle, C., "Le Tonkin ancien," *Bulletin de l'Ecole Française d'Extrême Orient,* vol. 37, no. 2, 1937, pp. 263-332.

Schafer, Edward H., *The Vermilion Bird: Tang Images of the South* (Los Angeles: University of California Press, 1967).

Tran Tu, *Hoa Van Muong* (Hanoi: Nha Xuat Ban Van Hoa Dan Toc, 1978).

Washburn, Dorothy K. and Andrea Petitto, "Southern Laotian textiles: Relationships between pattern structure and weaving technology," *Ars Textrina,* vol. 15, 1991, pp. 35-66.

54 Tai Muang *man bang* from Quy Chau District, Nghe An Province (woven in 1996).

215